MEN OF
GOD
MEN OF
WAR

THERAN PRESS

THERAN PRESS IS THE ACADEMIC IMPRINT OF SILVER GOAT MEDIA.

THERAN IS DEDICATED TO AUTHENTIC PARTNERSHIPS WITH OUR ACADEMIC ASSOCIATES, TO THE QUALITY DESIGN OF SCHOLARLY BOOKS, AND TO ELITE STANDARDS OF PEER REVIEW.

THERAN SEEKS TO FREE INTELLECTUALS FROM THE CONFINES OF TRADITIONAL PUBLISHING.

THERAN SCHOLARS ARE AUTHORITIES AND REVOLUTIONARIES IN THEIR RESPECTIVE FIELDS.

THERAN ENCOURAGES NEW MODELS FOR GENERATING AND DISTRIBUTING KNOWLEDGE.

FOR OUR CREATIVES, FOR OUR COMMUNITIES, FOR OUR WORLD.

WWW.THERANPRESS.ORG

This book was designed and produced by Silver Goat Media, LLC. Fargo, ND U.S.A. www.silvergoatmedia.com   SGM, the SGM goat, Theran Press, and the Theran theta are trademarks of Silver Goat Media, LLC.

Cover design & typeset by Jonathan Rutter © 2024 SGM

ISBN-13: 978-1-944296-26-1

A portion of the annual proceeds from the sale of this book is donated to The Rourke Art Gallery + Museum. www.therourke.org

MEN OF
GOD
MEN OF
WAR

NATHAN A. SMITH
STEPHEN A. SMITH

THERAN PRESS

To the few, to the fallen, and to our family.

.

CONTENTS

Part III — The Places I Have Been

ACKNOWLEDGMENTS

This story fluttered amorphously for twenty years in private scribbled notes from Iraq, raw journal entries, and hesitant blog posts, until friends and family convinced us it was worth telling. The narrative, dealing as it does with our experiences, displays the influence of hundreds who impacted our lives but whom we regretfully cannot include in a formal list of thanks. To those many generous and kind souls, we are grateful.

A smaller group who helped shape the finished work should be acknowledged here. To the friends and family who critiqued early drafts, you honored us with your time at a messy stage and made this manuscript better: Brian Boggs, Kristin Boggs, Ben Crenshaw, Christine Reilly Smith, Carol Smith, Christine Smith, Doug Smith, Rob Wolfe, Tom Wright, and Jordan Zandi. Sandi Glahn, thank you for your mentorship and zealously eliminating passive verbs. Thank you, Mark J. Lindquist, for the connection while you were volunteering in Ukraine. Peter Schultz, Cady Rutter, and the team at Theran: you brought boundless enthusiasm to this project, tightened the narrative, and gave us the gift of done.

This book grapples with themes of war, loss, and spiritual abuse. Yet, in our view, it is neither a dark book nor a hopeless one. The pain and challenges we faced provided the scaffolding upon which rose remarkable displays of love and generosity. Dr. Lane Kaplan, his wife, Joy, and children, Elton, Brandi, Beth, Josh, Amy, and Zak, opened their home and hearts to Nate during his last two years of high school when he had nowhere else to turn. Dawn and Ted Weber, and Ray and Sandy Lambert, welcomed Nate in Maine during breaks from school and military service and helped navigate important milestones, such as applying to colleges and scholarships, and buying a car. Dr. Mike Marsh, his wife, Jane, and their children, Drew, Joel, Seth, and Lydia, provided a refuge on their lovely farm in the Shenandoah Valley during weekends away from Virginia Military Institute (VMI) and Marine infantry training. John Bardis created and staffed Hire Heroes USA—among his many other astonishing philanthropic, business, and public service endeavors—the nation's most successful veteran employment program; HH USA provided Nate with a continuing purpose and profession when he left the Marines in 2010. To date, Hire Heroes USA has helped more than seventy-five thousand veterans and military spouses find new careers.

Any list of men who pushed Nate to be a better officer must necessarily remain incomplete. Yet, the following superb Marine leaders deserve special mention (ranks are accurate as of the time that Nate served with these men and may not reflect final career attainment): Lt. Col. Russell Rivers and Capt. Travis Homiak at VMI; Capt. Jeff Dyal at the Infantry Officer Course; Capt. Chris Ieva, Chief Warrant Officer 2 Robert Sipe, and Maj. Scott Leonard in Third Battalion Second Marines; and Lt. Col. Russell Hittinger at the Marine Corps Security Force Battalion–Bangor. Platoon sergeants provide mentorship and guidance to young officers from the perspective of enlisted Marines and ensure the welfare of the platoon; Nate's outstanding platoon sergeants included S.Sgt. Jeremy Martinez, S.Sgt. Tim Hanson, S.Sgt. Keith Thomas, Sgt. Wayne Odonnell, and Gy.Sgt. Darren Finney. Fellow platoon commanders provided camaraderie and healthy competition, most notably Marc Bullock, Joe Clemmey, Brian Stann, Charlie Walker, and Chris Doggett. Lance Corporal Brandon Puhlman and Sergeant Rajendra Singh remain some of the bravest men Nate has ever met. Capt. Ryan Kestle, Her Majesty's Royal Marines, was a remarkably gifted officer, athlete, and a good friend who provided one of the few bright spots during Nate's "time in the wilderness" while stationed in Washington. The Marines and sailors of Third Battalion Second Marines were magnificent during combat tours in Iraq in 2005, 2006, and 2007. Their courage, endurance, and selflessness were matched by supporting units and attachments. Warriors all.

To Mom, Dad, and Christine, we deeply love you. To Oliver, Josiah, Victoria, James, and Theodore, we wrote this so that someday you would understand. And to Christine and Teresa, thank you for being our partners in love and healing.

This narrative reflects the authors' recollections of experiences over time. The names and characteristics of some individuals have been changed to respect their privacy, and some dialogue has been recreated.

Men of god and men of war have strange affinities.

Cormac McCarthy, *Blood Meridian*

PREFACE

The world is full of men flung out on the far side of suffering, men who look back through a dark glass at regret, redemption, and the boys they once had been.

Our stories are no different, though we are twins.

One of us learned his lessons through war. The other learned his lessons through a twisted faith. Neither of these paths makes us exceptional. Like all men, we have loved, and we have hated. Like all men, we have suffered, and we have caused suffering. And, like all men, we have each been loyal to a nightmare of our own choosing.

Raised with the same values and observing the world with similar eyes, we were torn apart by dissimilar choices and hurled into parallel existences. Now, when each of us looks at his brother, we see the man who we each might have been staring back at us like a mirror.

This is our story.

PROLOGUE

Steve | 9 November 2006 | Cumberland, Maine

Wes sat stiffly by the window in the blue-and-white fabric armchair—my father's chair—and opened his Bible.

Pastor Wes never came just to visit. When he entered our house, he came like a prophet under compulsion, dark and brooding, the air growing thick like a summer thunderstorm.

Sometimes, Wes called before he came. The phone would jangle, my mother or father would answer, and then I'd hear their voices tighten with fake enthusiasm when they realized who it was. "Why, hello, Wes! Yes, of course, you can come over! Yes, now is convenient. You'll be here in five minutes? Very well. Yes, Steve is here. Yes, we'll let him know. Yes, yes, yes."

I don't recall us ever saying "no" to Wes.

Other times, the only warning Wes gave was the glide of his pale blue Buick into our dirt driveway, a turn in the barnyard, and the muffled slam of his car door. I'd watch him climb our porch steps, stern and erect, Bible wedged beneath his arm.

There's a scene in *The Pianist* in which the Gestapo comes at night for a family of Jews. When the Nazis arrive, Władysław Szpilman, the naive musician who has always blindly trusted human nature, looks confused. It is Henryk, his pragmatic brother, who senses danger at the first whine of the sedan, hissing to his family, "The lights! Turn off the lights!"

But in my family, there was no one to turn off the lights. We had cast out our Henryk—my brother, Nate—nine years before.

And yet, ironically, it was the crumbs of Nate's presence in our house that Wes came to judge.

Wes had discovered that my aunt had passed along some of Nate's emails from Iraq. Nate had written to other family members during his second deployment and my aunt thought that we'd like to follow his life from a distance. Not to support him, of course, just to keep informed. She thought we'd want to know.

Her offer thrilled me, although when my parents told me I wore a mask of indifference. I sat in my room for hours reading and re-reading Nate's notes, hearing his voice, feeling the dirt on his hands, the heft of his rifle. A lieutenant leading a platoon of Marines, Nate wrote of combat operations in Al Anbar Province. He spoke of tan ladybugs, forward operating bases, and cloth-blackening heat.

My mother—unbelievably—had also printed off a picture of my brother in his dress blue uniform, with his tan face grinning, white gloves held crisply in hand, medals gleaming. Behind him, the sun shone bright on green grass. Mom framed the picture and put it on top of the piano with the other family photos. She did it, she said, so she could remember to pray.

Unpardonable.

Now, Wes stared at us coldly, his Bible in his lap, and I realized that our sins were scarlet and that only blood could wash them away.

Nate | October 2008 | Naval Base Kitsap-Bangor, Washington

I remembered MATADOR today.

Not the whole operation, but bits and pieces, the sound and the fury.

It seemed incongruous to recall violent death in the stinking heat here in this cool, peaceful place. The Pacific Northwest, hollow with immense distance and towering heights, often seems capable of swallowing up the present and muffling the past. It appeared that way as I drove to check the base perimeter. To my right, the early morning sun flashed brilliantly through cedars and pines before illuminating glowing patches of icy diamonds on the forest floor. Autumn's first hoarfrost bristled like the bright lances of a drunken legion, then winked into submissive droplets on ochre stalks.

The road angled down a draw as it fell toward the water. Across the Hood Canal, a great leaping expanse of the Olympic Mountains sparkled with a dusting of fresh snow. It was a beautiful morning, so sharp and clear that the ridgelines seemed to cut the sky.

I slowed to turn near an industrial building when a solitary fighting position caught my eye. Sandbags were neatly pressed and stacked, but the position lacked a proper firing point. It was the work of Marines who had never been to combat and had carried out a task without understanding the "why." An amateur mistake, but one that would need correcting. I mentally added it to my list of tasks for the day.

I'm tired, I thought to myself. The constant need to supervise Marines; to correct the same mistake dozens, hundreds of times; to subordinate personal wants, physical needs, and comfort-based decisions to the requirement of "Setting the Example." These were the things that wore on me, exhausted me more than bad chow or lack of sleep. The constant burden of a leader who cared.

And I hated it.

But I couldn't stop. Bouts of harsh self-criticism paired with morose reflection weren't unusual for me. I hooked two gloved fingers into my throat protector and pulled my flak jacket away from chafed skin. *Were there childhood antecedents for this kind of disorder?*

"Shouldn't be driving the perimeter alone," I muttered to the slick blacktop. I stopped amid slimy potholes and fallen leaves. Then I turned onto a gloomy forest trail. Tires hissed against wet gravel as I drove up a steep hill choked with blackberry thickets and ancient trees.

Abruptly, the path leveled, the underbrush vanished, and the trees rose in a kind of huge, vaulted cathedral. Light filtered through leafy crowns and suffused the path with the green glow of ethereal stained glass. Rising above, great branches bearded with moss swept up and arched down, delicately dropping emerald tears onto a carpet of decaying leaves.

I slowed to a crawl. Every time I entered this hushed place, I was reminded of Stephen Crane's *The Red Badge of Courage*: Henry Fleming alone, separated from his unit, confronting a moldering corpse in an eerie forest chapel. The sense of otherworldly presence was so intense that I shivered and my eyes smarted. The feeling passed as quickly as it had come, leaving in its wake a kind of quivering sadness and regret.

I was alone—and not.

In the sepulchral quiet of the forest, faint echoes of war stirred, gained composition, and—in a rush of stark clarity—threw themselves before my eyes. Swallowing against the pain, I remembered.

PART I
AS SPARKS FLY UPWARD

Man is born unto trouble, as the sparks fly upward.

Job 5:7, KJV

They were men like other young men, unknown to themselves. So much that lay within them they were now traveling to meet.

Richard Flanagan, *The Narrow Road to the Deep North*

CHAPTER 1
The River

Steve | The 1980s | Eddington, Maine

My grandparents lived in a small, white house on the Eddington Bend where the Penobscot River shallows out, half a mile below the Veazie hydroelectric dam, and three miles north of the Maine river cities of Bangor and Brewer.

Water rolled over the dam's face in brown and yellow sheets, filling the air with a constant, elemental rumble. On midsummer evenings, the river seemed black against the far bank, which rose tangled and steep to a fringe of pines beneath a yellow sky. In the middle, deep water flowed, and the setting sun spun a sheet of wet gold all splattered with jewels. Across the current, circles bloomed as Atlantic salmon rose to suck down midges and damselflies bobbing like drunken crop dusters over endless acres of mercury. Following the feed, fly fishermen from the Eddington Salmon Club worked the shallows in their waders, torsos floating in silver pools, then in ink.

Our family often made the two-hour trip north from Cumberland to Eddington. In summer, Nate and I would spend hours roaming the river's hardscrabble banks. We skipped stones, built miniature dams in the puffy froth tossed up between boulders, and looked for arrowheads, gouges, plummets, and spear tips. Upstream from my grandparents' house stood Indian Island where the last remnants of the once mighty Penobscot Nation lived. We visited one August in my grandfather's beat-up Ford. I remember feeling disappointed to see wood-frame houses and children playing soccer in clothes like mine. I had hoped for teepees and perhaps a scalp or two.

Back along my grandparents' riverbank, I pocketed a nine-inch jag of flint, convinced that it was an Indian spearhead. For decades it sat on my bookshelf, a prize representing what I supposed was my own connection to an ancient race. My grandfather didn't have the heart to tell me it was only the river's rough counterfeit. Instead, he looked it over with a critical eye, fingered its sharp edges, then handed it back and said kindly, "Son of a gun, if that don't look like a spearhead."

At night, the deep sigh of the river sang us to sleep as it clattered over the falls and shouldered past the few boulders bold enough to stand against it. In the cool dark, through our upstairs window, I heard the throbbing rush of the water like the flow of distant traffic, endless and eternal. Untangling from hot summer sheets, I locked my hands behind my head and gazed up at the cream-colored ceiling, tracing World War II destroyers or Abenaki warriors with spears. I wanted to believe that I was courageous, and that someday I'd be a hero. Then I'd fall asleep feeling happy and brave.

It always shamed me when I woke from my nightmares having wet myself, calling for my mother.

———

My grandmother ruled a pleasant kingdom. It was inviting to children but deadly for gophers. Perhaps it was her bellicose English heritage? Streaks of auburn still burned like wildfire through her cream-colored curls. We called her Nana. She'd raised four children and served as a registered nurse before retirement.

One year, gophers got into Nana's cabbage.

She talked of it at lunchtime, clucking her tongue, *tsk-tsk*, in a faintly sing-song lilt: "Those gophers better watch out or I'll send my Donny after 'em with a rifle. Don't want 'em eating any more of my good cabbage. I've worked too hard for it, Stephen de-ah." She always turned "dear" into two syllables.

Later that afternoon, I saw a groundhog rooting in Nana's broccoli, its shiny back shuddering with joy. I dutifully reported the incursion. She rushed to the kitchen window, pulled back the yellow curtain, and shouted: "Donny! There's a gopher in my garden!"

My grandfather—we called him Gray—was sitting in his leather armchair, watching Tom Brokaw report the Iran-Iraq War. Without a word he got up, climbed the stairs, and trudged back with his .22 rifle. He stepped out the front door. Nate and I rushed after him, trembling with fear and ecstasy. I'd never seen anything shot before. Not in real life.

Gray stood beside the screen door on the front stoop. The gopher continued to forage just fifty feet away, his brown sides full of jelly. Gray raised the rifle and clicked off the safety. I held my breath. In that moment, the groundhog turned his head and looked directly at us, sprigs of broccoli sprouting from the sides of his mouth. Gray's finger tightened on the trigger. My heart stopped.

I'm not sure what I expected. An explosion of blood like a popping balloon, I guess. Instead, there was a sharp report, a blur of movement, and then nothing. Nothing at all. Gray clicked the safety and lowered the rifle.

4

"Son of a gun!" He shook his head. "I think I nicked him." He shouldered the rifle and started across to the garden. I noticed he was still wearing his tan, leather house slippers. We shadowed him, bubbling with excitement. I wanted to see gore, dead bodies, trophies.

"Looks like you missed him, Donny," Nana called through the window. "I was watching the whole time. Think he got clean away. Oh! My poor broccoli!"

Gray didn't answer. He just kept poking around the broccoli tops and brains of pale cauliflower until he found a few spots of blood. I was surprised how small they seemed. They didn't look like death. We followed the splatters out of the garden, across the abandoned lot next door, and into a hole dug beside the foundation of a rotting house.

"Well." Gray shouldered his rifle. "Let's hope the son of a gun bleeds to death."

But we never knew for sure.

It was an uneasy introduction to killing.

CHAPTER 2
The Hardest School

Nate | August 1999 | Lexington, Virginia

Boyhood evaporated in a Shenandoah afternoon.

With my eyes fixed forward and my flexed elbows spattering sweat against the faded concrete, I squinted at the "Rat Bible" held three inches from my face and yelled hoarsely along with my fellow rats: "It is the mission of the Virginia Military Institute to produce educated and honorable men and women, prepared for the varied work of civil life, imbued with love of learning, confident in the functions and attitudes of leadership!" Joined by 435 identically shorn and shouting unfortunates, I memorized VMI's mission and its Honor Code within minutes of our Hell Week inauguration as the lowest form of life in barracks. Hence "rats." Pillars of military, academic, and athletic instruction eventually rose from that moral foundation to bestow balance to our cadetship. But in that first, endless afternoon, the Institute's purpose seemed distilled into sweat, screams, and pain.

That night, long after "Taps" etched its mournful melody into the headstone of another day, I slumped onto a prison-made cot and choked back the burning in my throat. Our stifling room stank of unwashed bodies and new-issue clothing. Against orders, someone had thrown open a tall window in the back. I gazed longingly at Lexington's lights like beacons of hope in a terrible, new world. While I reckoned the direction home, one roommate said out loud what we were all thinking:

"What the fuck did we just get ourselves into?"

The sentiment lingered in the dark.

The Rat Line was an unforgiving, draconian system designed to wring out individualism and compel proper behavior in our Corps of Cadets. The Institute was welcomed by Lexington's scandalized citizens when it was founded in 1839 to reform carousing guards at the state arsenal, which overlooked a lazy bend in the Maury River. By the time Rat Nathan Smith was straining* his way through barracks, 160 years of accrued military discipline had shaped the VMI experience.

Discipline is just an idea if divorced from standards, so the VMI commandant's office distributed a thick sheaf of regulations to every room in barracks at the start of each school year. "The Blue Book"—imaginatively nicknamed for the color of its binder—was nearly a hundred pages of cause and effect, with penalties escalating in accordance with the grievousness of each transgression.

Appear at morning formation with scuffed shoes and brown brass? A paltry three demerits. Possession of intoxicating spirits in barracks? That called for the most severe penalty, the "Number One:" four months of room confinement and sixty hour-long penalty tours marching tediously with shouldered rifle in front of barracks, much to the delight of photo-snapping tourists. Cadets suffering under this penalty sauntered around the stoops sporting "#1" in duct tape on frayed bathrobes, enjoying their moment as minor revolutionaries.

Naturally, it was impossible to observe every rule, all of the time. No one—not even the saintly George C. Marshall, Class of 1901 and future head of the US Army in World War II—had escaped penalty free from "Mother I." The impossible system had birthed a timeless cat-and-mouse culture in which malefactors dodged the commandant's staff and the cadet officer of the day, who walked the halls, honor-bound to record every infraction. (A ring of blunted keys always jangled warning to us rats.)

VMI's aspirations were noble and good. But the Institute's reality was all too often dominated by a petty despotism of silly rules enforced on cadets by officers who should've known better.

Childhood idealism had foundered during the ten years I'd spent in a religious cult before fleeing my family as a junior in high school. My idealism returned once I fixated on the military as my path to meaning. But as my rat year dragged on, first with brown leaves swirling on the parade ground and then with the midwinter Dark Ages settling on barracks like a malevolent beast, my faith in VMI as an instrument to attain the heights of human glory crashed into the realities of its flawed system, then fizzled into bitterness.

Nevertheless, I remained focused and disciplined. A rat's existence was governed by an economy of pain. For six months, we lived under a tyranny of kicked-in doors and shouting gray shadows. Learning that a reputation can be made in minutes by tolerating hardship and disguising discomfort or disgust beneath a

---

*   "Straining" is a uniquely unpleasant form of exaggerated military posture where the chin is driven down to the chest and then pushed back against the throat, shoulders are thrust back to a point where the blades nearly touch, and arms are pressed rigidly against the body with thumbs tracing trouser seams. It is a painful and humiliating position endured by Rats in barracks for their first six months as cadets.

mask of indifference, I excelled.

My talent for subordinating my own personality to necessity was rewarded with selection as a cadre corporal for my Third Class, or sophomore, year. The transition wasn't difficult. I led by example, asking others nothing more than to meet my own high standards. Recalling respected cadre from my own Rat Line, I leavened instruction with humor, encouragement, and a measure of grace.

Quite unexpectedly, I was recognized at a springtime awards ceremony with the VMI Third Class Leadership Award. Voted by upperclassmen, peers, and the rats themselves, the award was the first time in my life I'd been marked as superior for simply being myself.

Second Class year introduced new challenges. I sewed on the stripes of a cadet first sergeant. My responsibilities included dealing tactfully with upperclassmen whose interests were more broadly civilian rather than military. I also watched with growing antipathy as the First Class struggled against the VMI administration to defend the integrity of the class system and Honor Court, a struggle that culminated in an unfortunately timed revolt shortly after the terrorist attacks of September 2001. The results were crushing. Respected members of the Honor Court and regimental system were demoted or expelled from the Institute.

It was all very disappointing. VMI couldn't function without cadet regimental and class systems, yet I observed the administration curtail those systems by targeting cadet leaders with threats, punishment, and expulsion. It seemed fiendish to entrust responsibility to a few outstanding cadets and then punish those same cadets for loyalty to classmates and subordinates.

Following 9/11—with smoke still curling from the rubble of the World Trade Center, days vibrating with tense excitement—it became apparent that the leaders I respected most at VMI were not part of the administration at all.

They were Marines.

So, when a Marine captain in VMI's Naval ROTC unit advised me to drop my four-year Navy scholarship for a Marine scholarship and go to war as "one of us," I mulled over the choice for a single night, then said yes. Six weeks at Marine Corps Officer Candidate School (OCS) in Quantico, Virginia followed in the summer of 2002. Upon completion of OCS, I returned to VMI for my First Class year and assumed the position of cadet captain, leading one of ten companies in the Corps of Cadets. It was, in my estimation, the best way to buffer one tenth of the school from the worst excesses of the VMI administration.

———

April 2003 | Lexington, Virginia

"You *knew* you were going to get caught! You *had* to have known!" The assistant commandant of cadets reacted to my explanation with a mix of indignation and incredulity, as if I'd just affirmed that I hated America or that I'd invented the snow cone.

Standing stiffly in his bleached office, a starched collar cutting into the razor burn of my afternoon shave, I felt sweat pool along my spine. Not once during my cadetship had I deviated from the Honor Code's strictures, which, among other things, meant that I hadn't told a lie in four years. Maligning my integrity felt like a punch in the throat.

I was furious.

"Sir," I began hotly. He cut me off with a wave of his hand.

"Got it," he patronized. "You inspected some of the younger cadets' packs at military duty and found they lacked waterproofing material and other required gear for the upcoming Marine FTX (field training exercise). You decided to leave Post to purchase the supplies, then eat dinner in town because you had missed supper roll call. So . . . ."

He continued, but I zoned out, falling unconsciously into a passive coping technique that I had learned in the cult as a kid. It seemed better to suppress emotions than to have them triggered by naked authoritarianism. I stared past the colonel's hunched shoulders to the bookshelf behind his desk. *Once an Eagle*. *About Face*. *We Were Soldiers Once... and Young*. He had all the right books. I wondered idly if he'd actually read them or just kept them for appearance.

" . . . and where the major saw you when he drove by. On a *Wednesday* night! When do you ever have GP (general permit) on a *Wednesday* night? Never!" The colonel leaned back triumphantly, surveying the effect of his devastating logic.

"Sir." I swallowed my anger. "I've never availed myself of GP during the week; there was always too much to do. So, I never paid attention to the exact rules. I assumed," wincing inside, knowing this would inspire further attack, but saying it anyway because it was true, "that because I was taking care of junior cadets and not seeking personal gain, that this wouldn't be an issue."

"Not an issue! Cadet Smith, are you trying to tell me that you've been at VMI for *four* years, attained the rank of cadet captain, and are unfamiliar with the rules for general permit off Post?"

Yes, that's exactly what I'm telling you.

I'd so dedicated myself to the Institute, and to my leadership responsibilities, that I'd never had occasion to learn the rules that governed off-Post authorization during the week. It had simply never come up. Should I have familiarized myself with the rules prior to leaving Post the night before? Yes. I accepted the fact that ignorance was no excuse. But this situation was so clearly a result of a senior cadet taking care of junior ones that I hoped the assistant commandant would apply judgment to the situation based on my proven character and performance over the years. Perhaps he would just give me a slap on the wrist? What was the point of a mauling less than six weeks before graduation?

The colonel peered menacingly over the penalty chit in his hands. Then, abruptly: "I don't buy it." He dropped the sheet, grabbed a pen, and scribbled across the bottom. "Number Five. Minus one penalty tour, which means that you may keep your rank."

I choked down a laugh. The *rank* was why I was here. Because I cared. Because I wanted to shield young cadets from the mindless enforcement of arbitrary rules.

Keep my rank?

I *wanted* to lose it.

"Dismissed."

"Dismissed. Aye, sir." The unauthorized naval terminology was as good as a curse. I saluted, executed a perfect about face, and strode out.

Leaving the colonel's office—and later, leaving the mustard-colored walls of VMI for good after graduation—I felt nothing but bitterness for an administration that had required sacrifice and loyalty without returning either. Paradoxically, the Institute inculcated an unshakeable sense of honor, gave me a score of brothers to replace the one I'd lost, and prepared me in a hundred ways to face the hardships to come.

CHAPTER 3
The Distant Sound of Guns

Steve | The 1980s | Eddington, Maine

We believed that my grandfather was great for no other reasons than that he'd fought in World War II and he talked about war in the Pacific like other people talked about a day at work. For this, we idolized him.

Around us, symbols of war littered the Down East Maine landscape. Every small town owned its faded memorial to fathers and brothers fallen on the field of honor. The moss-bearded Civil War statues drew Nate and me close to their gray-green chests, then thumped us with a sense of gravitas and our own melancholic need to serve a righteous Cause. We believed.

It was no wonder, then, that Nate and I sat slack-jawed at our grandfather's feet as he told stories about World War II, watching the blurred eagle tattoo on his left bicep flap its wings against a tan-and-speckled sky. *A man who has a tattoo like that has been somewhere,* I thought. He'd done something with his life. Someday, I wanted to sit in a chair with tattoos on my arms and tell brave stories to my own grandchildren.

Gray was an anti-aircraft gunner on a Landing Ship, Tank (LST). His stories came naturally, often after we'd watched segments of *Victory at Sea* in the living room. Sitting on Nana and Gray's green couch, there was something immensely reassuring about seeing the events of World War II play themselves out against a known ending and a carefully composed score. Listening to Leonard Graves and his apple-pie narration describing "waves of GIs advancing up the beach," or "the most formidable armada ever gathered in the history of mankind," gave me a manic sense of invincibility. Hollywood washed out the complexities of war. There was carnage, to be sure, but the floating bodies of Marines at Tarawa or Iwo Jima somehow made sense in the context of our greater victory.

At seventeen, my grandfather lied about his age and enlisted in the navy—literally jumping out a school window to run to the recruiter's office so he wouldn't miss the war. His older brother Teddy had already signed up. Gray shipped out for the Pacific in the spring of 1945. He was assigned to *LST-951*, a casualty evacuation control ship, for the upcoming invasion of Okinawa. He told us stories about diving off the fantail into the warm Pacific at Tulagi harbor in the Solomon Islands, shooting barrels floating in the surf, and stealing ice cream makers for the ship with his buddies. He talked about sunlight glittering on water, streams of phosphorescence in the night, and lazy dinners of pork and beans. He talked about "crossing the line" and turning from a Pollywog into a Shellback. He talked about the camaraderie of men on a ship at war.

Gray made combat sound glamorous. He shared how his vessel was converted into a hospital ship that evacuated hundreds of Marine casualties from the beaches of Okinawa. Sailors played cards with wounded Marines and offered cigarettes to men too far gone to lift a hand. Gray saw other ships cut in two by kamikazes, but he said the ships wallowed on, still afloat. When the fleet was hit by a huge typhoon, Gray spoke of seas as high as skyscrapers crashing over decks, huge pieces of metal twisted like Tinkertoys by the storm.

But even those perilous stories carried the sanitized chivalry of a twentieth-century Round Table. Like tilting knights encased in steel who fought but never bled, Gray's ships staggered but never sank. Tracers stitched into planes that splashed into the sea, but no pilots ever died. Marines formed an olive-and-red patchwork of broken bodies on the deck, but no one ever groaned. There was a cool cleanness about everything, a neat texture, a gauzy distance that made combat seem brave, bloodless, and mythical. World War II, Nate and I gathered, had been the time of Gray's life.

Every story made me and Nate want to enlist. Every tale was a rung on a ladder that led us to an idea of war as the greatest adventure a boy could ever want. War in the Pacific, we thought, was like a long summer vacation punctuated by bits of expert gunnery and occasional ice cream sandwiches.

I never stopped to consider why Gray filled garbage bags full of beer cans, or why he started drinking each day before lunch.

———

In Eddington, at my grandparents' house, day broke early behind the peach-colored curtains in the bedroom I shared with Nate. In the summer, Gray would wake at sunrise and raise the American flag at the nursing home up the street. He often woke Nate and me to help him. We bumbled out of bed, rubbing our eyes, blinking into the bright summer dawn. After walking fifty yards along the shoulder of Route 9 to Riverview Retirement Home, we fixed the flag to its stanchions and saluted as Gray hauled the Stars and Stripes up the pole. There were no bugles or cheering crowds, but it was a lesson that set in our souls like cement.

Back home, Nate and I ate cereal or toast and eggs at the breakfast table, but Gray always—always—had a single grapefruit while he read the morning paper that was splayed out on the table. He ate grapefruit because he'd lost all his teeth from scurvy during the war. Every night, he put his dentures in a clear plastic box on the sink in the bathroom, and he didn't put them back in until after he'd had breakfast. Then he'd smoke a cigarette. I loved the burnt coffee smell of his smoke; it permeated the house like a blue memory. Ever since, whenever I smell a Marlboro, I think of my grandfather and his morning grapefruit.

On rare days, Ronnie joined us to raise the flag at the retirement home. He lived in a trailer full of dogs between my grandparents' house and Riverview. He seemed like an old man, but he was probably less than forty. He had tired eyes, carried extra weight, wore whiskers, and walked with a limp. He was the right age for Vietnam. I imagined that he had been shot. I built up an elaborate narrative surrounding his wound and its heroic circumstances.

But I felt uncomfortable around Ronnie. He was quiet and looked sad and there was something about that limp. I thought he must be embarrassed, too, because he almost never looked at me. Sometimes I'd sneak a glance at him out of the corner of my eye. One time, he caught me looking and I blushed and pretended I was stretching my neck until I felt like a fool.

One morning, we raised the flag with Ronnie. As we saluted, I looked at him full-on and saw tears in his eyes. I don't think I'd ever seen a grown man cry. My father hadn't even cried when his mother died. Afterward, in Nana's sun-drenched kitchen, I poured a bowl of Fruit Loops and asked Gray why Ronnie limped. I waited for a jungle story full of explosions. Gray dug a spoon into his grapefruit, chewed for a minute, then said quietly, "Ronnie got polio, Stephen, same as your mum."

CHAPTER 4

Always on the Alert

Nate | June 2003 | Quantico, Virginia

After graduating from VMI, I reported to Quantico for six months of instruction with Delta Company in Basic Officer Course 04-03. At The Basic School (TBS), all new Marine officers undergo an intensive regimen of academic coursework, physical conditioning, land navigation, and infantry-focused field exercises that nominally prepare them to lead a Marine rifle platoon in combat.

Only thirty-three out of two hundred and twenty lieutenants in our training company would designate as infantry officers, but the corps' mantra of "Every Marine a Rifleman" means every Marine officer must prepare for battlefield leadership. And for good reason: History is littered with examples of support troops and officers called up into provisional rifle platoons when front line units failed to turn back the enemy. Beyond that, infantry is the defining element—really, the ethos—of the Marine Corps.

Our instructors were captains just returned from the war, which made their word gospel. One of their favorite tricks was to poll a classroom of eager lieutenants about our desired MOS (military occupational specialty)—the job we'd be assigned in the Operating Forces upon graduation. A grinning captain conducted the first such poll during our initial week of training.

"How many of you want to be infantry?" he asked, then chortled at the sea of raised hands that followed. Perhaps two-thirds of the class was eager to experience the corps' raison d'etre.

"Motivating," he said sagely. "But let's see how many still want it after First FEX (field exercise)."

He was right.

Fewer and fewer hands went up for infantry after grueling road marches or long field exercises in prostrating heat or desiccating cold. Officers who couldn't hack sleepless nights on the ground, or who struggled to maneuver through the five-mile endurance course, or who shot poorly at the rifle range, gradually discovered appreciable benefits of careers in air supply or logistics.

As summer gave way to autumn, student lieutenants closely followed the news from Iraq. In the final weeks before our career designation and graduation, casualty lists from the Ramadan offensive in the *Marine Corps Times* dampened our youthful exuberance.

Standing out from rows of enlisted soldiers—the army was taking nearly all the casualties in late 2003—were occasional portraits of lieutenants who had died in places with exotic names like Ninawa, Khaldiyah, and Fallujah. Some of the dead were less than a year out of similar seats at Infantry Officer Basic Course. Under the clean, fluorescent lights of our bloodless classrooms, their haunting images seemed unreal.

———

My raised hand never faltered during the captains' recurring polls. Infantry was all I wanted to do in the Marines. While I disliked dusty road marches and frozen mornings as much as the next lieutenant, I viewed deviation from the infantry as a personal defeat, an acknowledgment that I wasn't man enough to face the corps' hardest challenge. Despite the sweat, pain, and loss, I was fully committed to the infantry.

And I got it.

Other lieutenants—big, strong men—wept on assignment day when they were passed over for infantry and assigned to motor transportation or communications jobs. Secretly, I counted my blessings and then, with nothing but a piece of paper to separate me from my classmates, the creeping warmth of superiority blossomed in my heart. It was a shameful mark of immaturity, but I was young. It would be winnowed from me in a future threshing.

I graduated from TBS in December. Scout Sniper Employment Course followed in January, with its ghillie suits, field sketches, and six-hour, skull-dragging stalks through frozen briars to set up a single, perfect shot. Then it was on to eleven weeks at the storied Infantry Officer Course (IOC), which toughened me personally, sharpened me professionally, and prepared me for a humid day in July when I stepped in front of a rifle platoon in Third Battalion Second Marines (3/2) at Camp Lejeune, North Carolina.

———

In 2004, a burgeoning insurgency exploded in Al Anbar Province, Iraq. Scores of Marines died in chaotic urban brawls in Ramadi and Fallujah. In response to new enemy tactics, our pre-deployment training emphasized aggressive counter-insurgency operations and urban combat. By the time I returned to Maine in December for holiday leave, I carried with me an infantry officer's confidence, the weight of responsibility for dozens of lives, and a trained directness that bordered on belligerence. My tolerance for bullshit was at an all-time low.

So, when I picked up Grampie—my paternal grandfather—from his small house on Wilson Street and took him to a post-holiday lunch at his favorite restaurant in Brewer, a plaintive exchange toward the end of our meal set like molten steel in my heart.

"Your father returned the Christmas card that I sent him. Just like the birthday card. Carol returned hers. Your brother and Christine too." My grandfather was a strong man, not prone to much emotional display beyond some occasional, gruff enthusiasm. Now, his thick fingers twisted a napkin against the table and his eyes glistened with pain.

"Doug said that they couldn't accept anything from me until I acknowledged my sin of supporting you at your graduation," Grampie continued.

I was silent for a moment. I'd been surprised and delighted to see Grampie among the aunts and uncles who'd come from New England to attend my Marine commissioning and VMI graduation the previous year. It was the only time I'd received visitors during my cadetship, not because my loved ones didn't care but because it had never occurred to me to ask anyone to visit. I suppose I felt a need to prove that I could manage it all on my own. I hadn't seen my grandfather in six years. His powerful embrace and beaming pride during those few days in Lexington restored a part of me that I hadn't realized was lost.

"I'm sorry, Grampie," I finally said. "They shouldn't have done that. Their issue should be with me, not you."

After paying the tab and dropping Grampie back home, I drove in silence under a leaden sky. With a two-hour drive ahead, I suddenly made my decision.

I called home.

"Hello?" The voice was soft and melodic, warm hospitality extended to the world at large.

"Hi Mom, this is Nate."

"Oh. Hi, Nathan." The voice that had lullabied me to sleep fell into a deep sigh of disappointment and pain. I'd known it would be this way and had steeled myself to push through a bit of awkward small talk before my dad came on the line. When he did, his voice was the same as ever, edged with a firmness that followed from knowing he was right.

I cut to the chase.

"Dad, I just got done seeing Grampie. He told me how you cut him off after he went to my graduation." I ignored my father's attempt to interject. "It's wrong, Dad. It's unjust, and it dishonors him in a way that's totally hypocritical given the verses that you quoted to me in the past about honoring your father and mother. I'm a Marine. I've got broad shoulders. I can handle anything. But Grampie is a lonely old man. He didn't take sides when he went to my graduation; he was just being kind."

I didn't expect to achieve a positive result with my call and therefore wasn't surprised when the conversation teetered back and forth on the brink of civility and righteous anger. After a few strained minutes, Dad attempted a redemptive effort.

"Your Aunt Sally said you're scheduled to deploy to Iraq this winter. We'd like to talk with you before you go."

"We *are* talking." I was livid, fighting back the furies that rose whenever I confronted injustice.

"I mean in person. At our house. Maybe you could stop by when you get back to Cumberland," Dad responded. "We'd like to see you before you go."

The invitation was unexpected, but also incongruous. I didn't understand what was to be gained by such a meeting.

"Well, have you changed your view of me?" I asked.

There was a brief pause before Dad answered with calm assurance. "No, but—"

"Then we have nothing to talk about."

"I'm sorry that's the way you feel, Nathan."

"That's the way it is. Goodbye, Dad."

April 2005 | Haqlaniyah, Al Anbar Province, Iraq

In late February 2005, I found myself flung out to the western edge of Al Anbar, dropping gear with other members of Kilo Company 3/2 in an old train station at Al Qa'im. The next seven months would painfully reshape my sense of infantry superiority into a profound respect for all elements of the Marine Air-Ground Task Force.

At first, during those final weeks of the desert winter, we didn't do much, conducting an odd patrol here or route reconnaissance there to get a feel for our area of operations (AO). But as daytime temperatures notched higher, so did enemy activity. In April, our company journeyed east to embark on a six-day operation in the palm groves and dusty streets of Bani Dahir, a small town overlooking a pontoon bridge on the Euphrates River just south of the Hadithah Dam. Our mission was to block insurgent movement on the bridge and along the western river road, in support of clearing operations by a Marine Reserve battalion to the north.

At twenty-four years old I commanded fifty-five Marines, a squad of Iraqi Recon soldiers, and four amphibious assault vehicles (AAVs). Our brilliant and aggressive company commander had promised the regiment a nearly impossible series of tactical accomplishments, borne on the backs of young men who, by the evening of the second day, were dropping from exhaustion.

As the sun dipped behind embankments to the west, I decided to "go firm" with most of my men in a large house on the east side of town. To prevent insurgents from infiltrating our position through unobserved avenues of approach—and to provide overwatch for an Abrams tank parked menacingly in the street as a roadblock—I established several two-man security positions in the gardens and on a rooftop ringing our base. The tank had been struck by a rocket-propelled grenade (RPG) from a wadi the day before; I was determined not to let it happen again.

After completing security arrangements, I crawled beneath a thick Korean blanket on the roof of the firm base, leaned against my body-armor pillow, and prepared to doze off until it was my turn to man the radio. There was no moon; the town's electricity had been knocked out by an IED blast on the previous day. It was like drifting to sleep in a tomb.

"Sir."

I woke with a start to the tugging of Lance Corporal Dotson, my radioman (RTO). His face was a blur against the night sky. It was late, or very early, and shiveringly cold. Something was wrong.

"Sir, I can't get ahold of the guys on post. It's been over an hour since the last radio check." He was apologetic—no one likes to wake the boss with bad news. *Probably why he waited so long*, I thought.

"Where's Odie?" I asked, hoping this was something my acting platoon sergeant could handle. I was warm and toasty beneath my blanket, and the night air was frigid. The temptation to make a comfort-based decision was strong, until a nagging voice inside forced the next question.

"Which post didn't answer?" Before Dotson could reply, I saw Sergeant Odie's powerful shadow rise from his sleeping pad against the far wall. Dotson had woken him first.

Odie shrugged into his gear with short, jerky movements that signaled intense rage. He spat his response.

"All of them."

———

Rifle cradled against my chest, I followed Odie's squat silhouette as he picked his way to the first guard position. It was in a trench by some palm trees. An infrared chemlight glowed bright green through the lenses of my night vision goggles (NVGs), marking the location of the Marines. Instinctively, I stopped and took a knee about fifteen feet behind the position, allowing Odie some space. Both Marines were asleep. I heard rough whispering and a thud.

Odie stalked back to me and took a knee. If it'd been daylight, I knew the veins in his bull neck would be pulsing, and a long, jagged scar would show livid against his skull. Odie's Combat Action Ribbon bore a gold star from Afghanistan, and it was rumored he had a history of assault charges from before the war. Odie was not a sergeant you wanted to catch you asleep on post.

"They're awake now, sir," he said. I nodded and we moved to the next position. Same story. Same rough whispering. Same thud. This time, when he came back, Odie hung his head.

"It's my fault, sir. I should've known they'd be tired and toured the posts to check. I think we know what we'll find on the roof with the last team."

I said nothing. We'd both failed. The situation was serious. Even now, an enemy could be moving through an unobserved avenue of approach. We had to get to the last post.

I was a few steps behind Odie as he climbed the narrow stairs to the final guard position on a nearby roof. Warm, spicy air clung to me for an instant as I stepped out from the stairwell and paused to adjust my NVGs. An Iraqi soldier stared bemusedly from his position next to a chest-high wall running the length of the roof. Night vision goggles limit your field of view and distort depth perception, so I carefully lowered my head and began a search of the roof for the Marines who were supposed to be on watch.

Odie found them first.

It was like a snake strike. There was a flash of movement on the periphery, an animal growl, and then a Marine was being held by his throat over the edge of the roof. I glimpsed a twisted, terrified face, white against the dark background of empty space. Instantly I averted my eyes, focusing on the pile of blankets and loose gear that had been the Marine's cocoon. This was not something officers were supposed to see.

"You motherfucker," Odie hissed into the Marine's ear. "You fell asleep on post and let an Iraqi stand it for you? I ought to cut your throat! What if I was a muj? You think you'd be alive right now? Huh? Do you?"

The Marine gurgled.

This was not a movie. I had a responsibility to do something. Or did I? *Pretty sure that you do.* My moral dilemma was cut short by the Marine's panicked gasps for breath.

"Alright, Odie," I said. "That's enough." Whatever lesson had just been taught, I was certain it'd been learned well.

Odie swore and released his grip on the choking Marine, who collapsed in a coughing heap against the wall. The Iraqi soldier smiled awkwardly and gave Odie a wide berth as we stepped down the stairwell.

Radio checks went like clockwork the rest of the night.

CHAPTER 5
Church Split

Steve | 1988 | North Yarmouth, Maine

Tall and lean, with a pronounced Adam's apple, deep-set greenish-blue eyes, and an easy grin, Reverend Wes Harris bore a striking resemblance to his fellow Pennsylvanian Fred Rogers.

His decorum came from his posture: he carried himself like a Jesuit priest, whiplike with secret knowledge. Like braided wire, little about him betrayed his awful power.

Much later, I wondered what it was about Wes that held me long past the point of safety. If all he had was unshakeable confidence, I might have splintered off in a shower of sparks. But when Wes was gentle with you, or when he was pleased, or when he looked into your soul with the eyes of God, it was better than any drug. It was assurance and forgiveness and incredible joy. Needles of blind faith littered my life. Like an addict, I always returned for more.

There was also an endearing childishness about him, known only to the fully submitted, as though a stone statue had melted and underneath was an innocent, faithful six-year-old boy who believed in you more than you did yourself. On more than one occasion I'd seen fifty years' worth of frost melt away into that shy smile.

I loved him.

Yes, I did. He was beautiful in the way that a barbed wire fence is beautiful; he could be terrible, but you couldn't judge Wes as an ordinary man. Whatever he was, he was not common. What's more: he was willing to snuff out a flickering wick and break a trembling reed for the sake of his gospel. In a world of flitting shadows and unsteady alliances, he was concrete.

Four years had passed since Wes first appeared in our church. He had come in late December 1984, snow on the trees and lights in the windows. He arrived cool and pale, like a stick of ivory in a dark land. I was four years old at the time and had no part in the rancorous vote that brought him to our church, but if I'd been older I would have cast my vote for him.

He was a man unburdened by doubt.

———

The sanctuary at Faith Baptist Church in North Yarmouth, Maine, had buttery wood ceilings and white walls. Dark red carpet ran along the floor, worn to pink near the back foyer and in two spots where Pastor Wes stood for hours behind the pulpit. Banks of windows let in the light.

I sat next to my mother in our usual pew, sweat trickling down my back. The service had long since ended, but now the church was meeting in special session. There was gossip in the congregation. Divisions. Wes had called this meeting to enact biblical church discipline against the offending party. He believed gossip was a cancer that must be purged from the church. The Bible, he said, left no alternative but to deal decisively with such sin: "Expel the immoral brother or sister from among you."

Many of the brothers and sisters—immoral or not—disagreed with Wes's handling of the matter. Maurice was one of these. He sported huge mutton-chop sideburns, black hair slicked severely back, and a white-and-black plaid suit that he filled out like a puffy fruit. He stood in his pew, sweat shining on his forehead, jabbing a thick finger first at Pastor Wes and then at the assembled congregation. He was shouting but I can't remember what he said.

Someone else stood on the other side of the aisle and started speaking. Maurice kept shouting and the other man talked louder and louder until he was shouting too. His suit jacket was a beautiful claret red, which matched his face. He, too, was sweating. It was July and the sanctuary sweltered without air conditioning. Ceiling fans revolved slowly, paddle wheels in thick water.

I thought Wes was admirable because he stood quietly at the podium while his congregants shouted at each other. In the end, we only want to see the best in those we choose to save us. On that day, he wore a crisp plaid suit of tans and blues; his thin sandy hair was parted neatly to one side. Even though he stood beneath the spotlights, he didn't seem to sweat.

Maurice kept shouting.

It was two o'clock and we still hadn't eaten lunch. Mom gave me a wintergreen mint to suck and let me draw on the back of her church bulletin. She wore a cornflower blue dress and an opal necklace on a gold chain. She smelled like lip balm and eucalyptus cough drops. I tugged at her dress. She patted my head. Her hand felt cool.

I didn't like that Maurice was shouting. His face twisted and turned purple and flecks of spittle flew from his mouth. I liked that Pastor Wes remained calm. The man in red sat down. Maurice kept shouting and I didn't like it. I decided to go downstairs to the childcare attendants: Nikki in her pink poodle dress, dark-haired Amy, and Heather, who was especially kind to me and let me give her flowers. The girls would bring us outside on the church lawn where we'd pick violets and bluets and sit on moss in dappled sunlight. They gave us grape juice and saltine crackers. We sat in a circle and drank juice and ate unleavened bread while Maurice shouted and Wes stood unwavering.

That was the first of several special church discipline meetings Wes held that summer.

When I went back to school in the fall, Maurice and half the church were gone.

CHAPTER 6
Other Men's War

Nate | April 2005 | Haqlaniyah, Al Anbar Province, Iraq

It was a bad intersection, one of the worst in Iraq.

Curled up like a snake between a mosque, the river, and a handful of crumbling houses, the roundabout linked the desert road to the river road between Bani Dahir and Haqlaniyah. There really wasn't another way to move men and material to the Hadithah Dam: the upper river road was mined so badly it was considered a "black route" for coalition traffic. As our three-vehicle convoy closed the distance to the intersection, we kept twenty meters of space between us and looked hard for roadside bombs. Exploded curbs and twisted bits of metal and rubber marked the places where looking hard hadn't been enough.

That day, we were on a speed run to drop off detainees at the battalion's Advanced Logistics Operations Center in the desert fringe and extract a sniper team from their hide position covering the mosque. I was riding in the lead trac (AAV, also known as amtrac) and felt worried. Insurgents knew exactly where we were after three days of dismounted operations, and they knew what chokepoints we'd have to pass when we used vehicles to move. So, as we roared into the intersection at thirty miles per hour, I almost expected the jarring stop when it came.

"Hey, sir, looks like there could be an IED up by that curb. Better call EOD (explosive ordnance disposal)."

The trac commander's voice pitched flat in my headset. A novice might have mistaken his poise for unconcern. I knew better. Roadside bombs were the top killer in Iraq. Standing orders were for all IEDs to be cordoned and destroyed. On the first day of Operation OUTERBANKS alone, we'd found and detonated three IEDs in Bani Dahir. Even though this intersection was possibly the worst place in Iraq to be stopped, it didn't matter because we were here and there was an IED and that was that.

"Roger. We'll keep snipers in overwatch until EOD clears the checkpoint."

I hadn't finished the order before the tracs herringboned and took up appropriate positions with overlapping fields of fire. A dozen men remained standing in the troop compartments with rifles balanced on open cargo hatches, scanning their sectors with a combination of eagerness and uneasiness that's unique to Marines. They were ready for a fight, but unhappy that it might be here.

I understood their concern. Armored vehicles are notoriously vulnerable to dismounted troops in an urban environment. Two days before, a tank had taken an RPG from a gully after I'd failed to provide it with infantry overwatch. I didn't want to make the same mistake twice, but I was also hesitant to dismount Marines and clear houses to establish security positions. Two months into my first deployment, I still hadn't seen any combat. My natural preference for order, control, and limiting the decisions I had to make meant that roving teams of Marines were not yet in my playbook.

We waited. Men hunched down in turrets and hatches. You could only see darting eyes between dusty armor and Kevlar helmets. No known enemy snipers operated in the area, but it wouldn't take a trained marksman to let loose on automatic and hit us in the open.

We're being watched. The skin on my neck shrank. As I scanned buildings thirty yards across the intersection, I noted cinder block walls crumbled from repeated explosions, facades crosshatched by machine gun bullets, and severed electrical wires dangling like scalps from rusted poles. The evidence of previous violence was sobering.

Men who had expected to live had died here.

I wished I was someplace else.

———

The wait lasted more than two hours. It was unforgivably long in a cross-compartment danger area. In the decayed streets, the only movement came from tatters of plastic fluttering from scattered coils of concertina. I half expected to see a tumbleweed bounce past. This was unmistakably a bad place, and we were unmistakably not welcome in it.

Unmet responsibility added a growing sense of self-consciousness to my edgy nerves. I envied the men around me with their limited missions of covering avenues of approach or monitoring a radio. While equally exposed to danger, they suffered no angst about the next decision. *When should we reposition to gain better cover?* There were no better locations from which to observe the intersection while maintaining mutually supporting fields of fire. On the other hand, it was clear that bad things were bound to happen if we remained in place.

The sun climbed, driving the temperature into triple digits. Sweat pooled between my body armor and belt, then diffused into my green undershorts. A special kind of ache—part thirst, part stress, and part Kevlar helmet—throbbed against my temples. My feet felt squishy in dirty boots. I flexed my toes absently, disgusted by my own filth and depressed by the knowledge that we were less than halfway through the operation. My mind wandered to cooler, cleaner places.

"I've got movement to the south. About two hundred yards. Looks to be a MAM."

I jerked upright and realized I'd zoned out. There was no mistaking the urgency of the sniper team leader's report with its omitted call signs. *Had the snipers been lulled into a stupor too?* The thought unnerved me.

MAM. A military-aged male. We treated them differently from other Iraqis because the insurgency was fought almost exclusively by Saddam's former soldiers and by angry young men who freelanced as mujahideen for financial, religious, political, or personal reasons.

"Roger. What's he doing? Over."

A lone MAM poking his head out to observe us wouldn't be unusual in a town the size of Haqlaniyah. In fact, I was surprised we hadn't yet seen anyone during our time at the intersection. It was odd. Eerie, even.

"Uh, he's moving this way, over."

The trac commander in the hatch next to me cursed and stood up, accompanied by the hydraulic whirring of his turret-mounted heavy machine guns reorienting at the approaching man.

"Does he have a weapon? Over."

I was playing for time, processing information while trying to decide on the proper action. Of course, he wouldn't have a weapon. But at this stage of the war, every reasonable person in Iraq knew not to approach a cordon of Marines. *Why would an innocent man pop out of nowhere and stroll toward us down an abandoned street as we group around a known ambush spot?* On the other hand, it didn't make sense that an insurgent would approach us so brazenly. I was left with the thought that it was a ruse intended to lure Marines out of armored vehicles to expose them to attack.

"Negative. He's just walking. Over." Then immediately, "What do you want us to do? Over."

"Standby, over."

I had no idea what the sniper team should do.

Or the rest of the Marines, for that matter.

I wanted more information, but more information was a luxury I wasn't going to get. I could feel the weight of expectation pressing down from the men around me. It was my job to give them direction and make the situation turn out right. I needed to make something happen, to make the problem go away.

By now I was tracking the approaching man through my rifle optic. At four-power magnification he looked not much different from every other MAM I'd seen over the past few months. Perhaps a bit more disheveled—his dark gray jacket was dirty and stained, his hair unkempt. And his walk was unsteady and meandering. It occurred to me that he might be drunk.

I had an idea.

Shifting aim fifteen yards to the right of the man, I fired a single shot into a nearby wall.

"What do you see, sir? What's going on?" The trac commander pivoted toward me with an expectant look. In the troop compartment behind me, rustling movements and metallic scraping signaled Marines getting ready for a fight.

I cursed under my breath. It hadn't occurred to me to communicate what I was going to do. Marine Corps policy prohibited firing warning shots at people. The men around me knew the policy and naturally assumed I'd seen an overt threat.

"That was a warning shot, over."

I felt stupid and should have. Second lieutenants had to work hard against a stereotype of overeager inexperience. My rash action did nothing to diminish that reputation.

Embarrassed, I turned my attention back to the MAM. He had stopped but didn't turn to leave. Instead, he stood somewhat aimlessly in the middle of the street and stared vacantly at our security position with a half-smile on his face. This was not a reaction I expected from someone who'd just been shot at.

It dawned on me that, for whatever reason, this Iraqi wasn't going anywhere unless we made him. I knew with certainty the EOD team would not deal with the IED if they arrived on scene and found a random dude hanging out fifty yards from their position. He might be a trigger man. My uncertainty and embarrassment crystallized into frustration.

"Go snatch him up," I ordered a tall corporal waiting near the troop hatch behind me. In a rush, he and two other Marines were out the hatch and onto the street, moving quickly in a dispersed wedge. Gated windows, empty rooftops, and thickets of underbrush blurred. I expected the men to stop a few paces away from the

MAM, order him prone, and detain him.

They didn't.

Violently, the lead Marine slammed into the man and drove him into the dirt. I blinked. This was my introduction to kinetic energy applied to a problem, so different from my schoolboy track days or sand table exercises at The Basic School. For the first time, it dawned on me that I was a director of violence against other men. It mattered what I said, how I said it, and to whom it was said.

The Iraqi man lay crushed in the dust, unmoving.

I winced as the man was rolled onto his face, had a knee jammed into his back, and had flex-cuffs cinched around his wrists. Theoretically, the Iraqi was a possible enemy; therefore, our actions were well within the rules of engagement. But something inside me shrank from the force that had been used to subdue an unresisting man. I felt tension between my gentler sensibilities as a Christian and my professional responsibility as an officer to deal swiftly with possible threats to my mission and my men.

Fortunately, most Marines are inured to violence and comfortable with its application. Marine training is purposefully brutal to transform soft civilians into the hardened warriors required for success on the battlefield. Whatever my discomfort with the method, the Iraqi being jerked back to my position between two grim Marines was no longer an unknown, uncontrollable quantity in my battlefield calculus. Regardless of the reason he'd inserted himself into our situation, the man's removal by force simplified things. And his detention couldn't have come at a better time: EOD was just now rolling onto the scene.

Handing over tactical control of the perimeter to the senior EOD man, I turned to deal with the Iraqi being shoved through the troop hatch behind me.

"He's a retard, sir."

The corporal was right, if not politically correct. Orange food stains smeared the detainee's shirt. His hair was matted. He smelled of drool and feces. I lowered my gaze and noted a wet spot darkening his leg. The man was terrified.

There are times when shame and regret overpower one's professional adherence to duty. I suppressed those emotions. It would be weakness to release the man now, precisely when an EOD tech was examining a possible roadside bomb.

The appearance of a handicapped man in the middle of this intersection was not an accident. In fact, this was the first of many times that I would witness Al Qaeda's disregard for innocent lives, as mujahideen sent children, the disabled, and the unwilling to probe Marine roadblocks. Not infrequently, those episodes ended in death for the sacrificial lamb. Meanwhile, insurgents observed from the shadows and adjusted tactics. The technique was barbaric, but effective.

Feigning coldness I didn't feel, I ordered the trembling man blindfolded, searched, and seated next to other detainees for transportation to the detention facility. Since we didn't have a proper blindfold, a Marine grabbed an empty sandbag from the trac floor. As the bag went over his head, the handicapped man's eyes rolled, a mirthless smile frozen on his face.

You're nothing but a schoolyard bully.

I dropped my eyes and mouthed a silent prayer, hoping he'd be treated with kindness and gentleness and care—the opposite of how I'd treated him when I had the power and he was caught in the middle of other men's war.

CHAPTER 7

Preparing for War

Steve | 1990 | Cumberland, Maine

Between our grandfather's war stories and the clear-eyed assurance of Wes, Nate and I lived in a world of moral absolutes in which right always won—and in which we were always right.

To equip ourselves for conflict, Nate and I fought each other well and with fraternal vengeance. I trusted him completely. He loved me as himself. So I shot him with an air rifle. He threw a flashlight at me that missed and shattered gloriously through an upstairs window.

Our love was sweaty, tactile, unspoken. We pummeled each other with disintegrating dirt clods, homemade arrows, and young fists. We spent hours stalking through the fields and forests of Cumberland, dressed in camouflage and covered in mud. Cap guns, six-shooters, and, finally, pellet guns offered us a synthetic military experience.

Since we couldn't afford supplies for a fort, we scavenged the town dump for useful bits of plywood or particle board. Nate had already picked out the site: a rotting feed trestle in the middle of the field that bordered our property. It sat bleached and broken next to a cracked, antique bathtub. We spent an afternoon tacking broken boards together to form a stockade. Tall grass nearly hid the structure.

The finished fort looked like something after an airstrike. We didn't care. It was ours. We settled down behind rough boards and watched the grasses sway.

"This is a good fort," Nate said.

We'd barely spoken during its entire construction.

"We should play guns," I said.

Straightening the pins of hollowed-out steel grenades from a surplus store, we steadied them on the ledge and put red caps into our cap guns.

"Who's attacking?" I asked.

"The Japanese."

Together we nodded. The tall grass looked like something you'd find on a Pacific island.

"Get ready," Nate said calmly. "Here they come."

———

Our unwavering commitment to country and honor also came from the stacks of history books we consumed at our local library. The "We Were There" series inflamed our imaginations and made us believe that we were among the long lines of blue at Gettysburg, or splashing through red surf and machine gun fire at Normandy. A sense of martial duty came also from stories told about relatives long since dead, those who had been gassed in France in 1918 or killed seizing bridges in Holland during World War II.

But it was our living relatives who provided the strongest link to military service. During family reunions at my grandparents' camp in East Orland, between bites of potato salad and finger roll sandwiches, we heard our grandfather's lively tales of war in the Pacific. Our capable Uncle Ray had served on a riverboat in Vietnam. A second cousin was an Air Force colonel who'd later made general. Another flew Sea Stallion helicopters. Still another was in the Army Special Forces and had biceps the size of your leg. Though I'd never seen some of these relatives, they ghosted among the hamburger buns and coffee cakes, wraiths who took a commanding place at the table and occupied the best frontage in our minds.

When troops arrived home from Desert Storm in the summer of 1991, Gray took us to Bangor International Airport to get their autographs. Crowds cheered and whistled and offered cold drinks and phone cards as soldiers walked wearily past. Nate and I shyly approached tan servicemen with our pens and posters. They grinned broadly and wrote names, ranks, and units for us until our sheets were full. Other kids put up posters of Guns N' Roses or Cal Ripken on their walls, but when Nate and I returned home, we tacked up the signatures of men and women who had fought in the First Gulf War, dreaming of the day when we might serve.

Our love for country had never been stronger.

We would die for our nation.

———

"This is a Satanic nation," Wes said one Sunday, shortly after the first troops returned home from Kuwait.

The American exceptionalism witnessed in the crushing speed of Operation Desert Storm, combined with some lackluster scripture memorization efforts on the part of our congregation, seemed to have triggered Wes into a zealous rage. He was upset with our laziness. With our failure to follow his direct orders to memorize God's Word. We were just "playing" church, he said, and succumbing to a love of modern American culture that displaced our affections for the Truth. We could love our country, *or* we could love God. We could not do both.

"Satan gets people to put together their obedience to God and their patriotism to the State, and they become 'Christian patriots,'" said Wes. "But that is an incompatible union—that is light and darkness. No Christian, biblically defined, has patriotism to his natural country. His allegiance is to the Kingdom of Heaven and the Kingdom of Christ, alone."

Our church was small, Wes calmly explained, because "Deeper Life" movements are always small. To go deeper in Christ means that people fall away.

I sat in my pew and sweated.

While my love for country was strong, my fear of God's wrath was greater.

I didn't want to fall by the wayside.

Lest anyone miss his point, Wes spent ninety minutes each Sunday, for the better part of four months, on a series of sermons about Pastoral Authority. You can say a lot about a topic in twenty-five hours of pure lecture. Week after week, he stood at the pulpit elaborating from scripture about how he had been given authority by God and why we must obey him without question. It was a drumbeat designed to eliminate dissent through sheer obsessiveness.

Toward the end of one tedious message, Wes looked out over his church. "I think some of you believe that these concepts make us a cult."

Cult? I sat straighter in my pew. *Who thinks we're a cult?* The word had never crossed my mind.

"Satan wants us to think like this." Wes nodded. "And what is a cult, after all?" he asked. "A cult has a domineering, charismatic, controlling leader; a strong sense of community and cohesiveness; a sense of exclusiveness and paranoia; and very distinctive non-biblical beliefs or doctrines. Cult members are convinced they are *right*—but what makes them a 'cult' is that they are *wrong*."

Wes smiled out over his congregation. "But just look at Jesus and his band. They were a 'cult,' in Satan's terms. Look: strong leader, unorthodox teachings, cohesiveness, persecution."

"We're the same. We truly follow Jesus while other congregations just play church. In a Christ-centered church there *will* be different teaching than the norm. And there *will* be an us-versus-them mentality. And those who really follow Christ, if they lead with true spiritual authority, *will* be open to the charge of 'cult leader.'"

The sanctuary was silent.

"Yes," Wes continued, "true spiritual leaders will often be called 'cult leaders,' because they act so differently from the people-pleasing ways of this world."

I knew that Wes didn't care what other people thought, and that this was because he was closer to God. I, on the other hand, cared very much about the opinions of others. This was because I was sinful.

"If you are in a church led by such a godly leader," Wes continued, "you can expect to be persecuted. But you know what?" Here his face softened into the sublime smile of self-assurance that I always envied. "Suffering produces obedience. According to the Bible, if you don't suffer you cannot be saved."

I wanted to be saved.

Now it remained only for me to suffer.

CHAPTER 8

Into the Night

Nate | May 2005 | Camp Al Qa'im, Al Anbar Province, Iraq

It was Mother's Day and, coincidentally, the sixtieth anniversary of the Allied victory in Europe. Neither of those facts seemed ironic as I stumbled toward the chipped sink in an alcove of our one-room berthing area and prepared to shave. Only later, long after the coming day ached inside me, would I understand that war is the death of motherhood.

I stripped to the waist and splashed tepid water on my face. A brackish odor rose from the filthy drain. Wrinkling my nose, I lathered and *scraped my face*, then *brushed my fangs*—Marine idioms tend to brutalize the commonplace—then straightened up to examine myself in the cracked mirror.

The face staring back looked flat, hard, and bronzed from ten days of combat operations in Bani Dahir. Our company had arrived back at Camp Al Qa'im two days earlier after an eighty-mile, all-night drive, nursing NVG migraines and hoping for a few days' rest.

The regiment had other plans.

Operation MATADOR was planned as a seven-day, battalion-sized cordon and search of farming villages north of the Euphrates, from the meandering oxbow near Ubaydi to the crumbling cliffs and smugglers' caves that marked the border with Syria, fifteen miles west. It was ostensibly the Third Armored Cavalry's territory, but the army had bigger problems in Baghdad, Mosul, and Tal Afar; they left the far riverbank uncontested. Seizing the opportunity, jihadists flooded into Iraq from North Africa and elsewhere along well-established ratlines, which ended in safe havens north of our area of operations. Now, the river towns festered with violent, lawless terrorists. We were going to clean them out.

——

The desert night felt chill against my face as I walked to the company staging area.

It was pitch black. Unseen, but ever-present, were the razor wire, guard towers, and open desert that buffered the Al Qa'im railroad station from the bombings, rapes, and beheadings currently tearing apart Iraqi communities seven miles away. Our base was out of the fight.

To get back into the mix, we had to send hundreds of men across broken desert and crumbling roads in armored Humvees and tracs. Some of those vehicles huddled darkly against a dirt soccer field as I approached the staging area. I paused at the edge of the field to enjoy a brief, solitary moment of freedom from responsibility.

Ahead of me, cigarette cherries swung up, glowed brightly, then fell earthward where they jounced amid clusters of invisible Marines. Muted laughter echoed and was swallowed by the immensity of the night. Diesel fumes, the essential aroma of modern warfare, bit my nostrils.

The scene felt uncomfortable because it was anonymous. As a leader, I was expected to create order out of chaos, certainty from uncertainty. But in my heart, I craved direction and the comfort of being told what to do. It was my secret shame, one that I was forever afraid would be discovered by the men in my charge.

Fortunately, my sense of duty was stronger than my inclination to inaction. An officer isn't permitted the luxury of anonymity before a major operation. Decisions must be made. Reports must be communicated. Timelines must be met. Steeled for the demands of the coming week, I hitched up my assault pack and strode toward the Marines.

"Where's Second Platoon?" I asked.

Military men have an uncanny ability to recognize authority in the dark. Their response signals either respect or disdain, since the reply can always be excused by an "Oh, sorry sir—didn't know it was you." In this instance, a Marine promptly directed me to three nearby tracs.

Approaching the rear of the vehicles, I noted ramps were down and cluttered with supine bodies, crates of rations, weapons, and gear.

Warriors. Waiting.

One of the more useful benefits of rigorous field training at the small-unit level is the ability to identify a man at night by the set of his shoulders or the slouch of his hat. Scanning silhouettes, I recognized a corporal, who pointed me to Sergeant Orona's trac.

It took work to hoist my 190-pound frame, encased in seventy pounds of armor and gear, up short iron handles to the top of the trac. Once there, I slid into the

TC's (troop commander) hatch, staged my M4 and Kevlar, and lashed my assault pack to a cargo rail. After exchanging a grunt with Orona, I took a crumpled cover from my pack and slipped it on. Even in the dead of night, a Marine is expected to wear proper uniform.

Leaning back, I settled in for the inevitable wait. Orona would receive reports and updates on my behalf until the company moved to the departure point. In the meantime, I mulled over the what-ifs and worst-case scenarios that always stress a commander's mind the night before an operation. And I thought of home.

Stars glittered over Syria and beyond, the Mediterranean. Time passed in luminescent revolutions on my wrist.

———

"Sir, we're moving in five." Orona's quiet update shook me from blissful half-slumber.

It was just past 0400 hours. Muttered curses and scrapings signaled awareness from the sleepy squad below.

I buckled on my TC helmet with its soft padding and built-in headset. Through the set, I could hear other platoon commanders rogering up to the company commander. Captain Ieva was a brilliant, demanding man of short stature with a ferociously out-of-regulation mustache that he wore to impress the locals. I disliked him intensely.

(Genius is often guarded by quirks and plagued by impatience. In May 2005, I was a strongheaded lieutenant who chafed under Captain Ieva's exacting standards and intolerance of failure. Only later, after surviving a disaster of incompetent leadership during my second combat tour, would I look back with profound respect on this exceptional officer. The Bronze Star he won was well deserved.)

With accountability complete, six tracs and a dozen Humvees carrying two hundred men fired up their rumbling engines and lurched into place in a blacked-out column. I was effectively blind without an NVG mount on my TC helmet, but the limitation didn't concern me. Our drivers were excellent.

Another long delay awaited us at the entry control point (ECP). Even as a platoon commander, I was often left in the dark about the reason for such delays. So it was easy to sympathize with the Marines, who usually blamed "hurry up and wait" on the stupidity or maliciousness of officers and "pogues"—persons other than grunts—whose mission in life was apparently to sabotage the comfort of infantrymen.

After forty-five minutes, we gained permission to depart friendly lines. It was 0500.

"We're Oscar Mike!" radioed the lead vehicle.

On the move.

Tense excitement gripped me.

We rolled through the last wire defenses, gathered speed, and rushed into the night.

CHAPTER 9

Petty Despotisms

Steve | 1993 | Cumberland, Maine

Suffering came in a way I had not imagined.

Scattered across the North Yarmouth Memorial School playground were shriveled rubber rings the size of quarters and the color of tapioca. They were as alien to me as crop circles.

Inspired by a sixth-grade conservation talk, I spent several recesses collecting these strange rings from the parking lot, from behind the dodgeball wall, and from the forest's pitchy pine needles. Clutching two or three at a time, I'd walk to a trash can and dump them in.

On one such trip, Bobby Queen intercepted me. "Hey Steve, whatcha got?"

I held out my hand. "Trash." I figured Bobby would be impressed with my sense of environmental stewardship. He wasn't.

Bobby's explanation—the crop circles were condoms, and Bobby thought he knew how they were used—alerted me to a new dynamic of male-female relations that hadn't been covered in Sunday school. My face flushed. I threw the rings into the nearest trash can and went inside to wash my hands. But water couldn't erase the picture Bobby had painted. And I didn't want it to. The next time I saw a bit of latex on the playground, Bobby's story spread like a crimson stain across my mind.

I was glad, then, for summer break, which offered weeks of cold water and sunlight at my grandparents' camps in northern Maine. Lecherously, I ached for a baptism only beaches could provide.

Nana and Gray's camp sat at the end of a dirt road that offered little in the way of worldly education. The most you could expect was a glimpse of an elderly neighbor or the cry of a loon. But Beech Hill Pond was different. Grampie Smith owned a camp beneath huge fragrant pines on a populous shore. We often took a pontoon boat over to the teeming beach to throw frisbees and dive for colored stones.

That summer, I found the camp set strangely on edge. I walked through it as if born again, no longer a child occupied with childish things, my senses keen and sharp. A green bar of soap blazed from its footed porcelain. The aroma sent me reeling. When I looked at the black-and-white pictures of Grampie from World War II, each fine line demanded attention. Retreating to the outhouse, I brushed mosquitoes from my legs and noticed vintage posters on the walls showing families swimming in the 1950s. The busty women, with their poodle and pixie cuts, lounging in polka-dot swimsuits now intrigued me.

Though still full of the familiar scents of moldy canvas, pitch, and woodsmoke, the camp now rustled with the aching musk of desire. In the afternoons, sunlight flooded through the front windows and onto the beds' old quilts. I lay quietly in those blocks of light and listened to kids shouting and splashing from camps up and down the shore, but I no longer counted myself among them.

For the first time in my life, I felt my own lonely place in the universe. For the first time, I felt self-conscious. There was a tree loaded with knowledge out there, and its fruit looked delicious.

I wondered if it tasted as good as it looked.

———

Pastor Wes, knowing that the young adults in our church were vulnerable to the carnality of junior high and high school, decided to head off our sin by giving some special lectures at youth group on the evils of premarital sex. In the patient, clinical manner I'd come to expect from him—the same way he taught the books of the Bible on Sunday morning—he explained the spiritual and emotional requirements necessary for a healthy marriage. He also explained sex positions in jarring detail.

At the end of the final lesson, Wes singled me out. "Steve, do you feel ready to get a full-time job and spiritually lead your wife and children in the ways the Bible teaches?"

I was thirteen. I blushed and shook my head.

"Do you think there is a girl in your school who is ready to have a child, raise it, nurture it, and teach it to obey everything that God has commanded?"

Again, I shook my head.

Wes nodded. "That is correct. And that is why it is not God's will for you to date while you're in junior high or high school." He scanned the circle of awkward teens. "No girlfriends, no boyfriends, no proms, no premarital sex. The word of the Lord is clear on these matters."

When Wes left, I saw Austin, Kate, and Nate glance at each other.

At our youth group retreat in August, they huddled together and grumbled against Wes. I joined them, but without conviction. Wes's warnings had found their target. My own heart had caught fire that summer and Wes's blanket prohibitions were a foamy suppressant applied with the broadest stroke. The best way to avoid temptation was to cut fire lanes and light back burns to char my soul into safety. Besides, wasn't this all part of denying myself, taking up my cross, and following Christ? The strict rules didn't make my prospects for happiness any more hopeful, but at least they made my path clear: I would be the guy at high school graduation without a girlfriend, and I would never go to prom.

And that, I hoped, would make Jesus smile.

CHAPTER 10
First Contact

Nate | May 2005 | Four Miles North of Camp Al Qa'im, Iraq

Night movement in a trac was exhilarating. From my elevated position, the experience was like riding a rattling, jerking subway in pitch dark. Dusty, diesel-fumed air rushed past. From time to time, I smacked against the steel turret as our driver threw the machine into sudden turns.

We drove in single file to avoid mines, though we likely would've been better off driving alone. Early in the war, coalition commanders stopped riding in lead vehicles, which triggered mines and IEDs. Insurgents adjusted by placing mines in V-shaped holes. The result was that two, or sometimes three, vehicles passed over a mine before the next vehicle delivered the pressure needed for detonation. Delighted with their success, insurgents went one better by stacking multiple mines in each hole to enhance destructive effects. By the spring of 2005, well-placed mines were killing or dismembering luckless commanders riding several vehicles deep in convoy.

Briefed on the evolving kill-the-commander-with-a-mine game, my preferred location was in the lead vehicle where I had control over route and speed. The goal was to avoid mines altogether, not hope they'd explode behind me. I trusted Sergeant Orona for his uncanny ability to avoid hidden explosives; the reservist from Virginia Beach was an old hand in this area of operations.

Regrettably, tonight my personal preference was unsuited to the company order of march. We were fourth in a long line of armored vehicles snaking northeast toward a bridgehead on the Euphrates River. The plan was to link up at dawn with Army combat engineers just as they completed a floating bridge west of the city of Ubaydi. Once across the river, we expected a hard fight against Al Qaeda mujahideen.

Our blacked-out vehicles sped north on a deserted highway, past piles of industrial tailings from a looming phosphate plant. I was never able to integrate civilian imagery during missions. It seemed surreal that I should go about the business of death while others went on living. Even so, I took comfort in the bright industrial complex and its checkpoint of Iraqi National Guard soldiers. INGs were hardly known for military professionalism, but at least self-preservation made it unlikely they'd turn a blind eye to nearby insurgent activity. As we clanked past, two INGs in sandals and skivvy shirts stared sleepily from their machine gun position.

A few hundred yards past the checkpoint, we turned onto a dirt road and plunged into darkness. I glanced down at my Luminox and noted we were within our time-line, nearly halfway to the linkup point on the Euphrates. Blind without night vision goggles, I settled into the TC hatch and gripped the metal lip in front while jamming myself against the seat back to avoid being uncorked as we smashed into gullies and over dirt mounds. Marines riding in the troop compartment had likely nodded off despite the violent ride. In truth, my own eyelids began to droop: a normal reaction to sleeplessness, anxiety, and the strain of peering into the unseen.

No warning preceded a mottled orange flash in the darkness ahead, chased by a crushing, concussive thump. Instinct jerked my head behind the turret rim.

We shuddered to a stop.

The trac ahead of me had struck a mine. I noted that our section of vehicles lay in a slight depression below the surrounding desert, precisely the location favored for mines because insurgents avoided detection during the time required to scratch out a hole and wire munitions.

I shrugged out of shock.

What's the right thing to do?

No sound escaped the damaged vehicle. For some reason, I assumed everyone inside was unhurt, although they were just as likely dead or maimed. I expected someone to take charge, but as moments slipped by, no direction came from the radio and no movement came from the stricken trac.

After thirty seconds—which felt much longer—Orona reacted. Keying our internal frequency, he suggested diplomatically, "Sir, do you think we should go check on them?"

"Try them on the radio," I said. "We don't want to walk through a minefield." It was a weak answer referencing lessons from conventional war that hardly applied.

The reality was that I hoped someone else would act so I could remain hidden in the dark. It was the response of a man scared to walk into the unknown, terrified of doing the wrong thing.

Sergeant Orona paused; his thoughts were unspoken. I realized I had just lost a measure of his respect.

Before Orona could act, the radio crackled with a report from the third platoon commander that his last vehicle—the one in front of me—had struck a mine. A corpsman had suffered minor injuries, but the other occupants were fine. The trac itself was not fine. Tires, tread fragments, and twisted metal carpeted a crater measuring six feet wide by two feet deep. Worse, substantial damage to the trac's hydraulics and chassis meant we weren't going anywhere.

That changed everything.

I wasn't privy to the communications between Captain Ieva and the battalion staff at Al Qa'im as we sat immobile for the next four hours. Men slumped in fatigue; traded pound cake for jalapeño cheese; stretched and pissed on the crumbled rocks outside their vehicles while the sun crept above the horizon and our chance of surreptitiously connecting with the engineers slipped away.

I sat in my hatch, chewing a slab of MRE (Meal, Ready-to-Eat) meatloaf and waiting. Waiting while the injured corpsman was immobilized and evacuated. Waiting while gunny and first sergeant posed for pictures in front of the damaged trac. Waiting while updated timelines were given, revised, and rescinded.

Waiting and waiting and waiting.

All sense of urgency, of the energy and importance of our mission, fled like shadows before the rising sun.

I now know the battalion had bigger problems that morning than a slightly injured sailor and a lame vehicle. The engineers, despite their assurance that the river would be spanned by dawn, had not floated a single pontoon. The current was swifter, the riverbank softer than they'd anticipated.

There was no bridge, which meant there was no need to rush to the river.

Or so the planners thought.

But they were wrong.

Military dictums exist because they're proven time and again by men at war. One of the classic dictums states that when you lose initiative, the enemy gains it. So, when our column, minus one trac and one sailor, finally lurched forward at 0930, two things had changed.

First, we'd lost the element of surprise. The enemy knew where we were, suspected where we planned to go, and divined how we planned to get there.

Second, our battle plans were now irrelevant. The fight would happen at a time and place of the enemy's choosing.

CHAPTER 11
Running the Race

Steve | 1994-1997 | Cumberland, Maine

One doesn't simply wake one morning, pour a glass of orange juice, and say brightly, "Today, I think I'll kill my brother!"

But that was the effect.

Trauma didn't open me to religious fundamentalism. Instead, my extremism grew in creeping half-steps of acquiescence to petty despotisms made palatable by my own sense of worthlessness. It grew in quiet moments of weakness, where even doing nothing was a choice leading into the pit. And it flourished in an inner climate simmered by the minor grievances of junior high and high school, taking advantage of a soul both malnourished and pliable.

Our church entered a period of darkness—what Wes called "A Biblical Orientation to the Local Church"—just as Nate and I were beginning junior high. It was a 132-part series preached from 1994 to 1996 that excoriated our congregation for its lack of commitment to the Body of Christ. The world was a battleground not a playground, Wes said. If the church doors were open, then we must be present. That included men's fellowship on Saturdays, women's Bible study on Tuesdays, and any church social event or church softball game.

Sometimes, I spent up to nine hours each Sunday in church, and often another eight hours per week at various church-affiliated meetings. Family vacations and business trips had to flex around Sundays. Spiritual family was more important than natural family. We must hate both unspiritual pursuits and unsaved relatives with a holy hatred. Anyone who wouldn't devote themselves entirely to the health of their soul was unfit to follow Christ.

The tests came quickly.

Austin, a year ahead of me and six inches taller, dunked in the final minutes of the state championship basketball game as a freshman. Teammates carried him off the court on their shoulders. When Wes refused to let him participate in AAU travel basketball that summer, Austin left the church to live with his father. He was later voted Maine's Gatorade Player of the Year and eventually led the nation in scoring for half a season at UNH. His success, Wes confided to me later, was the devil's reward. I'd grown up playing H-O-R-S-E with Austin and once watched him break our wooden basketball pole with a monster dunk.

Now, I shunned him.

Other families left the church and were ostracized. It was a gradual exodus, coinciding with conflicts and unreasonable stipulations related to clothing, finances, and renunciation of holidays like Christmas. Wes said each rule was a litmus test for the remaining members, an obstacle in a course of unknown length with ever-harsher consequences. God, he reminded us, was very pleased with our suffering.

Depressed by these strangling regulations, Nate and I threw ourselves into running with an almost pathological devotion. As a freshman, Nate finished fifth in the 400 meters at Outdoor States. I enjoyed moderate success in cross country. We papered our bedroom wall with medals and ribbons and pushed each other through workouts that left us trembling. I never thought about Wes on training runs.

Conflict was inevitable.

———

I sat next to Nate at the men's fellowship table, feeling sick.

Across from us, Wes smiled and repeated himself: "Do you think it is God's will for you to go to an invitational track meet or to gather with his people and learn about his ways?"

It was fall of our sophomore year, two weeks before the big Catholic Memorial Invitational meet in Boston. Each year, our team drove two hours south to participate in the gigantic event. This year, the meet would fall during a normally scheduled men's fellowship.

"Cross-country," Nate replied tersely. "It's a cross-country meet. Track is next season."

Wes frowned. "My point remains. This meet does not impact your regular season. It's optional. There is no reason for you to miss men's fellowship for an optional race."

I didn't see it as optional. I'd improved since freshman year and had moved into the top five runners on our team. Moreover, for the first time I felt like I was starting to fit into high school culture, something I owed to my teammates on the cross-country team. I couldn't abandon them.

Wes turned from Nate to me. "Steve, you can see that it is God's will for you to attend men's fellowship when we meet on Saturdays, can't you?"

I thought of the hard-won currency I'd earned on the team. It was the only place I felt successful.

My lips quivered. I wasn't going to cry. Not in front of these men. Not in front of Wes. But I already knew the outcome. Wes's questions were a formality. He preferred to have us agree, but in the absence of obedience he'd mandate our actions. Wes wasn't going to let any kid's athletics get in the way of the trajectory of our church.

"Steve?" Wes asked. His voice was preternaturally calm.

I looked up. Gazing at Wes was like staring at Gibraltar. Hot tears rushed down my cheeks. I was starting to make friends in high school and I was respected by my team. With a stroke, Wes was about to cancel my efforts. And yet, in my heart, I believed that Wes spoke for God. Apparently, the Almighty hated anything to do with cross country. Or at least he mocked my pitiful efforts to blend in with my peers. Torn between social acceptance and divine wrath, a pulsing pressure lodged behind my eyes. My throat burned. A deep sob choked its way out of my throat.

Around the table, there was silence. A dozen men looked down at their laps. My father who, like me, believed that Wes was God's true servant, fidgeted with his notebook.

"You're bleeding," Wes said.

I touched my fingers to my nose. They came away red.

Beside me, Nate leaned toward the box of tissues on the table, rasped out three or four, and handed them to me. I grabbed the Kleenex and pressed them to my face. Embarrassment washed over me.

Will I always be so weak?

"Does this happen often?" Wes asked. "Do you bleed when you get emotional?"

I shrugged. "Sometimes. Usually, it only happens in winter."

Wes nodded sagely. "I see what's happening here," he said. "I think Satan has a strategy with you. It's a demonically influenced impediment to expressing healthy emotion."

I felt Nate's hand on my shoulder and looked up. Nate wasn't crying. Instead, his face looked hard as fuck.

Wes grew impatient. "Is your nose done bleeding?"

I didn't want to tell him that my bleeds could sometimes last an hour. I pulled the tissue from my face. Warm blood coursed down. I pressed the paper back into place.

Wes frowned. "Okay, let's take a break," he said. "Steve, kindly go clean up. We're done with this topic. I think we all know God's will in this matter."

———

Within every system of tyranny lies a counterfeit freedom.

This freedom can be poor, impoverished, stunted, but it's a type of liberty none-theless. In the worst cases, it's simply the freedom to no longer think for yourself. This may sound unappealing until you remember that part of the privilege of childhood is letting adults handle all your logistics while you go out to play. In the same way, Pastor Wes offered to drive the car of my life. All I had to do was sit in the back seat and look out the window until we arrived in heaven. The contract between us was clear: if I stayed in church, I was saved; if I left, I was damned.

So, it came as a gutshot a few months later when Wes declared me unsaved.

It wasn't just me. Most of us in the church were lost, he said, for the gate of salva-tion was narrow and we had been found wanting. The revelation came to Wes as he examined the criteria for salvation found throughout the New Testament and especially in Luke 13, which talks about the narrow way of salvation. "The Bible says that only a few are going to be saved," Wes said, "and it's clear that almost everyone in this congregation has just been playing church."

To emphasize the subtle deceptions of Satan, Wes required us to read an old Pu-ritan book called *The Almost Christian Discovered*. Written in 1662 by a humorless man named Matthew Mead, the book cataloged dozens of religious disciplines that meant nothing if you weren't saved. Mead wrote the treatise as a prophetic discharge of duty to stir up a "godly jealousy" in his reader, and as a reproach to his generation—most of whom he considered hypocrites. Like the whitewashed sepulchers of Jesus's day, few of us met the mark.

Wes measured up, of course. God had worked mightily in his life. And there were two older ladies who were also saved. They'd served as deaconesses for decades and were willing to shun their husbands when the men rebelled against Wes. Patricia's husband, a mild-mannered artist who painted brilliant landscapes of Acadia National Park, once keyed Wes's car and threw his Bible across the room.

When Wes picked the Bible up, the spine had broken with pages gaping out like white intestines from a wound. Wes used that Bible in the pulpit every Sunday to remind himself of what Satan could compel in placid men.

No one had to remind me of my own sin. Since that torrid summer after sixth grade when my eyes opened to girls, my own throttled passions had caused me unending shame. I knew that my only hope was to remain at Faith Baptist and wait for Wes to show me how to get saved. Who else but Wes had the words of eternal life?

In the meantime, I floated in limbo, a young man outcast from heaven, but forbidden the pleasures of earth. No longer did I think much about Jesus.

Why should I?

The arbiter of my salvation was Wes.

27 August 1997 | East Orland, Maine

In August, we ran four abreast up the dusty trail to the blueberry barrens on top of Great Pond Mountain in East Orland, Maine.

Nate, our cousin Matt, another friend named Adam, and I had come to my grandparents' camp on Craig Pond for a final break before classes and for some quality hill workouts. We wanted to burn up our quads on the granite ledges above the tree line.

Gray cooked us an early supper—his famous German dinner with Bangor rye rolls—then we swam and loafed on the dock for an hour before heading out for our run. I chose not to think about Wes, our church, or my soul. The only thing I thought about was dust rising off the road, sun throwing shadows through the trees, and my leg muscles coiling and releasing with each step.

My stomach felt tight and hard with joy.

The other guys pushed the pace, and I loved it. The road climbed up the side of Great Pond Mountain, shouldered it, then swung around toward Alamoosook Lake. On the other side of the crest, we spun off the road and up the trail to the top of the mountain. We ran loose—quads burning, slipping on rotten rock, letting our hands flap at our sides. Sweat poured down my back.

Adam drew up beside me, then Matt, then Nate. We ran abreast where the trail opened onto the granite blueberry barrens scattered with gnarly pines. Far below, I could see water sparkling between the trees. Then we broke out above the tree line and onto bare rock with black crusts of lichen scattered across it. Craig Pond spread out below us, gold and beautiful in the pink evening light. Beyond the pond were black pines and cliffs. Beyond those were more hills and ponds, hazy beneath the glare of the sun, until far off we could see the glittering flat expanse of the Atlantic stretching on and on forever.

"Such a great view," Adam said.

Nate hocked, spit, and raised his arms above his head to let the breeze wick away his sweat.

Adam flung his arms into the air and let out a shout. He capered for a moment on the rocks, took a long pull from his water bottle, then sloshed it at Matt. "This is so perfect," he said. "I wish we could stay here forever."

I felt the same.

Nate laughed. The sun coppered his face. Sweat slid down his chest. He looked at me without saying anything and I said nothing in return.

Because nothing needed to be said.

I thought I understood everything.

Three weeks later, I learned that I knew nothing at all.

CHAPTER 12

Alternate Route

Nate | May 2005 | Ten Miles Northeast of Camp Al Qa'im, Iraq

After the mine strike, we hurried, the column roaring toward Ubaydi in broad daylight. We quickly put the open desert behind us, heading north on a paved road that soon intersected with the main highway, Alternate Supply Route (ASR) Diamond, less than a mile south of the Euphrates.

Making the turn onto Diamond, I was struck by the deceptive ease of our maneuver. The usually bustling road lay empty of its normal contingent of civilian oil tankers, black Peugeots, and battered white Toyota pickups. Since the absence of civilians often indicated impending insurgent activity, the vacant highway seemed ominous.

The reality was that the enemy had taken charge of the battlefield and we now rushed in as latecomers. Fragmented contact reports filtered down from battalion; a much broader fight was coming. On a fifteen-mile axis stretching from Ubaydi to the Syrian border, other units began to run into opposition.

All the fighting was south of the river.

Ahead of us was a short bridge, which carried two lanes across a deep wadi that scored the desert from north to south. The span was an obvious chokepoint along an otherwise open highway. I surveyed a jumble of rock outcroppings on either side of the bridge, snatched up my carbine, and laid its stock on top of my shoulder with the muzzle canted to the front. If we were going to get hit before Ubaydi, this was the place.

In front of us, third platoon's vehicles roared onto the bridge at top speed. Nothing changed. No shadows detached from mounds of rock at the edge of the wadi. I breathed easier. The route was clear.

Lieutenant Clemmey's clipped Worcester accent crackled over the radio. "IED! IED! North lane against the rail. Get off the bridge!"

Fifty yards ahead, a bundle of artillery shells leaned against the guardrail, directly below the third platoon commander's TC hatch. His helmeted head was cocked toward the IED as he roared past, calmly reporting its characteristics as if it were a baseball score rather than a bomb. Instinctively, my right foot stomped on a nonexistent brake while I strained backward, expecting a mushroom of cement and shrapnel. Artillery shells will kill a man within fifty meters.

Inexplicably, the bomb failed to explode. I slammed against the hatch as our trac jerked from full speed into full stop, then into reverse again. We clanked off the west side of the bridge and regrouped with the rest of the convoy to work out a bypass to the northwest.

The broken terrain, jagged outcroppings, and vertical drop-offs bracketing the wadi looked completely impassable. I thought we might have to dismount and hoof it to Ubaydi while the trac crews cordoned the IED and waited for an EOD team to reduce the obstacle. Five miles was not terribly far to walk, but it would take time we didn't have, given the escalating fight along the river.

Sergeant Orona had a different idea. "We can make it," he assured the captain, who was eager to get into the fight. I hunkered down for a wicked ride.

Churning moondust, we led the column north for a hundred yards before Orona located a break in the terrain and angled us back toward the edge of the wadi. Captain Ieva was determined to detonate the IED by firing at it as we passed, thereby clearing the route for following forces. None of us held much hope for success, but Marines generally don't decline an invitation to use machine guns.

As we ground toward the bridge along the lip of the wadi, I heard a commotion behind me. Twisting around, I was surprised to see several Marines gesticulating from open cargo hatches and shouting fruitlessly beneath the engine's roar. I couldn't hear a thing. The squad leader keyed his radio.

"We just saw the triggerman!" He pointed. "He ran behind that rock!"

The trac stopped with a lurch.

I scanned the small escarpment. It was hard to see where a man could've hidden himself so completely. All I saw was sand and shale. Despite a sneaking suspicion the Marines were seeing things, I radioed the captain that we were dismounting a team to search for a triggerman. His response was sharp.

"If they saw the triggerman, why didn't they shoot him?" My shrug didn't pass through the radio. None of us had yet taken a life. I doubted anyone was eager to kill a man running away.

After a few excited minutes of searching, the dismounted team returned empty handed.

———

Looking back, I think it's likely the Marines did see the triggerman; we probably interrupted his final preparations to connect a trigger device to the hastily emplaced IED, which is why the bomb didn't explode when Clemmey drove by. The insurgent never would've expected a convoy to make an off-bridge wadi crossing. We caught him red-handed.

A pity no one killed him.

———

With everyone back in the trac, Sergeant Orona found an angle to unload a few rounds at the IED. Crouched behind the reticle of his .50-caliber machine gun, Orona thumped out a long burst—which utterly missed not just the IED, but the entire, enormous bridge. I heard a muttered curse and mechanical clicking as the trac commander adjusted his turret. He fired again. This time, chunks of concrete flew off the bridge a dozen yards from the IED. More mechanical sounds. Another long burst. For the life of me, I couldn't tell whether rounds impacted the IED, or just the bridge around it.

Captain Ieva radioed for a status report. I glanced at Orona, who looked back with mild disgust. "It's no good, sir," he said, punching a button to elevate his machine gun. "The sight alignment is off. We're never going to detonate it this way."

Keying the radio, I reported no impact on the IED and recommended that we push on. The column lurched forward raggedly, each vehicle wreathed in dust and scattered by the difficult terrain. As Orona maneuvered through a nearly miraculous route to the wadi bottom and up the far side, I pondered the wisdom of entering combat in a vehicle with a broken gunsight.

On the far side of the wadi, Clemmey's platoon retook the lead and pushed toward our linkup point with the engineers. The morning's misfortunes had distracted me, so it came as a surprise when we climbed an incline, followed a gentle curve around a low hill south of Ubaydi, and, suddenly, the river appeared: sapphire blue and silent between rush-covered banks. Even from a mile away, the Euphrates was impressive, glittering in midmorning glare.

We stopped short of our linkup with the engineers, screened from the city by a dirty hill crowned with a square water tower. This would be the company staging area, the captain announced. I felt confused. Staging next to Ubaydi was not part of the plan. At this point in the operation, we were supposed to cross the engineers' pontoon bridge and clear the towns north of the river. The only reason

Ubaydi was even mentioned during the operation order was as a major urban feature we could reference as we turned to head toward the bridge.

Now, scanning an agricultural floodplain that swept from the base of our hill to the river, my eyes traced a road to the bridge. Where the road intersected the river was a line of weathered skiffs held together by splintered planks and rotting cordage. It was optimistically labeled "Memphis Bridge" on our maps. Memphis was totally unsuited for military traffic and had previously been targeted by coalition aircraft and insurgent bomb makers. Armored vehicles couldn't cross it, hence the need for a pontoon bridge.

But the new bridge didn't exist.

I looked over at the riverbank and noted a clump of olive-drab vehicles interspersed with toy soldier figures. The engineers. They stood out darkly against blinding sand and baked mud. I indulged an infantry officer's contempt for their lack of security and dispersion. *No wonder they haven't put anything across yet. Look at that unmilitary goat rodeo.* My judgment was immediate and complete. I dismissed the entire unit as incompetent and wholly unsuited to support a Marine infantry battalion.

My disdain was short-lived. Spurts of dust and smoke blossomed around the toy figures at the river, followed shortly by the crump of explosions. My eyebrows shot up. It was accurate mortar fire—an oddity in this area of operations, where insurgents could reliably be counted on to miss. The washed-out sky seemed to darken as I comprehended the new threat.

"Holy shit, sir, you see that?" exclaimed an incredulous corporal from the back of the trac. My affirmative response was cut off by the distant rattle of a machine gun.

"Goddam, the army is *getting some!*" the corporal observed, eyes shining with excitement, his words tinged with jealousy. I shared his surprise, if not exactly his envy. Being mortared in the open was not my idea of a good time.

Sweating Marines, many of whom had been slumped despondently on benches inside the troop compartment, now jammed shoulder to shoulder in the open cargo hatches, craning their necks for the next impact while choking on oily exhaust. Several men clasped foil wrappers, munching contentedly on poppyseed pound cake or bean burritos and giving every indication they were at a drive-in theater instead of gearing up for a fight. Watching them eat, it occurred to me that I was famished. Rummaging in my assault pack, I pulled out a package of crackers and peanut butter and leaned back to wait.

I doubt many in our generation would've acted differently. We were raised on big-budget war movies and cable news stories of the Persian Gulf, Somalia, and Kosovo. In our world, America vanquished evil in two hours, tops. The reality was that not one of us believed he could die. Even our Infantry Officer Course visits to Washington, DC–area trauma centers did little more than grant me a distaste for sutures and drug users. Denial is a powerful opiate in youth.

All of that seems incredible now. But it's one of the reasons young men have always gone to war.

PART II
BURY THE DEAD

Let the dead bury their dead.

Luke 9:60

CHAPTER 13

Separation

Steve | September 1997 | Faith Baptist Church, North Yarmouth, Maine

I sat in my usual pew and stared at the yellow piece of paper on my lap.

It said: "Warning Signs of a Cult."

Around me, the rest of the congregation stared at the same yellow paper. The September sun had warmed the old sanctuary. Wasps practiced silent minuets in the rafters. Fall nights are cool in Maine. I waited for the evening breeze to lick through the window screens and wick the sweat from my brow.

"Does everyone have the sheet about cults in front of them?" Wes asked.

I nodded.

"Good," he said. "This is a very important night for our church. The Lord has much to teach us tonight about discerning truth from error. I know you all want the truth."

I nodded again. Indeed, the only response I knew in church was to nod.

"Let's pray."

I bowed my head. I guess I knew how to do that too.

As Wes prayed, my mind wandered over the events of the past few weeks. Even as I sat in my pew, I had to put my hands down to touch the red cushions to ensure that I was really there, that this was really happening.

———

Three weeks after we'd returned from Craig Pond, Nate argued with Mom at the dinner table about why he couldn't run for class office. Dad was away on business. Nate pushed tuna noodle casserole around his plate. Suddenly, he put down his fork with a clatter and announced calmly, "I'm leaving."

I almost threw up.

I knew that Nate wanted to run for class vice president. I also knew that Wes would never let him. But still, his words surprised me so much that I left my noodles half eaten and ran upstairs to cry into my pillow.

Polio and a half-dozen surgeries made climbing the stairs hard for Mom, but I heard her come up and limp down the hallway to my room. She sat on the edge of my bed. Her cool hands stroked my hair as if I were a child waking from a nightmare instead of a teenager walking into one. "It will be all right, honey," she murmured. "Everything will turn out all right."

But everything did not turn out all right.

Instead, Wes told Mom and Dad to ground Nate and to forbid him from participating in sports. Refusing to follow rules he thought cultic, Nate moved out of our house and in with a friend's family across town.

When Nate left home, there was no chance that I'd join him.

None.

While I had my own grievances against Wes and our church, I believed that my angst was mostly on account of my own sin. If I could just perform a little better, I thought, if I could just suffer a little more, God might look down on me with favor. What other chance did I have? Salvation was impossible outside the brick walls of our church.

The following Monday, I walked dazed through the halls of Greely High School, dumbfounded with loss. At lunch, to avoid the chance of seeing Nate in the cafeteria, I sat in a secluded carrel at the library and mindlessly leafed through a book.

Then, from the open area near the front desk, I heard girls' voices and the words "Nate Smith" and "cult." I strained to hear the rest of the conversation. One of the voices—I recognized it as belonging to a popular soccer player—said loudly, "Why can't Steve be more like Nate?"

A splintered trunk of pain plunged through my chest and lodged in my throat.

———

"Amen," Wes said.

I started out of my reverie. I'd failed to pay attention to Wes's prayer. That was a sin, but no one had noticed so I pretended to have heard the whole thing. I pulled my hand from the paper but sweat made it stick; it gave a tearing sound as I drew my palm away. The sanctuary was silent. I felt my face burn.

"As you all know," Wes said, "this checklist was passed on by Nate to his parents because he thinks our church is a cult. God wants me to walk through this list to explain why each item is wrong. This is a sobering business, but it is important lest anyone else in this congregation harbor doubts about what God is doing here." He looked around meaningfully at his people, some fifty souls. In the silence, I heard wasps bumping the rafters.

Wes's eyes shone. "You are all incredibly privileged—incredibly. God is doing amazing things here. The world doesn't understand this fact, because it is spiritually discerned."

I knew he was right. The world had rejected Jesus, and it would continue to reject his true followers throughout the ages.

Only a very few would be saved.

I wanted to be one of them.

From outside the open window came the sputter and roar of a lawn mower.

Wes spoke louder. "Scripture says, 'Now we have received, not the spirit of the world, but the Spirit who is from God, so that we may know the things freely given us by God, which things we also speak, not in words taught by human wisdom, but in those taught by the Spirit, combining spiritual thoughts with spiritual words . . .'"

I was having a hard time hearing him.

We should close the windows, I thought, *and turn on the fans.*

"'. . . but the natural man does not accept the things of the Spirit of God, for they are foolishness to him, and he cannot understand them, because they are spiritually discerned. But he who is spiritual judges all things, yet he himself is judged by no one. For we have the mind of Christ.'"

The mind of Christ.

I wanted that.

Yes! The mind of Christ can judge the world.

The mind of Christ will know how to disarm the feeble arguments of natural man. I wished that the mind of Christ could also figure out how to disarm that lawn mower. The throaty roar continued, reverberating through the chilly night. Through the window came the scent of cut grass.

Wes paused behind his lectern. "Let's ask the Lord to make that lawn mower stop," he said. We bowed our heads and prayed.

Close the windows, I thought.

"Lord, please have our neighbor realize that he is disturbing our service," Wes prayed. "Please give him the consideration to stop cutting his grass. Amen."

But the sound didn't stop. Instead, it continued for a long time. Long enough to cut all the neighbor's grass. Long enough to carry us through the whole checklist and why it didn't apply to us.

December 1997 | Portland, Maine

Nate sat across the table from us with his lawyer. She was a young attorney with a runny nose who sniffled nonstop into her Kleenex. "Sorry." She shook her head. "I can't seem to shake it."

Mom made gentle clucking sounds. She seemed altogether too compassionate toward the woman who was trying to rip my brother out of my life.

The goal of this meeting, Nate's attorney said, was to see if there was any way to reach a compromise. Per Wes's instruction, Mom and Dad had refused to sign Nate's permission slip to participate in sports at Greely. He was still seventeen and, thus, legally under their guardianship. Nate had missed the rest of the cross-country season while I co-captained the team. Now he stood to miss out on both indoor track and track and field. He had sued for emancipation so he could participate in sports.

Kevin, our lawyer, could hardly believe it. "You had a sheriff's deputy deliver a subpoena to your mother so that you could run track?"

The color rose in Nate's cheeks. "It's more than that. I want to compete for an appointment to the Naval Academy and sports are an integral part of who I am, what I bring to the table. Besides, I'm no longer accountable to Mom and Dad. They can't control me. I'm not even living at home."

Kevin looked at my parents. "Is there an easy way to handle this?"

Dad shook his head. "The only way we'll sign is if Nate repents of his sin against his pastor and his parents."

If anyone thought it was odd that Dad spoke woodenly in the third person about himself and Mom, no one showed it. I understood where his language came from. We'd already met with Wes for three hours the night before, and he'd fed us our lines. That had been the real meeting. Today's meeting with the attorneys was just a formality to regurgitate our talking points.

"Repent?" Nate emitted a humorless laugh. "Well, that's not gonna happen. Repent of what? Leaving a cult?"

His lawyer intervened. "Perhaps there could be some sort of mediation? You know, with a Christian counselor or someone you both respect. Nate's not asking you to do something immoral. He just wants to run track. Surely that's not unreasonable." She looked up through watering eyes. "If you agree to sign for him, we can avoid going to court and can hire a mediator to work on options for reconciliation."

Her argument sounded reasonable, but reason had nothing to do with our situation.

We were operating on principle.

———

Wes invited himself to our final meeting with Kevin on December 30, the day before the hearing. He didn't believe my parents could adequately convey the sobriety of the situation, the grievous nature of my brother's sin, or the hard, principled stand we needed to take. He'd also promised that the church would defray our substantial legal expenses. For that reason, he felt ownership.

It made sense to me. The lawyers were nominal functionaries, but Wes was our true advocate in God's eyes. And as Wes frequently reminded us, God had uniquely gifted him with training and abilities unavailable to the rest of us.

In Kevin's office, I found myself sitting again at the shiny wooden table. Kevin turned to my mom. She looked awful. "How are you holding up?" he asked. Mom started to cry. Kevin looked uncomfortable and passed her a box of Kleenex. To give Mom time to recover, he asked me how cross-country had gone.

"Okay," I said. We'd finished a disappointing third at States. "But we won the Ellsworth Invitational back in September." I remembered the race fondly as the last good thing to happen before Nate left.

"Wow," Kevin said. "You guys beat Ellsworth on their home turf? That's no easy feat. They always have a competitive team. One of their guys is national caliber. I remember when I was in high school . . ."

Wes cut him off. "Let's get down to business. We've got a hearing tomorrow that will decide the fate of this family. I'm not sure sports are relevant." He flipped open his notepad and uncapped his pen.

An uncomfortable silence fell on the room.

I glanced nervously at Kevin. His jaw muscles pulsed, and a vein popped on his forehead. Had Wes just interrupted our lawyer in his own office, the man we were relying on to defend our family and church against the charge of spiritual abuse? The room seemed to spin.

Wes continued without missing a beat, oblivious to Kevin's anger. He explained again why we couldn't compromise. He explained why Nate had to return home. He explained why the judge would respond favorably to such loving parents and a concerned pastor. We had to stand our ground. It was simply a matter of principle.

Kevin nodded and jotted a few notes. Then he slapped down his pen. "Listen. The Smiths have retained me to represent them and I'll be the one arguing before the judge. Is it too much to ask that I lead the discussion in my own office?"

I thought Wes would explode.

"There's no need to get angry, Kevin," Wes said, as if soothing a naughty child. "The church is helping to pay your legal fees, and the meter is running. I would rather not waste money talking about the Ellsworth track team. Time is short."

Cross-country, I thought darkly. *It's cross-country, you stupid jerk.*

Kevin leaned forward in his chair and took a deep breath. I thought he was about to order us all out. Then he seemed to change his mind and shook his head slightly. "All right," he said curtly, glaring at Wes. "Then I'll make this quick."

When we finally got up to leave—exactly on time—Kevin motioned us out as a group. As I reached the door, he clapped a big hand on my shoulder and looked me in the eye. "It's a tough situation, son," he said. "A tough situation."

It looked like he was about to say something else. Then he just shook his head and squeezed my shoulder. "A real tough situation."

31 December 1997 | Cumberland, Maine

The next morning dawned cold and gray.

I woke with a headache and an upset stomach. I'd gone to Walmart the night before to buy a tie that matched my light brown shirt. Though I didn't own a suit, I wanted to look as professional as possible in front of the judge. I believed my credibility depended on it. I laid out the shirt and tie on my bed and went downstairs to eat breakfast. Mom and Dad looked exhausted. There was little to say.

The phone rang. Dad answered it. "Hello? Kevin? What? Really? Today? Okay." He hung up.

Mom and I looked at him.

"Kevin has decided that he can't represent us," Dad said, his face a careful mask of composure. "He's calling the judge to ask if the hearing can be stayed so we can locate different counsel."

"What?" Mom said. "Why?"

"He didn't say. He just said that he didn't feel he could represent our position in good conscience."

I knew why.

We all did.

Wes had hijacked yesterday's meeting. Apparently, Kevin now believed that Nate had a case against us, that Nate really did come from an abusive church. I felt heat spreading beneath my collar. This was all Wes's fault.

Screw Wes.

There was a flurry of phone calls. Dad called Wes, then Wes called Dad. Wes was going to come over. We would devise a plan. All would be well.

I put my shirt and tie back in the closet.

The phone rang again. It was Kevin. He told Dad that the judge had refused to stay the hearing. Nate had waited too long already, the judge said. Indoor track season had already begun. The judge wouldn't tolerate a delay just because defense counsel got cold feet.

I took out my shirt and tie. I began to button the shirt.

Wes called. He was furious. Kevin had sabotaged our case. The hearing couldn't possibly continue, he said, it wouldn't be fair. The judge was prejudiced against us based on our own lawyer's request for recusal.

I unbuttoned my shirt.

Dad called Kevin. The hearing would continue, Kevin said. There was nothing we could do now but show up and do our best. If we didn't appear, the judge would hold us in contempt.

I buttoned my shirt and put on my tie.

——

A few hours later, we drove home in silence.

Garlands decorated light poles and a huge spruce tree blinked with strings of colored bulbs in the middle of Cumberland.

I wanted them all to explode.

The judge hadn't even let me testify. When Kevin put me on the stand and asked his first question the judge raised his hand and halted the proceedings. "I will not have twin brothers testifying against each other in my court."

I felt heartbroken. I wanted to defend my family. Instead, I clambered down from the witness stand and trudged back to my seat.

The judge, husband to one of the teachers we'd known in grade school and father of a boy with Down syndrome, seemed to be a kind man. The case genuinely appeared to puzzle him. He called my parents into chambers. Both Nate and my parents seemed like fine people, the judge told Mom and Dad. He'd never seen a court case like it. An upstanding set of parents against a son who wanted to enter the Naval Academy? Totally unique. As a father, he wanted to rule on behalf of my parents, but as a judge the law favored Nate. Was there really no way to compromise? None at all?

"No," Dad said. There wasn't.

So, the judge ruled for emancipation.

When we got home, I went upstairs, took off my shirt and tie, changed into my running clothes and went back downstairs. Mom and Dad were sitting in the living room with the lights off. Mom was crying; she made a little noise when she saw me and then started up as if she were going to fix my lunch.

"I'm not hungry," I said. "I'm going for a run."

Screw them.

I plunged outside as snowflakes fell, running hard and angry. God had failed us, I thought. He'd let my brother leave home and now he'd orchestrated this sham of a hearing to drag our whole family through the mud.

Screw God.

I ran through the swirling snow up to Main Street, then down Lawn Avenue and up Dews Trail over packed snow, dodging trees and leaping from rock to rock.

Snowflakes clung to my eyelids and kept freezing. I had to blink them away, then rub them out of my eyelashes and off of my nose with a gloved hand. I ran faster. Up Greely Road Extension and then down a side road to where a large house stood at the end of a quiet cul-de-sac.

The house where Nate was staying with one of our best friends from school.

I wanted to keep running right up the driveway and through the front door and into whichever room in the house Nate lived so that I could punch him in the face.

Screw him.

Instead, I jogged around the cul-de-sac and stopped on the other side and watched snow sift down onto the house where my brother now lived.

I stood for a long time.

Screw me.

CHAPTER 14

Into the Fight

Nate | May 2005 | One Mile South of Ubaydi, Iraq

Accurate mortar fire at the river was a problem.

I'd just squeezed peanut butter into my mouth and chased it with a broken cracker when "Shotgun" crackled over the radio, indicating that officers should be prepared for follow-on orders. I hastily stuffed crackers into my pack as Captain Ieva directed staff and officers to the brow of the hill. "Bring a map. You have two minutes. Black, out."

At the hill's base, I linked up with my platoon sergeant, Staff Sergeant Hanson, and climbed through fragments of windblown plastic and lumps of discarded metal. A knot of men had gathered around a map just below the crest. Clemmey gave a half-smile as we joined the group.

Pleased to have his legs after a morning of mines and IEDs.

Captain Ieva was all business. He rapped out the situation, fixing each officer with a penetrating stare and underscoring key points with jabs in the air, as if insurgents lurked in the ether:

The bridge was behind schedule because of unexpected fire from Ubaydi.

Without a bridge, there could be no operation north of the river.

The engineers needed breathing room to finish their job so we could begin ours.

We stood silent, absorbing the information and what it meant.

Motioning for us to follow, Captain Ieva crouch-walked to the crest of the hill and took a knee. America's astounding superiority in advanced communications and space-based technology had been trumped by the fact that we lacked any imagery of Ubaydi to guide our planning. Instead, as commanders have done for thousands of years, we surveyed the enemy town with our own eyes while the captain reviewed the assault plan.

He pointed toward the urban complex, visible for the first time in its entirety. Compared to the ramshackle villages and Bedouin tents of our first three months in Iraq, Ubaydi was huge. I glanced down at my map, hoping the city looked more manageable on paper.

It didn't.

Ubaydi was a gray square crosshatched by roads, spanning two kilometers from west to east and one kilometer from south to north. It had been built during Saddam's regime to house workers from the superphosphate plant we'd passed six hours earlier. From a distance, Ubaydi faintly resembled Eastern European housing projects. *But dustier.* And lacking the charm of Communism.

Speaking quickly, Captain Ieva laid out operational details. Second Platoon (me) and Third Platoon (Clemmey) would assault from west to east to clear the southern half of Ubaydi, while a company of Marine reservists from Ohio—Lima 3/25— simultaneously assaulted the northern half. First Platoon (Lieutenant Bullock) and Headquarters Platoon (Captain Ieva) would occupy an attack-by-fire position on the hill to support the maneuver element by destroying insurgents fleeing the assault.

Armored units had moved to cordon the city to the south and east, while the Euphrates River cordoned it to the north. In simple terms, Second and Third Platoons were the brooms that would push insurgents into a dustpan of machine gun, cannon, and chain gun fire from supporting units.

One piece of information above all others struck me from the captain's order: "The battalion estimates that twenty insurgents are using the city to fire mortars and small arms at the army bridging unit."

In operation orders, the enemy is the critical factor. Everything else is predicated on the enemy's composition, disposition, and probable course of action. As the small knot of troop commanders broke up to return to our men, I felt sanguine. Twenty muj were manageable. Hell, twenty dudes wouldn't even stay to fight when they saw what was coming for them. The pending assault, like every other assault we'd done in Iraq, was going to be a full dress rehearsal for the real fight, whenever that eventually happened.

Thumbing my personal role radio (PRR), I briefed squad leaders on the assault plan as Hanson and I trotted back to the tracs. There was no time to issue formal orders; my final instructions were shouted over the roar of a revving engine in the troop compartment. The Marines' knitted brows and repeated calls for clarification did not bode well for comprehension. When the trac lurched forward, I gave up trying to shout over engine noise. I was leading sixty men into an assault, and all they knew was that the vehicles were moving and that, at some point, we'd drop ramp so they could rush into a fight.

It was 1130. Third Platoon swept around the western edge of the hill and roared toward the city. My tracs followed at twenty-five-yard intervals. We followed a broad, concrete boulevard that ran south to north on the western edge of Ubaydi. Scanning ahead, I noted a drainage ditch choked with trash and brambles that divided the highway between road intersections. The city appeared abandoned. Not even a stray dog nosed the roadside garbage.

Movement from hill to city took less than two minutes. Rows of drab apartments loomed, their narrow windows set far apart. I'll always remember those windows, black and vacant as we closed the distance.

Then they began to sparkle.

Firing started as soon as Clemmey's tracs came within small-arms range of the city. At first, I assumed his gunners were softening up target houses in preparation for the infantry assault. From my vantage, standing chest high in a TC hatch, I observed heavy machine gun fire chew into concrete walls and flail trees and bushes in backyard gardens. The rhythmic hammering of .50-caliber machine guns was so intense it was impossible to hear any return fire. Live-fire ranges at IOC had taught me to shift to eyesight as the primary sensory input when gunfire overwhelmed hearing. But in training we wore ear plugs. An actual firefight was magnitudes louder.

Sergeant Orona's .50 cal opened up beside me, a bowel-jarring clatter. My heart, already pumping, thumped harder. To the tinkling accompaniment of brass casings spilling over the trac's nose, I squinted at the buildings ahead. Orona was too experienced to fire at nothing.

There it was. A tiny sparkle, nearly lost among puffs of concrete dust raised by impacting rounds. Then again, winking brightly in a window corner. Clued in, I apprehended a shifting constellation of muzzle flashes throughout the urban landscape.

So, we were in it.

Combat was not at all what I had expected. Nowhere could I see a head-and-shoulders silhouette. No black-clad men rushed between firing positions, or popped over walls, or peered out of windows. A glance around revealed no dead bodies at all. I found myself doubting that we were being attacked.

My doubts were short-lived.

Clemmey was tasked with gaining a foothold in the first two rows of apartments while Second Platoon supported and then seized its own foothold on the left flank. The two platoons would move in parallel to clear the town's east, block by block. Ubaydi was built along a linear design, which meant rows of apartments lined streets that ran west to east and intersected the boulevard at right angles. In effect, we faced blank walls at the end of each row since courtyards opened onto side streets rather than the main boulevard.

Still focused on target identification in the middle distance, I was caught off guard when the trac in front of me veered right, oriented directly down a side street, and halted. It continued to fire as we passed. This marked Third Platoon's left flank, which meant Second Platoon was now the forwardmost element in the hostile city.

The sensation was one of utmost exposure. In a self-conscious rush, I realized that behind every muzzle flash was a man who wanted to kill me. The idea that someone who didn't know me—who in fact was completely unaware of my childhood joys, love of nature, and kind disposition—could be capable of lethal action against me, felt wrong. More than that. It felt unjust.

Twenty-five meters beyond Third's dismount point, Second Platoon executed an identical maneuver. We were on the west side of the boulevard. In front of us, a shallow drainage ditch separated us from the eastern boulevard, a concrete sidewalk beyond it, and the apartments we were ordered to assault.

Almost before the trac stopped moving, I tore off the TC helmet and reached for my Kevlar. Until I linked up with Lance Corporal Dotson, my radio operator, I'd be out of communication with the tracs, other platoons, and the company commander. It was imperative I get on the ground and physically take charge of the situation.

As I pulled myself out of the hatch and kneeled on top of the trac to sling my M4, I picked out a new sound amid the hammering of the heavy guns: a hissing, electric snap and crackle of bullets zipping by. The sound was familiar from pulling targets in the "pits" at stateside rifle ranges and from overhead machine gun fire at Twentynine Palms. I cataloged the sound as one more distraction to be ignored while I did my job.

By the time I reached the ground, Marines had taken up a kneeling, semicircular security posture oriented to our rear. I paused for a moment to gather myself. The machine gun and small arms fire was so intense it acted almost like a physical restraint.

Up to this point, I'd been carried along without volition, first by the captain's order and then by the trac. From now on, I realized, forward movement was my responsibility. Fighting through sensory overload, I achieved calm based on res-ignation: *I'm going to get hit.* With that conviction came a degree of freedom that enabled me to focus on making one small decision at a time.

Meeting the expectant eyes of the squad leader at the back corner of the trac, I motioned to the ditch in front of us. Instantly grasping what I intended, he shouted hoarsely, gave up when no one heard him, and went from man to man, grabbing their shoulders and directing them to take up firing positions in the depression. Dotson ran up in a crouch, radio antenna slanting prominently out of his pack, and gave a nod when I pointed him to the ditch.

I followed.

CHAPTER 15

A Breath of Wind

Steve | 6 June 1998 | Bangor, Maine | State Class "B" Outdoor Track and Field Championships

Wind fluttered the standards on the pole-vault uprights.

From the pee troughs under the Bangor grandstand floated the unmistakable smell of buttered popcorn, Gatorade, and urine.

"Fifteen minutes to the men's 4 x 800m relay," blared the announcer's voice. "Fifteen minutes!"

I jogged with Adam and Matt into the damp gloom of the piss chamber and took a corner position close to the wall. Other runners in warmups and singlets jostled for space. The tripping rhythm of Lynyrd Skynyrd crackled from an athlete's headphones. I poured my nerves against the steel wall. Tried to shut out the commotion around me. Tried to impose a confidence on myself that I didn't feel.

It still seemed wonderful that our relay team had entered the state meet undefeated. On the rainy, two-hour bus ride from Cumberland to Bangor, I caught myself guiltily daydreaming about what it might feel like to stand atop the awards podium instead of down in the grass. I had never placed first at a state meet. Then I chastised myself. I'd learned that happiness was a dangerous feeling and not to be trusted.

Six months had passed since I stood in the snow outside the house where Nate had moved. Since then, nothing had shaken my conviction that God had abandoned me. Meanwhile, I shunned Nate as much from a sense of personal betrayal as from biblical principle. And since our relatives supported Nate, I shunned them too. Just like that, seventeen years of warm family history fossilized into dark amber. Nana and Gray, my aunts and uncles and cousins, our family legacy of military service, all were dead to me. Pastor Wes—perhaps regarding my pain as a worthy sacrifice for Christ—left me mostly to myself.

Now I stood in the dungeon-like dimness near the pee troughs while a terrible thought stretched insect wings: *What if I am really cursed by God?* Would God blast our entire relay team to punish my earlier sense of pride on the school bus? I thought I'd repented of my joy, but now I wasn't so sure.

Was there a way I could somehow make myself more miserable, and thus more acceptable to God? What penance could I perform that would avert His accusing eyes long enough for our relay team to sneak beneath His upraised fist?

I shook my head. There was no time.

To my left I noticed a short, dark-haired athlete in a maroon tracksuit. Louie Luchini of Ellsworth. He was the anchor leg of the Eastern Maine championship 4 x 800m team, seeded two seconds ahead of us. Louie was a standout runner who'd go on to place second at Foot Locker Nationals a few months later.

In my stomach, butterflies danced.

An hour earlier, as we'd streamed off our yellow school bus in the stadium parking lot, Coach Dowling pulled me aside. "Steve," he said gruffly, "you're our lead-off runner today. It's not good enough to hang with the pack. Break it open so Ellsworth can't draft off Adam or Matt. When Zach gets the baton as anchor, I don't want Luchini within fifty meters."

I shared little of his confidence in me. "But they're seeded ahead of us," I said. "Shouldn't Zach or Adam go first?"

Coach frowned from beneath his Tom Selleck mustache. "We're better than them," he said. "Break it open."

"Ten minutes until the men's 4 x 800m race," crackled the loudspeaker. "Ten minutes!"

I took one last glance at Louie Luchini before jogging out into the light. The multicolored pageantry of dozens of track teams, the smell of hot dogs frying, and the commotion of the crowd made me feel for a split second like a gladiator arriving in the Colosseum. *Come on Steve,* I thought. *You've done this before. Get your head in the game. Focus!*

For a few minutes, I jogged easily behind Adam and Matt in the final stages of our warm-up. Zach joined us—tall, lanky, and grinning—and I tried to forget about Ellsworth and Louie Luchini, forget about my responsibility to gain us a lead, forget about my broken family and my broken life, forget about my unshakeable sense of incompetence.

Then I saw Nana.

Oh shit.

She wore celery-green slacks, a flower-print top, and a cream-colored cardigan.

I knew I was supposed to shun her—that she was supporting Nate and that any affection I felt for her must be put to death. I tried to slip behind Adam but it was too late. Nana had already seen me. She rubbed her hands together nervously and walked straight toward me.

"Stephen, de-ah, can Nana have a hug?" She raised her arms and, before I could stop myself, I leaned into her, short as she was, and let her engulf me, the familiar scent of her perfume and age combining like rose petals and fresh cauliflower. All the happy memories of summers and Christmas at her home and World War II and Craig Pond and raspberry picking by the Penobscot River came tumbling back. I could no more refuse her hug than I could stop my heart. I knew that I was sinning—knew that Wes would disapprove—and yet I couldn't stop it.

I'm the worst kind of coward.

Nana hugged hard. I was surprised by her strength. As she clung to me, she spoke into my chest. "Oh, Stephen de-ah, it's so good to see you! Nana misses you so. Gray wished he could be here but his back's so bad, you know, and he just can't sit in the car like he used to. Tell your Mummy and Doug that Nana says 'Hi!'"

She let go quickly, stepped back, turned to Matt, and gave him a hug. "Good luck, de-ahs. Nana's so proud of you. You go out and beat those Ellsworth boys, you he-ah? They've got an awful fast team, your Aunt Sally tells me, especially with that Luchini boy. But I know you can beat 'em. You're all such good boys."

The other guys bounced up and down, staying limber, but I stood rooted to the grass, as if Nana's hug had manacled me to the earth.

I am a son of dust, not heaven.

And this proved it.

Nana wiped her eyes. "All right, de-ahs," she said, "good luck now. Nana loves you." And she bustled off, probably to look for Nate.

"Final call for the men's 4 x 800m relay," crackled the loudspeaker. "Final call!"

I tried to still my reeling mind, but all I could think about was how great God's wrath against me must be.

In that moment, I knew that we would lose.

———

In the quarter second it took to register the sound of the starter's pistol, I noticed the Ellsworth runner on the inside lane hesitate. I darted out and cut him off.

To my right, a tall Maranacook runner moved in fast. I accelerated. A riot of jerseys splayed around the curve. Lots of shoving and bumping. I sprinted to keep from being engulfed. Scarborough, Ellsworth, Gorham, Gray-New Gloucester, Fryeburg, Hampden. I ran faster and faster. My pace, I knew, was unsustainable. I could see it in my mind: I'd take the lead for the first lap, the other runners would draft off me, and then I'd falter and choke on the homestretch.

I would fail and we would lose.

Someone elbowed me and I felt a stinging pain in my shin. In my peripheral vision I saw a runner go down and then heard the sharp report of a pistol.

False start.

An excited voice crackled through the megaphone: "Runners, return to the starting line! Runners, to the starting line!"

Forty meters deep, we were already halfway around the first curve. I slowed, then turned and jogged back toward the clot of coaches and officials milling by the starting line.

My muscles shivered with adrenaline.

One of the runners made a wisecrack about the new 840-meter race. Another cursed under his breath. I felt a hundred beating wings in my chest. From my right leg, a trickle of blood ran where someone had spiked me. All my nervous energy seemed to drain onto the track with those crimson droplets. Whatever confidence I'd mustered for the start was gone. Now I felt flat and forsaken.

As officials worked to restart the electronic timing system, I jogged down the homestretch feeling sorry for myself. Other runners in red, black, green, and purple sprinted back and forth or hopped up and down with nervous energy. They all looked tall, fast, and intimidating. There was no way that I could beat them.

Don't worry, came a voice. *Everyone's in the same boat. Go out fast this time. You can do it.*

I turned around. Who'd said that?

Other runners jumped up and down flapping their arms, trying to channel their nerves. Fifty feet away, Coach Dowling joked with Zach while Matt and Adam ran sprints on the infield. Across the track, Louie Luchini ran back and forth in a blur of wiry legs and arms.

You can do it.

The voice came again, clear and low. It wasn't anyone standing nearby. I stood alone at the fifty-meter mark.

Go out fast? I thought. But I already feel spent.

You can do it, the voice said. *I'll help you. But you must go FAST.*

A breath of wind blew across the infield and ruffled my hair. All my butterflies flew away. In their place flooded a warm rush of energy.

"Runners," blared the bullhorn, "return to the starting line!"

I jogged over. *Go out fast?* I thought again. *I guess I can try.*

The starter raised his left hand. Around me other runners leaned forward along the waterfall start. I tensed on the line and noticed for the first time that it was a beautiful morning.

The gun cracked.

This time I easily avoided the crush as runners from the outside lanes collapsed toward the center. By the time we sorted ourselves into a colorful chain, we were on the backstretch, and I was in fifth place, running fast and easy. Ellsworth's lead-off man was just a few feet ahead.

Go now, the voice said. *Don't wait.*

I went.

Accelerating past two runners, I felt the simple pleasure of my body obeying my head's commands, each muscle playing its part in a seamless flow.

Ahead of me, kind-hearted Lucas Churchill of Gray-New Gloucester set the pace, his big stride rolling along and his long hair flapping in every direction. A runner from Gorham trailed just steps behind.

"... 57, 58, 59 ..." Coach Dowling counted as I ran over the starting line and the bell clanged. "Go get 'em, Steve! Open it up!"

Around the curve I passed the Gorham runner and then saw Lucas's shoulders tighten. Something inside me clicked. Churchill was done.

Go now, the voice said. *Turn it on.*

My legs had started to go numb as they usually did around 550 meters, but I could see that Lucas felt worse than I did as I passed him on the backstretch. Around the curve, my peripheral vision told me that runners were strung out well behind me.

Go hard, the voice said. *Bring it home.*

As I rounded onto the homestretch the sound of the crowd in the grandstand swelled and I could hear individual voices cheering. As if through water, I heard Nate bellowing at me to go faster.

I started my kick.

Twenty meters out, I saw Matt on the inside lane shouting and gesturing for the baton. Race officials were frantically rearranging runners on the starting line. Greely, Gray-New Gloucester, Ellsworth.

We have our lead.

I shoved the baton into Matt's outstretched hand and then stumbled off the track and sprawled on the infield grass. I let the soft blades itch me as my chest heaved.

I couldn't catch my breath and I couldn't feel my legs.

I had never, ever been so happy.

A sweaty hand reached down and pulled me up. It was Lucas Churchill. "Get up brother," he said, smiling and brushing hair out of his eyes. "Great race out there today. Wasn't that fun?"

Yes. I grinned shyly. *It was a lot of fun.*

Twenty minutes later, a track official guided the top six relay teams to a spot on the infield in front of the grandstand.

Coach Dowling caught my eye. "Told you we'd win." He pointed at his watch. "Six seconds!"

I looked around for the podium.

"Sorry fellas," the official said. "You're the first event. They haven't had time to set up the podium yet." He glanced sheepishly at the assembled teams. "You'll have to stand on the grass. I hope you don't mind."

I felt the breeze on my cheeks and smiled.

Mind?

Not at all.

CHAPTER 16

Ambushed

Nate | 8 May 2005 | Ubaydi, Iraq

Now that we were stationary, the volume of fire notched higher, like a cloudburst. The ditch was a poor substitute for cover and offered zero concealment, but I was grateful for its waist-high defilade within the boulevard's tabletop surface.

Glancing up and down the ditch, I realized only two squads were prone, firing selectively at targets to our front and flank. Where was second squad? Swallowing my frustration, I turned to Dotson and told him to raise the other squad.

"White Two this is White Actual, over. White Two this is White Actual, over." Dotson's repeated calls went unanswered.

The noise around us was terrific. It hammered against my skin and lodged inside me like a shaking possession. Given the rush from order to full-on assault, it wasn't surprising that a squad was misplaced. I'd have to go get it.

Figuring his radio would slow us down, I left Dotson in the ditch.

"Monitor the company tac (tactical network) to see what Blue (Third Platoon) is doing." He nodded, but was too professional to look relieved. With one gloved hand splayed against scorched earth and the other grasping my carbine, I paused below street level and squinted through stinging sweat at a trac parked twenty yards away. Gunsmoke edged around the flat scent of bleached dirt. Sonic boomlets crackled overhead, and an occasional flit of dust marked where a string of rounds skipped off the concrete.

The moment felt familiar, somehow: a young boy with sun-bleached hair lingered on a dock grayed by summer waves. A pause in August warmth, tilting forward, then a running leap into frigid, black depths. Hesitation stretched out pleasure on the edge of discomfort.

Weakness.

I took a long pull from my Camelbak. In the desert you drink not to die; there's no relief in it. Thumbing the cap back onto its tube, I shifted into a crouch.

The cloying inertia of anticipated pain can be overcome by one act: *moving*.

I went in a rush, footfalls crashing. The olive-drab trac bounced crazily in my narrowed field of vision as I angled toward its back hatch, then leveled as I slowed to maintain the appearance of control. *Bearing* is one of the fourteen leadership traits enshrined in Marine Corps training, and incidentally, it was something I valued more than not getting shot.

The trait had been forged long before my first day at Officer Candidates School. As a teenager, I sheltered behind false calm to manage difficult situations without exposing fear and indecision. Later, shorn and sweating, my bearing had been burnished in the bedlam of the Rat Line. Self-control was now as integral to my identity as anything inherited from genetics.

At the back of the trac, several Marines faced outboard with rifles at the ready, the universal posture of trained men awaiting orders. Beneath alert eyes, they frowned in concentration. The rest of the squad was crammed tightly in the troop compartment. It seemed incredible that no one had thought to link up with the rest of the platoon. Then again, we'd likely only been halted for a minute or two—time elongates in extremis. Raising my voice only enough to be heard above the gunfire, I directed the men hunkered inside to leave their false security and occupy the ditch.

———

By the time I linked back up with Dotson, members of the wayward squad were snapping off rounds at targets in the ville. During my absence, a machine gun team and clutch of snipers had bellied through trash and animal waste to a point where the ditch culverted beneath a road intersection to the north. Using the embankment as cover, they set up in tandem, with the snipers calling out targets and the machine gunners laying down disciplined bursts at insurgents in the city center on our left flank.

Well-trained gun teams operate within a carefully choreographed dance of *shoulder tap–bap, bap, bap–shift target, shoulder tap–bap, bap, bap, bap, bap*. I watched with pleasure as crimson tracers arched into windows, spattered rooftop satellite dishes, and punctured water tanks three hundred yards away.

Pleasure.

It was an unexpected sensation, but it shouldn't have been. After two years of arduous training and dull routine, it was deeply satisfying to shoot at *things* in a foreign town rather than at targets in Camp Lejeune. Generations of Marines have trained to go to war and war never came. It was like being in the National Football League and never leaving the bench. Hunger for action must be managed or it can lead to excess, but even a civilian might understand why Marines feel fraudulent until they've fought in service of the country they've sworn to defend.

It seemed like we waited in the ditch for an hour. Third Platoon was working to gain a foothold in the two streets to our right; only then could we shift from a support element to an assault element. My view of Third Platoon's progress was blocked by a row of ugly apartments, their rooftops sporting water tanks freshly perforated with bullets. Substantially in the dark, I shifted uncomfortably on one kneepad, swiveled my head in a dutiful parabola, and felt useless.

There was no need for me to move up and down the ditch, an activity synonymous with good combat leadership according to war movies. Hanson and Sergeant Odie were managing their squad leaders with ease and were quite obviously enjoying themselves. I suppressed an urge to engage targets alongside riflemen and grenadiers. My job was to stay in contact with Captain Ieva, maintain situational awareness, and ensure Second Platoon was ready to move when signaled.

It wasn't a pleasant job. The longer we remained exposed, the more uncomfortable I felt. Gunfire gusted along the boulevard in rattling sheets; I marveled that no one had been hit. The captain's plan depended on a solid front of Marines assaulting into the city along its western edge. But ten minutes into the attack, I was still waiting for Lima 3/25 to shore up my exposed left flank by hitting the northern half of the city.

Several hundred yards separated my position from Lima's objective. In between was a block of apartments, set back fifty yards to the east by a curve in the boulevard, which opened a beautiful field of fire between Lima's unmolested target buildings and the sweating Marines scattered around me.

Judging by the muzzle flashes and the increasing volume of fire that crackled by us, insurgents had taken up positions in those apartments and were using the standoff to their advantage. In Lima Company's absence, my push into the city ran a significant risk of being enveloped by insurgent teams darting around our northern edge. No matter what my platoon strength looked like on paper, on the ground my flank ended in just one man. It was a sobering thought. Whoever that flank Marine was, he'd enter an urban fight with absolutely no support to his left.

My brooding was short-lived. Occasionally combat reminds you why basics are the basics. Ever since I ordered Second Squad into the ditch, every Marine had been focused on targets in the city center. My own attention was split between Third Platoon's progress on our right and our exposed left flank. No one was oriented to the rear. It came as a jolt when rounds suddenly sparked off the rear armor of our far left trac.

We were in a three-sided ambush.

Before I could react, a rocket-propelled grenade ripped overhead and slammed into a trac thirty feet away, detonating on a pack strapped to the gear rack. A second RPG skipped off the street and clanged against the treads of another trac but failed to explode.

Choking on the nitric tang of HMX fumes, I slid a few feet through the ditch and found Odie, who was already fixated on a low-slung warehouse about 150 yards to our rear. Fringed by scraggly palms, feathery tamarisks, and rubbled buildings, the warehouse presented an ugly foreground to a sweeping panorama of lush green fields that stretched nearly a mile to a farming village beyond. The warehouse could easily contain a dozen insurgents.

Odie knew what to do. Turning to the men around him, he gruffly reoriented them to the rear. Pointing a stubby finger at the warehouse, he gave a simple order.

"Light it up."

Rifle and light machine gun fire stabbed out from the ditch and stitched into the warehouse. To our left, I watched with glee as two tracs pivoted to the rear and coughed out cascades of 40mm high explosive from their Mark 19 grenade launchers, then riddled the smoking building with hundreds of heavy machine gun rounds. Fire from the warehouse slackened considerably.

"Sir, Black wants us to cease fire!"

I looked at Dotson in disbelief. The captain couldn't be serious. "What, like it's a range? Why?" The radio operator shrugged and offered me the handset.

"I say again, White: Cease Fire! Over." It wasn't Captain Ieva. Rather, John Hayes, his XO, was so excited his words ran together.

I felt confused and put off. Weren't we supposed to return fire in a gunfight? John was apparently relaying the captain's order, but it made no sense. If we stopped firing, insurgents in the warehouse would likely engage again.

"Roger, Black. We're in a three-sided ambush, break." I paused to consider a response on the un-court-martialed side of insubordination. The tracs' .50 cals clattered throatily above the higher-pitched popping of M16s and chattering SAWs (squad automatic weapons). "Need to understand why you want us to cease fire, over."

Hayes was furious and abandoned any pretense of radio protocol. "You have friendlies passing to your rear. Lima is moving on the road beyond those fields. It's geometry of fire: you are shooting right into them! CEASE FIRE, goddammit!"

Craning my neck, I could just make out armored vehicles moving amid clouds of dust in the village beyond the warehouse. It was the reservists, nearly fifteen minutes late to the fight. For a dark moment, I had to quell a surprising desire to keep firing. After all, Lima's tardiness was one reason why the men I loved were nearly surrounded by murderous insurgents.

Inhaling deeply and letting it out slowly, I issued the order without emotion. "Cease fire" rippled down a ragged row of parched throats and somehow made it to the armored vehicles, where trac commanders looked disappointed and elevated their guns.

"Hit them with the Mark 19s if they start firing again," I ordered the trac crews. Friendlies or no friendlies, I'd be damned if insurgents were going to shoot at us unscathed. Leaving Third Squad oriented to the rear, I once again turned my attention to our objective.

The quality of firing in the city had changed. Rounds still whip-cracked overhead, but now measured patterns of assault gunfire and explosive breaches reverberated within the streets and courtyards in Third Platoon's sector. Across the open area to our north, fire slackened and then swelled as Lima approached. No movie surround sound can do justice to the symphonic texture of an urban firefight.

It was the change in sound from Third Platoon's area that alerted me to the seizure of their foothold. Pushing through the ditch, I gathered Hanson and Odie, took a knee, and pointed to the two streets in front of us. High courtyard walls shouldered against sheet metal gates. Not a soul was in sight.

"It's time for us to go." They nodded, waiting to hear my plan. At that instant, two mortar rounds crashed down barely twenty meters away. *Holy shit.* A quick glance. No one hit.

"We need to get out of the open *now*. Into the apartments, where we have some protection from indirect." In clipped sentences, we agreed that Hanson would lead Second Squad to seize a foothold in the street to our right. He'd be followed immediately by me and First Squad. Sergeant Odie would cover our movement with Third Squad, the machine guns and snipers.

Orona's tracs hulked behind us as we readied to push across the fire-swept street.

CHAPTER 17

What is Best in Us

Steve | 29 June 1998 | Portland, Maine

If Wes had learned of the arrangement, he would've forbidden it.

That summer, I worked at a warehouse in South Portland with Adam, Josh, and Nate. (Josh was the friend whose family Nate had moved in with.) I was supposed to shun Nate completely, but I wanted to see my brother. Wes didn't know because I didn't tell him.

Each day, in the sweltering heat, we sat for hours reworking products from a diet supplement company. It was mindless, repetitive labor—which ensured we could spend the whole summer talking. With Nate on the other side of the table, I felt once again complete. It was an illusion that couldn't last, but for two months I willingly suspended judgment in the name of comfort. When I stopped to think about it, I felt like a hypocrite. So, I didn't think about it.

Buoyed by our relay win in Bangor, Adam and I ran nearly every morning before work. Rising at five, we'd run an easy six or seven miles with my cousin Matt. Safely away from my house, Josh and Nate sometimes joined us. After work, we often ran five or six miles more. Once per week, we pushed out even farther to ten, twelve, or even fifteen miles.

On a hot, dripping evening in late June, Adam staked out a winding, ten-mile course from Park Street in Portland to the fire station in West Falmouth. We left one car in Falmouth and then backtracked the course and spray-painted mile markers on the side of the road. Every three miles I threw water bottles into the grass.

After dropping off one car on Park Street, the four of us—Adam, Josh, Matt, and I—headed out. It was full dark when we arrived at the fire station. Soaking wet from the run, we hopped into the car and drove back to Portland. Park Street lay abandoned, a few dim streetlights its only illumination.

As I crossed the road to Adam's maroon Saab, an old man approached. He had long hair and wore grungy clothes and walked with a limp. Deep lines creased his face. I tried to ignore him, but he veered toward me. "Hey buddy," he mumbled. "Got a dollar?"

I did have a dollar in the car. I shook my head. "Sorry," I said. "I don't carry cash."

The man wheezed and turned to Adam. "Spare some change, son?"

Adam shook his head. "We just finished a run."

The guy grunted and shuffled off toward Congress Street. The shadows swallowed him.

Adam fumbled with his keys and then cursed. "I forgot my water bottle!" he said. "Hey, Josh, wait a minute!" Then he dashed across the street.

Alone in the dark, I stood with my hands resting on the cool metal roof of the Saab, feeling a thin layer of condensation form. From the corner of my eye, I saw two men walking along the sidewalk from the south. One carried a glass bottle. They seemed to move with purpose. I tried to lean out of sight behind the car. Then they were past me. My heart hammered.

Suddenly, someone shouted, "Shut up, old man!" There was a sharp *pop* and a groan.

I looked toward Congress Street and saw the homeless man crumple to the sidewalk. Shards of glass sprayed across a circle of lamplight. The two men had just broken a bottle over Homeless Man's head. Unlike the movies, the two men said nothing as they beat him. They panted as one kicked him in the face and the other stomped on his chest.

In my schoolyard fights, this would've been the time to stop. Instead, I heard a succession of small pops and wondered sickly if they were Homeless Man's ribs cracking.

A brave man, I knew, would rush over to help. He'd throw himself into harm's way to aid the helpless. But I was not a brave man. I was just a scared kid from a quiet neighborhood who liked to read and run. I didn't belong here.

On the Saab's roof my fingers described small circles in the condensation.

The homeless guy curled into a fetal position. The man kicking his chest screamed in frustration—"Fuck!"—then repositioned himself and started kicking the man's head. I saw the old man's long hair tremble from the blows.

Part of me wished that I was brave, but most of me just wished I was someplace else.

The kicking continued. *Thunk. Thunk. Thunk.* Cars whisked by on Congress Street. In the distance, I could hear the raucous call of gulls. I wanted the beating to end. I wanted to go home. I wanted to feel brave, but instead I only felt afraid.

"Stop!"

The shout startled me. I looked around. Had someone come to the rescue?

The two men stared in my direction. One of them had his leg drawn back mid-kick. Why were they looking at me?

"Stop!" the voice said again.

I realized that it was my own.

Oh shit.

The two men glared at me. For the first time, I noticed how big they were. I thought I ought to take command of the situation, to say something to make the street thugs go away, but no words came. My legs, as confused as the rest of me, moved me out from behind the shelter of the car and toward the three men.

The street fighters broke away from their victim and strode toward me. I realized that this was about to hurt.

I wished Nate was here.

Think of something intimidating to say! I told myself. But the only thing that came out of my mouth was a timid "Stop hitting him!"

The man on the right wore a goatee, black ear gauges, and had biceps the size of softballs. The other guy had a shaved head and wore a dirty black tank top. A snake tattoo coiled around his arm with the jaws opened as if they wanted to swallow his hand. He trembled with adrenaline.

"He started it!" Snake Tattoo said. "Guy tried to rob us!"

His friend nodded vigorously.

Behind them, I could see Homeless Man dragging himself into the shadows of an alley, groaning.

Why are they explaining themselves to me? I wondered. *Why don't they just hit me?* Then, from the corner of my eye, I saw Josh draw even with my elbow. A well-built gymnast, he was shirtless and sweating. Not far behind him came Adam and Matt. I wasn't alone.

"He tried to rob us!" Snake Tattoo said again.

My mind, an unwilling observer to the whole episode, froze. *That old guy needs an ambulance.*

As it happened, a chance occurrence saved us.

On Congress Street, a car shrieked to a halt. From the open window a woman shouted, "We see you! We called the police!" The car drove off.

Snake Tattoo and his buddy disappeared into shadows. Homeless Man was nowhere to be seen.

A distant siren wailed.

"Let's get the H out of here!" Adam yelled.

We jumped into our cars and screeched down Park Street onto Spring Street. In Adam's passenger seat, I hugged myself to keep from shaking.

Shouldn't we call an ambulance?

I never asked the question out loud.

20 May 1999 | Greely High School, Cumberland, Maine

In late May, I sat alone in Dr. Stone's Contemporary Novel classroom feeling embarrassed by my own presence.

Senior Skip Day had dawned rainy and then turned to sun. There was hardly a senior anywhere on campus except for me. When I had asked Pastor Wes if I could go with my friends to the beach—foolishly believing that I might receive some sort of guilt-reducing benediction—he simply said, "Do you want to be a friend of God or a friend of the world?" Then he folded his large hands and stared at me. Blue veins spidered beneath his parchment skin. His way or no way. Binary and bruising.

So, I sat alone watching *Apocalypse Now*, feeling sorry for myself. The movie served a purpose: in class, we were reading Joseph Conrad's *Heart of Darkness* and Dr. Stone said *Apocalypse Now* was based on the book.

At lunchtime, I walked out to a picnic table near the track, trying to shake my sense of isolation. A single seagull soared above the fields, then dropped down next to a trash can and stabbed at a hotdog bun. White pieces of bread scattered like shrapnel. Underclassmen looked at me curiously, wondering why I was there.

I opened the book to where I'd left off. It was the scene where Marlow first encounters an acolyte of the renegade ivory trader Kurtz deep in the African rainforest. Marlow had been sent as a representative of the trading company to discover why Kurtz no longer supplied them with ivory. Strange rumors floated downriver of a rogue white man who'd set himself up as a godlike figure in the villages. On the way, Marlow's jungle packet was attacked by a rain of arrows—an ambush ordered by Kurtz.

The acolyte admitted that Kurtz had directed the attack but seemed untroubled by the violence, satisfied that Kurtz sat morally apart from other men. Indeed, all the natives did the bidding of Kurtz as if he were a demigod. "You don't talk with that man," said the cringing follower, "you listen to him."

Near the riverbank, Marlow saw a row of shrunken heads on sharpened stakes. Kurtz had punished rebels to make them an example to the remaining savages. The acolyte excused such behavior. "He could be terrible," the man said, "but you can't judge Mr. Kurtz as you would an ordinary man."

A burst of laughter jarred me from the story. I looked up. Three freshmen girls from the track team ran to catch a classmate who'd stolen one of their lunches. The tanned girls were beautiful in bright pastels—pink, yellow, blue. I had a crush on one of them. My heart caught in my throat. I wished the girl would come talk with me. I wished I were at the beach with my friends. I wished that obeying Wes's commands felt as good as it did to sin. The girls recaptured their lunch and the group settled again like butterflies on the lawn.

Kurtz's methods had ruined the district but he still had followers, disciples who'd never leave him. They accepted the destruction he wrought as a necessary judgment on the unworthy. Of this sadism the acolyte said, "I did not betray Mr. Kurtz—it was ordered I should never betray him—it was written I should be loyal to the nightmare of my choice."

With a yellow highlighter, I marked *nightmare of my choice*.

When Marlow finally encountered Kurtz himself, the renegade was pale, sick, and dying, yet eerily confident and lucid. "I had to deal with a being to whom I could not appeal in the name of anything high or low," Marlow said of Kurtz. "There was nothing either above him or below him, and I knew it. He had kicked himself loose of the earth."

After Kurtz's death, Marlow journeyed to France to report the news to Kurtz's fiancée. The woman, Marlow perceived, had "a mature capacity for fidelity, for belief, for suffering." Marlow understood Kurtz's power over his Intended because it was the same power Kurtz had exercised over everyone else that he'd met. "Who was not his friend who had heard him speak once?" Marlow said. "He drew men toward him by what was best in them."

This sentence struck me too. I highlighted it. *He drew men toward him by what was best in them.*

I threw the book in my backpack and took one last look at the sunny fields.

Kurtz is a tyrant. But only to those who chose him. He was a projection of their own ideals, a distortion of what was best in them. Kurtz was a tyrant not because of his own power but because of the power that his followers willingly gave him.

And therein lay the horror.

3 June 1999 | Cumberland, Maine

Wes arrived unexpectedly at our house three days before my high school graduation.

It had been Class Day at Greely. Nate had read a funny poem in front of the whole school and I'd felt guiltily proud of him. Later, we'd had a team dinner and pool party for track. Birds sang in the trees and fair-weather clouds floated in a bright blue sky. I felt almost giddy with pleasure. I came home feeling sunburned and happy, surprised by my own nostalgia.

Then Wes arrived, solemn and unsmiling.

Someone is about to die.

Wes waited for us to sit, then he settled stiffly on the couch. His face looked composed and stern like pictures I had seen of Roman gods or of the Caesars.

"God has sent me here for a reason," Wes said. "I know that Steve has Candlelight on Friday, the State Track Championship on Saturday, and graduation on Sunday. I know that he has done well and has been honored in various ways by the school and by his peers."

Across the room, I saw my mother plucking at her dress the way she always did when she was anxious. *Does she know what's coming?* In his chair, my dad sat impassive and silent.

Wes turned toward me. "Steve, high school graduation is a time when the world applauds eighteen-year-olds and tells them that they can do anything. It is a time when success and acclaim can easily go to your head. God doesn't want that to happen."

He looked at me frankly and without malice. I knew that this conversation cost him nothing because he had kicked himself loose from earth. I also knew that it was going to hurt me a lot because I still had a heart full of world-love. I knew that Wes wanted only God's best for me. I was a terrible sinner and I'd become a friend of the world because I loved to run and because I liked girls. This was God's just punishment. I should welcome it as a wound from a friend.

Wes leaned toward me. "Remember that the Apostle Paul was caught up into the third heaven and that God gave him a thorn in the flesh that tormented him to keep him from becoming conceited. You are a very privileged young man, Steve. Do you want to be free from conceit?"

I gulped and nodded.

Wes looked first at me and then at my parents; I could tell that he loved me. Then he smiled. "Very well," he said, "then consider this a blessed torment."

For the next hour, Wes told of terrible things that had happened in my own mother's life, the memories of which had been recovered in counseling sessions with himself.

Since October, Wes had shared church members' dark secrets with our congregation, awful events that supposedly had been recovered from repressed memories. He used a technique called "theophostic counseling," which involved guided imagery, demonic deliverance, and accusations of Satanic ritual abuse.

The tales were so horrible that I felt they could only have happened to a very few unfortunate people.

Wes believed otherwise. He thought such abuse was common, even universal. And now he wanted me to know that my own mother was a victim at the hands of evil men.

As he talked, my dreams of a happy family crumbled and fell into the dark. When Nate left home, my future had exploded. Now, with news of my mother's alleged abuse, my past seemed stolen too. All that remained for me were the few slipping grains of the present. Futureless, rootless, the sands in my glass bent toward Wes's gravity with a dark magnetism that was irresistible.

On the other side of the room, my mother wept silently in her chair.

Dad said nothing.

When Wes finally rose to leave, I stood quickly to shake his hand. My joints hurt from sitting straight during the session. I'd wanted to show that I was alert, that I welcomed the pain Wes gave as a gift of love, something that would further my pursuit of salvation.

Thank you for destroying my high school graduation, I thought.

And I meant it.

In the doorway Wes paused, and I felt a breath of cool evening air puff past him, loaded with lilac. "Steve, I hope you remember these sobering things as the pageantry and foolishness of your graduation happen tomorrow," he said. "Remember what Jesus told his disciples, 'The world will laugh while you mourn and weep.'"

I couldn't bear to look in his eyes, so I stared at his nose that looked strangely like a beak. Wes inclined his head and his Adam's apple jogged.

"Now is your time to weep."

CHAPTER 18

Urban Assault

Nate | 8 May 2005 | Ubaydi, Iraq

With tracs covering our rear, I added Third Squad's reinforcing fire to the gun team and the snipers still engaging targets on our left flank. They'd suppress enemy positions to the north while the rest of the platoon dashed across the eastern boulevard and seized a foothold in the apartment blocks.

There was no room in the ditch for elaborate staging. Instead, Hanson lobbed a smoke grenade to screen our movement from the marksmen in Lima's target buildings. Then he grabbed the nearest fire team, pointed at a street corner opposite us, and sent them running. When they arrived, gasping but unhit, he followed with a second fire team. Marines disappeared around a high wall, leaving one kneeling rifleman as a connecting file.

It was a relief to feel like we were finally moving. In a moment, Hanson swaggered back into view, flashed a grin, and gave a thumbs-up. I turned to Corporal Rooks, the First Squad leader.

"Let's go." One after another, his three teams echeloned out of the ditch. Dotson and I sprinted with them across the boulevard. Third Squad's covering fire was effective; only a couple rounds snapped over our heads as we crossed twenty yards of open pavement.

Rounding the corner, I saw that Marines on the left side of the street had their weapons covering rooftops on the right side, while their counterparts on the right side covered rooftops on the left. Point men covered courtyard gates to the front. It was textbook urban security; I nodded with satisfaction. We were out of a difficult spot.

Time to go to work.

Now that we had the numbers to do it properly, we proceeded confidently with urban clearing. It was a skill rehearsed hundreds of times in stateside tape houses and executed scores of times during previous operations in Iraq. With practiced efficiency, an assault man slapped a quarter stick of C-4 plastic explosive on a locked gate, smoothed olive-drab tape on each side of the charge, then jerked the metal ring of an M60 fuse igniter.

"Fire in the hole!" He trotted past a team stacked for the clear and ducked in behind them.

One thousand three . . . one thousand four . . .

I knew the fuses on doorbusters were intentionally short but couldn't remember how many seconds I should be counting.

. . . one thousand six . . . one thousand seven . . . one thous—

The explosion was more violent than I expected, focused by the high walls that amplified its decibels and angled its shock wave back into our soft tissue. A smudge of black smoke hung in the air. Instantly, a clear team rushed forward, then stopped. After a moment of fumbling, the point man reared back, front-kicked the gate. The sheet metal gave way with the sound of cookie trays crashing to the floor.

Marines flowed through the breach, rifles covering every angle of the courtyard. The space was empty but smelled powerfully of goat urine and gasoline. Flowing forward again, the team stacked beside the front door of a single-story apartment. The point man tried the door handle . . . shook his head . . . another demo charge was set. *One thousand six . . . one thousand seven . . . .* Again, Marines poured through the shattered door in a halo of smoke and dust.

Within the apartment, the team crunched over glass and splintered metal as they quickly cleared two front rooms. The midday sunshine was muted by dirty windows, but here and there it burst through shrapnel holes and flung tiny spotlights against the wall. The air was redolent with curry, khubz, and cheap perfume.

Working their way down a gloomy hallway, Marines discovered the apartment occupants in a stuffy back room. Children huddled together on a thick carpet next to women whose upturned faces were masks of contempt. Two glowering, military-aged males stood apart in dirty shirts and track pants. Body odor whipsawed through the room as the MAMs shifted slightly to square up to us as we entered.

It was a scene repeated dozens of times over the next few hours: Marines quickly searched the men, then herded everyone out to the courtyard. Women and children were directed to one side; men were directed to the other side and then questioned by an interpreter. The questioning was useless. Iraqis went from insurgent to civilian simply by leaning their weapon against a wall, picking up a child, and waiting for Marines to kick in the door.

"No! No muj. Muj gone!" The line was repeated smugly by men who knew our rules of engagement and viewed American fairness as an article of faith. During several house clears Marines found AK-47s with expended magazines and barrels warm to the touch. MAMs found in those houses were flex-cuffed and blindfolded before being led off to a detainee collection point.

Once we were in possession of the first few apartments on the street, enemy fire slackened considerably. I ordered Third Squad out of its support-by-fire position so it could commence clearing houses on the street to the north, representing our left flank. A fire team from First Squad trotted over to reinforce them.

Between our two streets was a double row of apartments, each with ten units from west to east. Within each row, apartments were connected but were without internal access between adjacent structures. Separating the rows was a narrow, tree-choked gap, divided by a dozen concrete walls.

It was impossible to see Third Squad's street from my position. With Dotson in tow, I ducked through a gate and headed toward the entrance of the second house we had cleared.

"Where are you headed, sir?" asked a sweating team leader. He was staged to leap-frog around the next team once it had cleared the adjacent building.

"To the roof. Third is on the next street and I need better SA (situational awareness)."

"There's no roof access, sir." The lance corporal jerked a gloved thumb toward the house he'd just left. "The stairs are blocked. No way to get to the top."

I stopped in my tracks.

He nodded slowly. "I think they are all like that."

This was bad news. Having the high ground taken from me in the first minutes of a major fight was disorienting. Trying to manage the dynamic and often chaotic process of urban clearing at street level was not unlike an NFL offensive coordinator trying to manage his team's end-zone drive from the depths of a locker room tunnel.

If I'd taken a moment to ask for clarification, I would've found that the team leader had meant the stairs were blocked with bags of UN humanitarian rice and slabs of cement. The obstacles were unhelpful, but not impossible to clear.

Instead, I took the information at face value. Turning around, Dotson and I returned to the street.

With my Third Squad working its way down the street to our north, Second Platoon was clearing four rows of apartments. Forty structures. There was no other way I could see to do it since the Marines clearing one side would be exposed to enemy fire from the uncleared side unless fellow Marines kept pace across the way.

The midday sun was scorching and its heat, radiated by concrete streets and courtyard walls, created a convection oven effect. Sweating Marines baked as they assaulted each apartment wearing close to seventy pounds of gear and armor. Pressing on despite the discomfort, teams cleared with as much shock and speed as they could muster. But, as they worked their way down the street, it was evident from flushed faces and hurried gulps from Camelbaks that the heat was taking a toll.

For some time now, the enemy had gone strangely silent. We still heard occasional small arms fire from uncleared buildings to the east, but none of it was accurate. After the maelstrom of the open boulevard, we all but ignored bullets crackling overhead. My perspective was limited to a narrow slice of town less than half a football field long, at the end of which was a small open area hemmed in by the wall of another apartment row. I assumed the insurgents who'd met us with heavy fire as we entered the city had now gone to ground all around us.

There was nothing to be done but root them out and kill them.

———

"What should we do with them all, sir?"

I glanced over the perplexed team leader's shoulder. Behind him was a crowd of civilians whose faces seemed frightened, furious, or masked with feigned indifference. The first courtyard we'd cleared had become a de facto collection point—not only for suspected insurgents but for all civilians yoked up—as Marines worked their way through the row of apartments. I shrugged internally but maintained an imperturbable mien. This wasn't necessarily something we'd covered at IOC.

"Keep them here. We can't let them stay in a house once it has been cleared. If one of them is an insurgent, he could link up with his buddies." My solution was only temporary, as we couldn't possibly funnel every citizen of Ubaydi into one courtyard. I vaguely sensed we had an obligation to protect civilians but hadn't worked out what that looked like in a full-scale urban fight. For now, the presumed innocent were allowed free range of the courtyard, while a knot of presumed guilty were flex-cuffed, blindfolded, and seated under guard off to one side.

"I'll take care of it, sir," offered Staff Sergeant Hanson, returning from supervising house clears on the other side of the street. By doctrine, detainee handling was the platoon sergeant's job, and I was happy to turn over the logistics to him.

Back on the street, I monitored the radio and observed the clearing of the last two apartments on our block. With the street secure, I positioned a medium machine gun team on a corner to cover the long axis of a street to the east.

"Fire if you see someone with a weapon or demonstrating hostile intent." I'd barely gone ten paces when the gun rattled off a short burst.

"Got him!" sang out the gun team leader with glee. "They're running between buildings, sir," he explained without looking back.

"Roger. Keep the street clear."

"Roger that, sir." Cocking his head slightly and pursing his lips, the team leader expertly jetted dip spit onto the pavement, then settled comfortably against the side of his gunner. I'd rarely seen a man whose talents so perfectly intersected with the moment. It was combat Zen.

Shaking my head in admiration, I turned and walked slowly toward the detainee collection point to confer with Hanson. As we moved, Dotson reported that Third Platoon had finished clearing its block of buildings and was tied into our right flank. That was good news, since it meant the only thing preventing us from pushing forward was Third Squad's unfinished clear on our left.

"Dotson, get Odie and let him know we're tied in with Blue. Waiting on him to finish his clear to the open area so we can consolidate and push east." Dotson conveyed the message to Odie, then listened for a few seconds, fingers on his earpiece.

"Sir, they're about two-thirds of the way through," he reported. "They've got two or three more clears on each side."

"Roger."

As we approached the courtyard with its mass of detainees, an automatic weapon opened up inside. The high walls amplified the staccato blast of explosions and reverberated their echoes after the weapon itself fell silent. A long, keening wail pierced the air.

We just committed a war crime.

Closing the distance to the courtyard gate in a stride, I crossed the threshold fully prepared to see a pile of maimed innocents at the hands of a deranged Marine. What I would do if that was the case, I had no idea.

Instead, Lance Corporal Roberson and Staff Sergeant Hanson looked up wide-eyed from their position about five paces inside the entrance. Roberson—a "dark green Marine," as we say in the corps—was white with shock. His huge hands cradled a SAW, its barrel still smoking. A fine cloud of concrete dust rose from a series of divots in the pavement at his feet.

"It just went off, sir!" blurted Roberson.

I said nothing.

Sweeping my gaze left and right, I scanned the courtyard for casualties.

Seeing nothing but civilians huddled in shock, I turned to Hanson. He arched his eyebrows and shrugged.

"No one's hurt?" I asked.

They shook their heads.

In the Marine Corps, a negligent discharge is extremely serious—the ultimate in poor discipline or lack of attention—and earns nonjudicial punishment or worse, depending on its effects.

But we aren't on a range.

Instinctively, I decided that Roberson and Hanson needed to be brought back into the fight after their brush with disaster.

"Roberson, you're a dumbass."

"Yes sir!" he agreed hurriedly. Then a huge, shit-eating grin spread across Roberson's face as he realized that life would go on.

After updating Hanson on our position in relation to Third Platoon and the approximate timeline associated with our next push, I stepped back into the street to watch two tracs clank past and set up behind the machine gun team. Their up-guns were a welcome addition to the platoon's firepower.

We were in a lull.

It wouldn't last for long.

CHAPTER 19
Nothing to Lose

Steve | Summer and Fall 1999 | Cumberland, Maine

After my spoiled graduation, very little captured my attention.

Wes had already told me I couldn't go to college unless I got saved. And since my salvation depended exclusively on him, I waited in a black haze for God's servant to take an interest in my shattered life.

But besides a short meeting, during which Wes told me I could no longer wear jeans to church and that I needed to go to his favorite barber to get the same haircut as him, my pastor left me entirely to myself.

When summer ended, my friends went off to college. I stayed home.

Mom and Dad both worked day jobs, and my older sister, Christine, was now attending college in Illinois. Once Mom left the house each morning it was just me and the heavy silence of empty hours.

The house needed painting, so I painted it. I leaned a ladder against the cedar clapboards and scraped for hours. The days shortened and frost bit the air. My fingers grew stiff with cold. I painted one wall, then another. The bushes needed trimming. The lawn required mowing. I sat on the tractor and circled the lawn as I had done a thousand times before.

In that familiar place, I let memory play over the years and the many changes they'd brought. Nate and I used to split the outside chores. I remembered him on the riding mower wearing fatigue pants and a boonie hat, shirtless, his muscles glistening in June sunlight.

Far out in the field, a deer grazed in tall grass, ears alert, tail flicking. When it heard me come around the corner on the mower it raised its head and stared at me with liquid eyes. I felt a brotherhood with the deer—a quiet tenant of this world who meant no harm. I allowed my heart a few moments of wonder. But when I parked the mower inside the barn and shut the big sliding doors . . .

I feel dead.

Every day was the same. Each morning I read, then worked for a few hours on the house. At noon I made myself a small lunch of cheese and crackers or vegetable beef soup, then watched some TV.

I became amazed by my own thoughts. I considered myself a philosopher, a man distant from the world and thus able to make pronouncements about it. I read the newspaper and snorted at the petty trifles of community life, the slinging mud of politics, the smoke of wars, and rumors of war. I was a man who knew suffering, I thought. Surely this drew me closer to the marrow of life.

As October lengthened, Dad asked me to paint and stain the front of the barn. It was cold, so the stain took longer to set. My knuckles scuffed the rough boards and my nose dripped endlessly.

On Mom's birthday, I baked a carrot cake from scratch. I grated carrots, blended pineapple with batter, then mixed cream cheese frosting and layered the cake. It took a whole afternoon. When it was done, I stood back and admired my work and thought about the effort and my mom. I felt pleased and happy. Mom came home, looked at the cake, and smiled. She didn't like carrot cake. She ate a small piece anyway and remarked on its moistness. Dad and I ate the rest.

By November, I'd reached the peak of the barn beneath the gambrel roof. Resting at the top of the thirty-foot ladder, my hands felt numb. A bead of moisture clung to the tip of my nose. I hadn't spoken to anyone all day. I felt tired and I missed my brother terribly. Wretchedly I remembered that according to Wes I was still unsaved.

Perhaps, I thought darkly, *I am unsavable.*

I looked down at the cement thirty feet below.

Little drops of red stain spattered its surface. Suddenly I recalled the gopher that Gray had shot so long ago, its spattered blood on the broccoli. A flight of happy memories sparrowed through my brain: warm summer nights at Nana and Gray's listening to the river and hearing Nate breathing in the next bed; a Christmas tree covered with tinsel and hot, colored lights at Grampie Smith's house; riding bikes and playing guns with Nate in the fields and forests of Cumberland; carefree hours lounging on the dock at Craig Pond while little waves slapped beside us and the sun stapled us to our beach blankets.

Now those days seemed like ornaments from another boy's life.

What ever happened to that kid?

My brush fell from my hand with a clatter. It glanced off the ladder and onto the frozen ground below. A red stain spread on the grass. Little droplets sprayed against white-painted cinder blocks.

I don't care.

I looked again at the cement and wondered idly if it would hurt very much to fall. My nose dripped, and I watched the silver drop plummet to the ground. It was cold. So terribly cold.

I stuck my foot into space.

With one hand, I let go of the ladder; when I tried to release my other hand it wouldn't loosen. I tried again and failed, and then a loud voice said "Stop!" and told me to climb down the ladder.

So, I did.

A glorious sunset flamed up behind pine trees to the west.

When I turned to see who had spoken there was nobody there.

CHAPTER 20
KIA

Nate | 8 May 2005 | Ubaydi, Iraq

Gunfire in our section of the city was now largely limited to occasional bursts fired by machine gunners at targets of opportunity in uncleared blocks to the east. From time to time, the crack of a lone rifle shot rang out, indicating that snipers had engaged an insurgent somewhere to the north. Except for three teams finishing up their clear of the street on our left flank, the platoon had settled into static positions and was preparing for a big push into the next block of apartments.

I had a dehydration headache and my feet throbbed. I was tired. My adrenaline rush from the ambush had worn off, leaving me feeling depleted and sluggish.

Trac exhaust and the stink of sour skin wafted as I paused in a courtyard entrance to lean and shrug my body armor a few centimeters off my shoulders. The relief was fleeting. A clatter of machine gun and small arms fire from Third Squad's street jerked me upright. Nothing followed the gunfire; no shouting or radio reports indicated anything unusual had happened.

Must've been a target in the next block.

Motioning to Dotson, I stepped out of the courtyard to check on positions farther down the street.

Everything is going according to plan.

I was naturally a linear thinker, so I took comfort in the methodical progress of an operation executed along clear lines of advance. It gave me the same, easy sense of purpose and immediate gratification that I felt whenever I mowed the lawn. A part of me believed that the fight was over. Surely the insurgents had realized they were outgunned and outnumbered; their best tactic was to fade away and live to emplace the IEDs that accounted for half of coalition fatalities in Iraq.

A flash of motion ahead.

Framed by the tawny wall of an apartment block to the east, a lone rifleman rounded the corner from Third Squad's street. I did a double take. Men do not move independently in uncleared sections of an urban battlefield. Rifle hanging in his right hand, the Marine walked stiffly toward me without any sense of tactical awareness. A red-star cluster burst in my mind, the same unease I'd felt when I encountered a sick raccoon, swaying and mewling, on a forest trail as a boy.

Something's wrong.

In moments, the Marine approached within five paces of me and stopped. It was as if he bore a pestilence and had quarantined himself to avoid spreading the disease.

"What's going on, Puhlman?" He was from the team that had gone to reinforce Third Squad. Brandon Puhlman was a cutup, someone genetically programmed to meet every situation with a devil-may-care grin and wise-ass comment. He was also recklessly brave. Now, as I peered into Puhlman's blue eyes, it struck me how serious he looked.

Inclining his head to the side for a moment as if turning over his response, Puhlman furrowed his brow. "Sir, uh, I think we have some KIAs."

I stared at him. Blank. What I'd heard did not compute. Puhlman's tone was a cross between calm statement and question.

"KIAs?" I repeated the word mechanically.

Killed In Action.

"Ours? Or theirs?"

My mind felt fumbling, slow. It hadn't occurred to me that any of my guys could get killed. Death in battle was, of course, a well-known risk in Marine infantry. But until this moment, with the world spinning slower and my vision narrowing, casualties had been part of a separate history, populated by the legends of Tarawa and Hue City. With surprise, I realized what history really looked like: a dusty side street in a second-rate city on the outskirts of Iraq's western desert.

Puhlman sounded apologetic. "We've got a whole team down, sir. I think they're all dead."

In a moment like this, a platoon commander with a warrior's heart would do two things: he'd plan a way to kill the enemy that had just taken out his fire team, and he'd communicate concise orders to put that plan into immediate effect. Marine infantry officer training focuses on getting inside the enemy's decision cycle and imposing one's will on him. In this instance, the aggressive and unexpected thing to do was to maneuver around the fixed position where the fire team had been

100

shot down and destroy the insurgents before they could retreat to other positions deeper in the city. If we didn't kill them now, they'd surely repeat their successful tactic.

But none of that occurred to me.

Lacking visibility on the other street or information about what had happened, I was unable to formulate any kind of plan, except the simplest.

"Okay, show me."

———

The memory is fragmented, yet perfectly clear. I walked east, then cut left at the cross street that served as Second Platoon's current limit of advance. Puhlman and Dotson were with me, and it was midday, but my impression was one of solitude in a world of glowering darkness.

Ahead, a small square that served as the terminus of Third Squad's street, hemmed by uncleared apartments to the north and east. Brooding windows, rooftop water tanks, and open angles between streets created a kaleidoscopic danger area. My senses sharpened, casting the world in sharp relief: every detail, every nuance of color rushed through dilated pupils into decision centers in my brain. As I approached a stand of low palms, I sensed the spectral presence of evil.

For the first time since we'd arrived in Iraq, I felt afraid.

Ducking past a drooping palm, I saw men scattered on the ground at the base of a cinder block wall. Private First Class Nelson, dazed and missing his Kevlar, was propped in a sitting position against the wall, a bandage wrapped around his arm. A few feet away, Doc Alfaro applied a pressure dressing to the leg of PFC Kern, who lay motionless in the dust amid a drifted pile of bloody bandages. A dark stain seeped through Doc's utility trousers at the calf. Kneeling an arm's length away from him was Lance Corporal Sanders, eyes darting above the sights of his SAW, which he pointed toward the last apartments on the north side of Third Squad's street.

Casualty collection point (CCP).

The realization came with cautious relief that some of the men I considered dead were not. There was no time to dwell on the good, however. A palpable sense of vulnerability prickled the nape of my neck. In the wall's shadow we were shielded from the area of immediate danger on Third Squad's street, but we were completely exposed to the uncleared city on two other sides. Brushing aside an urge to move to better cover, I knelt by Sanders and asked him where they'd taken contact. Sanders was relieved to see me.

"We got hit going into that second house from the end." The SAW gunner looked at an open gate across the way. Like the street I had just left, a tall cinder block wall ran the length of apartments, broken at intervals by sheet metal gates opening to courtyards.

"Kern got hit in the leg. Nelson in the arm. I got grazed," added Doc with clinical lack of emotion. "Philippon is dead. He's still in the house."

I processed this information. If a Marine was unaccounted for, then we'd go get him. It wasn't even a decision. But knowing that Philippon was in a house held by insurgents complicated matters. Clearing houses with an entrenched enemy is the most dangerous of all urban tactics. We were virtually guaranteed to lose more men.

"Sir," Doc continued. "We need to medevac Kern or he's going to bleed out. I've got a tourniquet on the leg, but he needs surgery."

"Right," I said, glad for a concrete problem to handle. "Dotson, call Staff Sergeant Hanson. I need him to deal with casualties." Standing up with a show of certainty I didn't feel, I set out to find the rest of Third Squad and to organize an assault to recover Philippon.

"You're completely exposed to the rest of the city," I added over my shoulder as I headed toward the other side of the street. "Sanders, reorient across the square until Staff Sergeant brings more guys."

"Roger that, sir." Sanders pivoted to cover the new direction.

Shame rose in me.

The only decisions I can make are the small ones.

———

Across the street, Dotson and I crouched against a wall and scanned west, trying to locate other Marines. Puhlman had rejoined his team during my stop at the CCP. The street now appeared vacant. Hoping to avoid a two-person patrol past insurgent positions, I glanced down to twist a knob on my PRR. Each squad used an assigned channel for internal communications. My PRR was set to the command channel, monitored by all key leaders in the platoon. I fumbled to find Third Squad's frequency.

It seemed a long time since Puhlman had found me. Each second that ticked by added to my sense of responsibility. I had to make something happen, to fix the situation, and to somehow make all things turn out right. The pressure, as I fiddled with my radio, seemed overwhelming. In this role of ultimate authority, I'd never felt so alone and inadequate.

As I flipped channels, scattered bits of dialogue from Marines in nearby buildings and courtyards crackled through my headset. One of the PRR's benefits was a level of informality not permissible on the company's tactical network. When I found Third Squad's channel, I caught breathless directions and choppy responses flung in rapid succession.

Marines were on the move.

I looked up, hoping to find the men I was hearing on the radio. At that moment, Sergeant Odie exited from the next courtyard and paused in the street. For an instant, his chin dropped to his flak. Then, as if shaking loose from an enormous burden, Odie jerked his head up, swiveled it around slowly, and saw me. Without any visible emotion whatsoever, the squat sergeant strode forward, his bearish forearms folded over a carbine on his chest.

With Odie here, an important piece of my command environment clicked back into place. Here was someone of great personal bravery, self-confidence, and experience who could advise me on the right course of action. I was relieved to see him.

Obviously disdainful of any danger in the street, but mindful that I was on a knee, Odie lumbered up and eased himself down beside me. Then he gave his report in clipped sentences that cut through the fog of my uncertainty.

"Hey, sir. Philippon's dead. They had a PKM (medium machine gun) set up behind bags of rice and rolled carpets at the end of the hall, plus two guys in the front rooms with AKs (assault rifles). When the team made entry . . . ."

As Odie spoke, I noticed movement over his left shoulder. An awkward cluster of men shuffled out into the street. Four Marines, their weapons slung, some of them bareheaded.

Each grasped the limb of a sagging body.

CHAPTER 21
A Portrait of the Artist

Steve | November 1999 | Cumberland, Maine

I didn't hear the voice again.

At night, I stared out my bedroom window and watched radio towers blink near Portland. Nate used to stare out that same window. His absence—what I still considered his betrayal—filled me with pain that felt like an amputation.

My world consisted of unimportant things drawn out over empty hours to the point of exhaustion.

Meanwhile, under sanctuary lights, Wes hinted darkly that awful things were afoot. "We've only scratched the surface," he said one evening to the fifty-six souls left in our congregation. Satanic ritual abuse was rife among us, he said. Unless we exposed it, unless we familiarized ourselves with enemy tactics, it would destroy us entirely.

Week after week, Wes counseled several women in the church who he said had suffered terrible things. During those sessions, he methodically jotted notes on index cards so that he could eventually recount them to us. To parents who complained that their children were too young to hear such horrors, Wes replied that God had told him to teach the whole counsel of God's truth; this was the world we lived in.

Wes loved the dark process of uncovering abuse. It animated him and gave him a gleeful sense of manifest destiny. Other churches might loiter on the surface of Sunday School stories—but, on Sunday evenings, Wes bypassed scripture altogether and delved deeply into our hidden darkness. He was special. Anointed. A Crusader of Light called to do battle in the backwaters of Maine against the hordes of Darkness.

Yet, it was our own church that grew dimmer every day.

In sessions that lasted late into the night, Wes would sit in his office while women sobbed uncontrollably in front of him, describing weird rites they believed they'd been subjected to, black violations and intimate betrayals. Allegedly, many of the perpetrators were fathers, brothers, or husbands of the victims. And in all instances, the very horror of the crimes created a protective amnesia in the women, which only counseling with Wes uncovered.

In addition to the menagerie of grotesque sexual images and macabre cultic practices that Wes unveiled to us, he spent dozens of hours describing the demonization of victims. Satanic abuse opened pathways for demons to gain control of our lives, Wes said. Thus, our every waking hour was a pitched battle between light and darkness. No moment was safe, no soul secure.

Seduced by his spell, this alternate reality thrilled us with a pungent sense of dread. We hung on Wes's words, if only to learn how horrible our fate would be. Our sense of dependence on God's Servant grew with every revelation. It was to Wes that God had given these keys of knowledge, we thought. Only Wes could unlock the secret wisdom that would set us free.

———

Adam and I sat parked in my cousin Matt's driveway. Brown oak leaves lay scattered across the front lawn.

"Just like old times," Adam said.

He honked his horn.

I stared listlessly out the window. Thanksgiving was two days away, and I felt anything but grateful.

Adam honked again.

The front door opened and there was Nate.

I blinked with surprise. I didn't know that my brother was back in town, and I wouldn't have met him if I did. Adam had tricked me. He told me that we were going to lunch with Matt.

Instead, it was Nate who bounded down the steps and jumped into the back seat with his contagious grin. "Hey brother!" he said, slapping my shoulder.

I fought a rising tide of panic that battled an equally strong wave of pleasure.

"What's new?" Nate said.

Suddenly, I wished that something *was* new. That something—anything—had happened in my life. I was staying home from college so that Wes would save me, but instead I was worse off than before. I didn't want to tell Nate stories about family abuse or demons or how the red droplets spattered like blood on white cinder blocks when I dropped my brush from the top of the ladder.

"Not much," I said. "How about you?"

He laughed and told me about the Rat Line at VMI and how miserable it was and how the rooms were Spartan—truly depressing, right out of the Soviet bloc—and ranked worst in the nation.

But to me he sounded happy.

He sounded alive.

Nate saw that I was wearing black leather driving gloves and asked for them. I handed them over. He tucked in the bottoms, then passed them back and said, "Try that."

They were too short. Nate laughed and said that was how to blouse my gloves.

We ate lunch in Falmouth and Nate paid for my sandwich. The whole time that Adam and Nate chatted I looked out the window and didn't hear a word. I could only think about how badly I was sinning and whether anyone from church would see me and tell Wes—then my life would be over.

"Hey," Nate chided. "Did you hear what I said?"

I shook my head. "Sorry, I was looking out the window."

He cleared his throat. "I said, 'When are you getting a job?'"

I felt ashamed. "I'm working part-time for Mom and Dad."

"Careful," Nate snickered, "or you'll end up working grocery at Shop N' Save."

Suddenly, I felt quite good about myself. "Don't worry," I said. "I've got plenty of options before I work at Shop N' Save."

———

In the break room at Shop N' Save, I sat eating my turkey sandwich and reading Plato's *Five Dialogues* because I felt a self-conscious need to better myself. I also hoped that other supermarket employees would see my reading material and be impressed by my intelligence.

None did.

I soon grew tired of Plato and switched to James Joyce because I'd heard that he was the best novelist of the twentieth century. I figured I ought to have read something by him before I went to college. (I did this secretly because I had also heard that Joyce was dirty.)

From a Falmouth bookstore, I bought *A Portrait of the Artist as a Young Man* and brought it home in a brown paper bag when my parents were away. I read it in two breathless sessions in my room at night, shrouded in quilts and blankets, scarcely sensing the passing of time or the winter cold.

For those two nights, I lost myself in nineteenth-century Dublin: I was bullied in the schoolyard cliques with Stephen Dedalus, terrorized by Jesuit priests with their patty rods, religious devotion, and moralizing homilies on sin. Like Dedalus, I walked in fog beneath shrouded street lamps and felt the same burning lusts. As I read, I rejoiced in Joyce's perfect placement of noun and verb to build a world into which I could enter. An ocean away and generations gone, the book read like my own dim life.

In the final pages, when Stephen walks clear-eyed to the ocean quay and watches green seaweed waving like anemones as he loses his faith, I walked with him. I sampled the same salty air, felt the bracing wind of atheistic humanism, and with him gazed detached at the pale boys bathing in the sea. I stood upon the jetty where waves broke against rocks and thought and thought . . . .

I stood there for a long time.

But when I put down the book, rather than laying down my faith as Stephen had, I picked up my Bible and began to read with new purpose. Stephen's scuttled faith filled me with terror. His vision of demonic goats ambling through shitty fields, the long homily by a priest about the torments of hell, and his dalliance with prostitutes all rang a sympathetic chord in me. The ringing was a knell.

I could become like Stephen Dedalus.

It wouldn't take much to swing me over the line.

Joyce recalled the priest's warnings about hellfire with irony as an example of religion gone sour, but the very dogma that drove Stephen from his faith filled me with credulous fear.

Stephen doubted, but I believed.

I would do whatever it took to keep myself from burning in hell.

———

Wes sat between me and the only exit. "How do you feel?" he asked. "You haven't been in a counseling session like this before, have you?"

I shook my head.

"There's nothing to be afraid of," he said. "You want the truth, don't you?"

I nodded.

"Good," he said. "You know that I have counseled extensively with your mother and you've heard about some of the things that have happened to her. You know that you are not immune."

I nodded again.

Wes sat straighter. "I don't mean to suggest anything to you," he said. "I'm just setting out reality. For this process to work, it has to be organic. Just settle down into yourself and ask God to show you the truth. There's no rush. We have all the time in the world."

I did feel rushed.

I felt pressured to produce vivid memories. I wanted to be healed and to get saved. If terrible things had happened to me, then I wanted to know about them. A quick mental slideshow rattled through my brain, all the different memories that other people in the church had recovered that had been shared from the pulpit.

Have similar things happened to me?

Wes thought that they had. "Do you see anything?" he prompted.

Behind my closed eyes, I felt how hot the office was. It was just Wes and me and the uncomfortable silence. I didn't see anything in my mind. I shook my head. "Not yet," I said. I felt that I ought to have seen something already. I felt that I was letting Wes down.

"That is okay," Wes said. "Take your time."

I wriggled in my seat, tried to will myself into the past. Surely, if something bad had happened to me there would be telltale signs. A fractured partial memory, perhaps, or some deep-seated feeling of anger or pain associated with one of my relatives.

But I felt nothing.

I could hear Wes's fingers drumming softly on the yellow arm of his faux leather chair.

"Anything yet?" he asked. "Do you have the sense of being in a certain person's house? Do you see anything associated with a particular relative or acquaintance? Anything at all?"

I didn't. I felt shame that I couldn't produce anything for Wes. I didn't want the session to prove fruitless.

"Lord," Wes prayed suddenly. His calm voice was loud in the still office. "Reveal to Steve what you want him to see. And if there are demons in the room who are interfering, I pray that you bind them and keep them from harassing Steve. In Jesus's name, amen."

My ears filled with a loud buzzing. Then came crisp silence as though I'd pushed through a tangled forest of screaming cicadas and suddenly came upon a blue lake. My body felt light and free, and in my mind's eye I pictured a scene.

"Do you see something?" Wes asked. I could hear his eagerness.

It thrilled me.

"Yes," I said proudly. I felt happy and scared, and I realized suddenly that I was about to become worthy.

Perhaps I can even go to college.

From across the room came the scratching of Wes's pen on a notecard.

"Very well. Let us proceed."

CHAPTER 22
House of Evil

Nate | 8 May 2005 | Ubaydi, Iraq

It was the most terrible thing I'd ever seen. Nothing in life or the movies had prepared me for that shattered corpse swinging between a sweating quartet of stricken men. Their deliberate movement conveyed almost an ecclesiastical reverence for their burden that transcended all other considerations, even personal safety.

Odie's report continued in the background.

". . . Philippon was lead, so he got it point blank from the machine gun and AKs when he kicked in the door. If he wasn't so big, the guys behind him would have been killed. When we heard it, I grabbed Borch . . . ."

The words buzzed meaninglessly in the breezeway of my brain.

Before joining our unit, Lance Corporal Larry Philippon from West Hartford, Connecticut, had spent several years in the straight-backed marching platoons at Marine Barracks, Washington. I recalled that he had borne the national colors at the front of President Reagan's funeral procession, a parade I had watched with some interest on a mess hall TV at the Mountain Warfare Training Center in California's High Sierra during Infantry Officer Course.

Had that golden season of surging adventure and clean mountain air passed less than a year ago?

The distance between Larry's flint-faced visage framed by folds of Old Glory and the unfolding nightmare of his broken body carried from a stinking Iraqi courtyard was so enormous my brain defaulted to denial.

No.

The sun, street, and sand-colored walls around me froze and faded, leaving only an advancing horror.

Watching me closely, Odie broke off his account of how he and several other men had smashed through a window and ran to Philippon's body over a skittering carpet of shell casings and glass, prepared for an explosion of gunfire that never came.

"You okay, sir?" he asked suddenly. The question—compassionate to the point of tenderness—carried with it unspoken assurance. Like the outstretched hand of an older brother, I snatched at the humanity proffered by the tough sergeant and pulled myself together.

"Yeah, I am." Turning to Dotson. "Get Black on the radio."

———

"White Actual, confirm you have one, *friendly* KIA, over." Captain Ieva, sitting in an armored Humvee overlooking the city, seemed struck by the same disbelief I'd had moments before. Or perhaps my carefully unemotional report made him question if he'd heard me correctly.

"Affirmative, Black. White platoon has one, friendly KIA and three, friendly WIA (wounded in action), over." Sucking a deep breath, I exhaled slowly to ensure my voice remained flat. Dozens of men engaged in combat operations throughout the AO were monitoring our tac net, so it seemed vitally important not to convey that things were falling apart.

"Here you go, sir." Startled, I looked up from the radio to see a hatless sniper handing me a rifle. His face bore the smudged black outline of a skull. Behind him, Philippon had been lowered to the ground and covered with a poncho. One gloved hand, partially shot away, flopped in the dust. I stared dumbly at the rifle until I noticed twisted metal handguards and realized that it was Philippon's weapon. I wanted nothing to do with it.

"Put it over there." I gestured to the wall and went back to the radio.

Lacking Philippon's "kill card" with its numeric identifier—a way to transmit casualty information anonymously—I reported his name over the net. This would ensure that the official notification process could begin. It would end, I supposed, later that night or early the next morning with a knock on the door of a middle-class home in Connecticut. We'd still be here, in the sand and the stink and the heat, while other Marines in dress blues mourned with grief-stricken parents in their barren home.

Home.

The thought introduced a duality I was unprepared to deal with. I needed to focus on the present. Hearing the radio key, I cringed, certain I was about to receive a browbeating from the commander we all knew was intolerant of failure or mistakes. As it turned out, my sentiment was unworthy of the man.

"Okay, buddy. We'll take care of the medevac. Gunny and First Sergeant will link up with your platoon sergeant. You focus on the fight. What do you need?" Captain Ieva's concern was an arm around my shoulder. I found myself marveling at the common decency, perhaps "fraternity" was the better word, elicited from hard men when life's veil is torn asunder and we stood together facing eternity.

"Roger, sir. I could use a tank."

———

Sergeant Odie departed to gather the rest of Third Squad and finish clearing the street. Before they could do that, however, I needed to deal with Larry's house.

Walking back to the other street, I marshaled a brace of assault men and a SAW gunner and led them to the casualty collection point. It was now abandoned, save for wafers of blood crusting in the dust and a sterile wrapping or two. I pointed at the house where Philippon had died.

"Hit it. Guinn, lay down suppression while the assault team gets in position. They'll be most vulnerable right before the launch. Keep firing until they get back to cover, or they'll be totally exposed." Sleepy, silent Lance Corporal Guinn had surprised me by instantly volunteering for this dangerous task. At a motion from the assault team leader, Guinn stepped out from cover, shouldered his SAW, and opened at the cyclic rate. Rounds pummeled concrete walls and shattered windows of the target house as the assault men rushed forward with their rocket.

"Backblast area all secure! Rocket!" The excited gunner shouted the right words but failed to check over his shoulder. I barely had time to sidestep before the rocket's concussion blasted a swathe of dust and shredded vegetation behind us. Standing next to a rocket launch was like falling hard on ice; my insides tingled for several seconds after the initial jolt.

"Hit it again. Try the other window." I was unimpressed by the rocket's effect. Guinn continued to blast away as the assault men prepped and fired a second rocket. Frustrated, I realized the SMAW (shoulder-launched multipurpose assault weapon) was no match for a concrete house. Although Odie and Corporal Borch had cleared part of the first floor to get Philippon, I didn't want anyone else entering a structure with prepared defensive positions. Maybe I would have to wait for the tank.

"Sir."

I glanced around and saw two combat engineers peering curiously from behind a wall. One, a friendly corporal wearing flashing spectacles, casually sidled up.

"Sir, we can help. Those rockets won't penetrate interior sections." He squinted knowledgeably at the high courtyard wall. "And the angle isn't right to get good blast effect in the front rooms. But we have satchel charges." His buddy walked over with two, olive-drab bags the size of purses slung across his body.

"Twenty pounds of C-4 will bring that house down." The engineer paused. "But we'll use both, just in case."

It sounded like a great solution, but I wasn't clear on the method.

"How will you get them inside? There could still be insurgents in prepared positions."

The engineers looked at each other and shrugged. Then, with West Virginian simplicity, the corporal spoke.

"I guess we'll just run up and toss 'em in."

And that's exactly what they did. Providing their own suppression, the engineers sprinted up on either side of the front door, pulled primers, and flung the explosives down the hall. I had relocated outside the courtyard wall to ensure Third Squad was clear.

"Sir, you're gonna wanna move!" shouted the corporal as he rushed by. In seconds, an enormous shock wave pulsed through the street, followed by a tremendous roar. Chunks of concrete and twisted rebar crunched down around us, followed by a spatter of gravel and sifting clouds of gray dust. Gingerly, I peered around the courtyard wall and saw daylight beaming between ugly structures to the left and right.

The house of evil was gone.

———

Back on the street we'd first cleared—it seemed days ago—I picked my way to the rear of an Abrams tank. During our reduction of the enemy house, the tracs had left with our casualties and been replaced by this seventy-ton monster. Sickly sweet exhaust poured out from Honeywell turbines. The tank's 120mm main gun and frontal armor were oriented east toward uncleared streets with its hatches shut tight. Instead of an easy back-and-forth with the tank commander in the turret, I'd need to use the grunt phone.

At Twentynine Palms, during IOC, tanker veterans of Iraq had enthusiastically reminded us of the many benefits we could expect from tank support in an urban environment.

"Yeah, we have a sweet main gun, .50 cal, and a 7.62mm coax machine gun that uses the same thermals as the cannon—but don't forget we're a mobile armory too." The tankers were well-versed in infantry-armor tactics from the "march up" to Baghdad.

"If you get in a fight," an impossibly salty, one-eyed gunny had continued, "and need anything—extra batteries, frags, or even boxes of 7.62-linked—give us a call and we'll drop you a resupply."

We grinned appreciatively and cast envious glances at his black eye patch.

"Oh yeah," the gunny continued, almost as an afterthought, "if you're taking fire, better use the grunt phone in the back. We'll be buttoned up." He crooked a finger at his deformity and said flatly, "RPG."

Now, standing next to the whining turbines, I reached for the tan phone on its hook and placed it to my ear. Over the engine noise, I couldn't hear a thing.

Do I need to press a button or dial something?

No, a careful inspection of the phone box revealed nothing of the sort. I decided anything labeled "grunt phone" must be simple to operate and self-consciously began to shout into the mouthpiece.

"This is Lieutenant Smith. We need grenades to finish our clears on the next street. Do you have any?" There was no response, at least none that I could hear standing next to the turbines. I tried again. Again, there was no response. Frustrated, I slammed the phone on its hook and stepped back, looking for a way to climb on top of the turret.

Suddenly, the commander's hatch popped open and a grimy head appeared over the rim. Peering down at me, Lieutenant Dan—the Forrest Gump reference was inevitable, given the tank platoon commander's first name—was genuinely solicitous.

"Hey man, heard about your Marine. Sorry for your loss. What can we do to help?"

I nodded. The tanker's sympathy was unexpected but appreciated. In an unusual departure from the norm, Lieutenant Dan had graduated from the US Merchant Marine Academy and commissioned into the Marine Corps rather than assuming command of a civilian freighter. None of us really understood how it'd happened. He was fine-boned and bore a gentle demeanor that was out of character in the Marine Corps' meat-eating officer culture.

"Thanks. We're clearing the rest of the street and need grenades. You have any?"

Lieutenant Dan thought for a moment. "We sure do." He dropped from view, then reappeared shortly with three black, cardboard grenade canisters. I was disappointed there weren't more but didn't want to look a gift horse in the mouth.

"Here you go." He tossed them down one at a time. I looked disbelievingly at the label of one, then another.

"Dude. I don't need red smoke, I need frags."

Lieutenant Dan shrugged and looked embarrassed.

"Sorry, it's all we have."

So much for a mobile armory.

I shoved the grenades in my man purse without further comment and turned to rejoin my Marines.

————

The remaining house clears were uneventful, save for Private Lockwood's scuffle with a suspected insurgent that sent a blast of buckshot into both from the Marine's slung Mossberg 500. Lockwood shook his fist and roared at the man while blood trickled from a double-ought-sized hole in his boot. For his part, the unwilling detainee—crimson smeared across his thighs and torso—seemed considerably chastened and submitted quietly to a blindfold and plastic cuffs before receiving medical treatment from a corpsman.

The fighting seemed to have moved to the north and east. From time to time, we heard great, rocking explosions and long bursts of machine gun fire from Lima's area. Haze-gray Cobras and Huey gunships made occasional passes at a cement tower several hundred yards to the east, their miniguns whining and rockets flashing through the hot afternoon with a sound of tearing bedsheets.

At the end of Third Squad's street, we took up positions in the last houses and prepared to move into the next block.

But the order never came.

Instead, as the sun crept toward the horizon, Second Platoon pulled back from our limit of advance and returned to the tracs on the boulevard, leaving machine gun teams and snipers to hold key positions. I was nearly unconscious with fatigue and dehydration when I dropped into the TC hatch next to Sergeant Orona.

"You look tired, sir," he observed kindly. "Why don't you let me monitor the net while you take a break."

Pushing aside a flash of guilt, I gratefully accepted his offer and promptly passed out.

Orona woke me some time later. Blinking, my eyes bleared with dust and dried sweat, I ran my tongue around the foul taste in my mouth and felt defeated. Orange light slid across pockmarked buildings and shot-up palm trees, as if the setting sun begrudged any respite to this godforsaken desert.

"We're moving back to the fuel point by the water tower," Orona said. Snipers and machine gunners echeloned back to the tracs as big engines coughed to life, sending pleasant vibrations through my aching body. By the time we made it to the low heights south of the city, the sun was gone and the sky had deepened from pale blue to sapphire.

While the tracs refueled and NCOs drew water and chow for their exhausted teams, Orona passed word that two Marines had been killed in the northern part of the city: one shot down by Chechens in hidden positions beneath a staircase, the other killed in an attempt to recover the body.

I took the information silently. Orona didn't press me for a response.

Why should he? There was nothing to say.

CHAPTER 23

We All Fall Down

Steve | August 2001 | Taylor University, Upland, Indiana

Leandro stood big and rangy in the hallway of our dorm. He had sweet tats, huge biceps, slicked-back hair, and a voice like a crowbar. Because of this, the other guys nodded when he said, "Hey, let's make our own version of *Fight Club*. It'll be a great way to bond as men."

Sure, they said. Let's beat the crap out of each other.

It made a lot of sense—if you were Leandro. He'd boxed on the amateur circuit and grew up in the ring. He also had a broken nose and the reach of a gorilla. For him, smacking down an opponent was part of the bond of brotherhood. No one at our small Christian college could possibly beat him.

And so, "Trailer Club" was conceived at Taylor University in Upland, Indiana, in late August 2001. Guys sat around shirtless and sweating, planning the intricacies of the meetings. What was the purpose? Who could come? And of course, what were the rules? Because the first rule of Trailer Club was . . . well, you couldn't copy *Fight Club* word-for-word, could you? The guys sought their own punchy epigram.

Leandro said he wanted to galvanize young men who'd grown up in a culture of affluence and who'd mostly avoided suffering. He wanted us to take up our cross and follow Christ. From our suburban, white velvet Leandro wanted to create saddle leather. By suffering together, we could move toward community nirvana.

I felt I already knew something about suffering. The idea of being knocked around by an amateur boxer carried little appeal. For a few minutes, I listened to Leandro outline his vision, watched the sweat glisten on his forehead and drip down his nose, saw the circle of eager, upraised faces.

Then I quietly backed away and shut my door.

Two weeks later I sat in US History class, waiting for Dr. Jones to arrive. The clock on the wall read 9:06. According to the *TU Student Handbook*, we could leave if a professor was more than ten minutes late. Several students put their heads down on their desks. I tapped a mechanical pencil against my binder.

At nine past nine our professor strode into the classroom, coattails flapping, sweater vest askew. "Two planes just flew into the World Trade Center. Go find a television."

No one moved.

Outside, I could hear birds singing. From somewhere down below the dining commons a lawnmower roared. Cornstalks bent in the breeze. It was a gorgeous day.

"Terrorists are flying airplanes into buildings," Dr. Jones said. "Our country is under attack."

Back in the dorm, I stood on a chair behind two rows of guys huddled around Dave Ayres's widescreen television. We watched replays of the second plane dissolving into glass and steel as a fireball bloomed from the other side of the South Tower. Papers fluttered like wounded birds in the smoke.

Then the North Tower imploded.

"Oh, my God!" one of the guys said. I could hear shouts coming from rooms up and down the hallway. Far away a girl screamed.

Over and over, we watched the towers fall.

"It looks like a movie," Dave said.

Nothing about it seemed real. Not until a reporter said that over three hundred firefighters were missing.

Three hundred?

It was such a hideous number that the enormity of what was happening finally clawed into our packed dorm room.

Three hundred firefighters dead?

That was obscene.

I stood on the chair and knew instantly that we would go to war.

And then I thought about Nate.

———

To his credit, Leandro dissolved Trailer Club and instead led a trip to Ground Zero to help feed first responders.

It never occurred to me to go.

Disasters, I thought, were something that other people handled. My job, as Wes had told me repeatedly before I left for college, was to attend every single class and get perfect grades. This would bring God's pleasure. It was also a requirement to retain the substantial scholarship my church had granted me each semester.

In mid-October, I sat nursing a migraine in the study rooms at the library, eating handfuls of almond Hershey Kisses and drinking cold coffee past midnight. A pile of foil wrappers blossomed beside me.

Every few minutes, I checked the latest CNN headlines about Afghanistan. The previous summer, I had fantasized about becoming a missionary to that brown and blasted land.

A thought struck me.

I typed "Missions to Afghanistan" into my browser. Which Christian organization could I join? I wondered. One serving orphans? Or perhaps amputees? But the first dozen hits were all about B-2 bombing missions in northern Afghanistan.

I canceled my search and returned to my books.

Closing my Greek grammar, I decided to check my email once more before trudging back to the dorm. The subject line at the top of the queue said simply "Hi."

It was from Nate.

Blood thumped in my ears. I looked over my shoulder. It was a silly gesture. The room was empty, and the nearest member of my church was a thousand miles away. No one would report me to Wes.

"Hey Steve," the note read. "Hopefully this is the right Steve Smith. How are you? How do you like school? This year has been my busiest yet, for a lot of reasons. And now with this war, things are getting even busier. Hope you are well. I'd like to hear from you if you get a chance. Love, Nate."

I hadn't seen Nate since we'd crossed paths accidentally in Cumberland back in May. We'd run past each other on Main Street, turned, then stared at each other without saying anything. After a brief argument about who was right and who was wrong, we turned and ran off in opposite directions.

Now in the study room, softened by loneliness and the distant guns of war, I wanted to reply to him.

I will reply.

He was my twin brother, wasn't he?

My hands went to my keyboard and then fell away.

Nate probably thinks that I shunned him just because Wes told me to. And now that I'm a thousand miles across the country he thinks I'll throw all that away.

But that wasn't true. Nate had gone out from us because he wasn't one of us, and if I had fellowship with him, it showed that I actually hated his soul. The very pain of rejection was supposed to drive him toward Christ. The Bible said so.

I knew that I should report Nate's email to Wes, that I should let my pastor know that my brother was trying to contact me without his oversight. My hands rose again to the keyboard, and I started to type another email. Then I canceled it and let my hands fall to my lap.

I couldn't do it.

I couldn't do anything.

A few weeks later, I dashed off an email to Nate. God was working deeply in my life, I said, and the Lord could change Nate's heart if he let him. There were only three things Nate needed to do: he had to give up everything, return to our church, and obey Wes completely.

What could be simpler?

CHAPTER 24

Burning

Nate | 8–9 May 2005 | Four Hundred Meters South of Ubaydi, Iraq

We spent the night in skirmisher trenches on a low ridge south of Ubaydi's mosque, while tanks and light armored vehicles (LAVs) scanned the smoking city and joint direct-attack munitions (JDAMs) crashed down from the starry sky. Task Force—a secretive group of Tier-1 operators whose beards concealed hard faces accustomed to killing—flitted through abandoned streets making house calls in the dark. The fight in Ubaydi was over for Second Platoon, but insurgents continued to die as they prepared to repel a new assault in the morning.

The assault never came.

Shaken awake by a tired radio watch in the chilly half-light before dawn, I watched the eastern sky slowly separate from desert while the captain issued a warning order: be prepared to mount up and cross the river at daybreak. The regiment's plan to clear north of the Euphrates would proceed.

It seemed odd that we'd leave the city to insurgents and start searching for them in hamlets on the north bank. The planners must have compelling intelligence to direct us so. Frankly, it was a relief to know yesterday's bloody seizure of an urban foothold wouldn't have to be repeated.

I hadn't spoken to the platoon about Philippon's death, but while tired men stowed gear and stumbled into darkened troop compartments didn't seem like the right time. I was loath to manufacture a poignant moment minutes before we embarked on a new series of house clears and cache sweeps. For now, I wanted the men focused forward.

The engineers still hadn't managed to construct their bridge. We crossed the surging Euphrates an hour after sunrise on a floating road section used as a raft. On the far side, we churned past swaying thickets of reeds and thin-leafed cattails, up a steep embankment, and broke through a fringe of tamarisks and low palms at the edge of a broad field. A dirt road ran through the field and wandered into a village set behind an earthen berm half a mile away. According to my map, the village was Battalion Objective 1.

We dismounted and hit it at 0730.

———

Over the next few days, Second Platoon pushed toward Syria, clearing towns nestled between desert heights to the north and the broad Euphrates to the south. Small stone houses jumbled together in the comfortable disorder of agrarian hamlets. Roosters and clay-oven cooking fires woke us before dawn. At night, the yips and howls of feral dogs echoed over trash heaps in a millennia-old melody as we drifted off beneath a blanket of stars.

Sunny days slipped by without incident. As they passed, the memory of Ubaydi's savagery blunted and lost a measure of its horror. The earthy smell of melons and cucumbers, shadows stretching across crumbling stone walls, and the hungry cattle lowing in the gloaming were all remarkably healing. The timelessness of the land seemed an elixir for the soul. I drank in great draughts of country air and felt nearly whole again.

Despite the bucolic scene, we remained disciplined. We moved only under the watchful eyes of our fellow Marines, who provided overwatch from rush-covered rooftops. When we mounted up between villages, Sergeant Orona found creative routes that avoided intersections, choke points, and other areas likely to be seeded with mines and IEDs. Sometimes, we carved broad gashes through swaying fields of waist-high crops. I felt bad about the destruction and told Orona so.

"We're not taking that road, sir," he stated flatly as the sweet smell of onions exploded from beneath our treads. "They've had days to prep for us. I'll cut through every field in Iraq if it'll save one Marine."

His logic was sound, but the locals were unlikely to view our actions so philosophically.

If this farmer didn't support the insurgency before, I thought cynically as we burst from the field in a spray of brown earth and green onions, *he does now*.

———

By early afternoon on the third day, we'd slogged through hundreds of houses in four battalion objectives and discovered little more than a few wires, one old antipersonnel mine, and an Iraqi National Guard officer's Chicom (Chinese Communist) grenade. In contrast, Captain Ieva confirmed rumors of hard fighting to the west, where two of the battalion's mobile assault platoons had been ambushed south of the Golden Gate bridge.

After losing a tank and tank retriever to suicide attacks, the mobile assault Marines had fought through the ambush and were now holding the southern approach to the bridge for several days against spirited attacks. Importantly, it was the only span between Ubaydi and Syria that could support vehicle traffic. Enemy gunmen in slit trenches and insurgent mortars on the north bank of the river were relentless.

Now we were approaching those enemy positions from the east. Everyone, from the captain to the regimental planners, thought we were about to get into it. Second Platoon went firm to wait for tanks, LAVs, and Third Platoon reinforcements before launching an assault against the positions that had been most troublesome. I squatted on a rooftop plotting the platoon's next movements when Staff Sergeant Hanson appeared at my shoulder.

"Hey sir," he said excitedly, "I heard Ollie North is embedded with the battalion staff for this next objective. He's going to film the action for Fox News. The jump (battalion commander's mobile command group) has collocated with Captain Ieva."

The news was of slight interest to me. Any propensity to hero worship had died in Ubaydi, where real heroes looked remarkably like filthy young men in need of sleep and a smoke. The fact that the famous host of *War Stories* was at our position struck me as a needless distraction from the business at hand.

"Great," I grunted. "At least he's a Marine. If things get bad, he can join in."

Fortunately, things didn't get bad. Perhaps because of low-altitude passes from British Tornadoes; LAV chain gun fire at suspected vehicle-borne improvised explosive devices (VBIEDs); and machine gun, rocket, and tank fire that demolished an Iraqi police station used by gunmen to target the bridge, the insurgents chose not to defend their positions and melted away without a fight.

During the assault, while a nearby LAV hammered a parked vehicle with 25mm rounds at twenty yards, I happened to look down into the alley separating my building from the next one and saw a cluster of kneeling men. Hunkered down like a command group beneath the cliffs of Normandy, several battalion staff members gestured excitedly while speaking rapidly into handsets. Crouched next to the staff was a figure that looked conspicuous in clean desert utilities and a flak jacket free of ammo or grenade pouches. *That must be Ollie North.*

A broad, red face glanced up.

"Hey, sir," the battalion sergeant major rasped out, "come on down and tell Colonel North what your boys are up to!"

I shook my head.

"No thanks, Sergeant Major. I've got a platoon to lead." My tone hinted at belligerence, and I fully expected a tongue lashing from the battalion's famously short-tempered senior enlisted Marine. Instead, Sergeant Major barked out what could have passed for the cry of a wounded animal, but was presumably his version of glee, and rejoined the command group without another word.

I turned back to the roof in confusion.

Then it dawned on me: *He's treating me like a peer.*

The idea seemed absurd, until I realized with sudden clarity that a few hours in Ubaydi had washed away my greenness and established me as a man who had seen the beast and not come undone.

Hardly a war hero.

But the corps puts great stock in those baptized by fire.

———

Residue of previous fighting gave abandoned houses a sinister air as we swept through our objective. Mortar fins lay haphazardly against gray walls spattered with shrapnel starbursts. Upended platters spilled profusions of rice and beans across floors floured with cement dust. In one alleyway, a cloud of flies clung greedily to a brown puddle that smelled of corruption.

The late afternoon smothered beneath a hazy sky. Stepping out from between buildings, I found myself on the edge of a dirt road that ran north to south and marked the limit of our advance. Across the road stood a low stone wall and beyond that, thin groves screened a series of fields interlaced by irrigation ditches. Turning south, I squinted through a mirage and made out the road passing through an open area before disappearing over a bluff and then rising to meet a nondescript line of pontoons.

"Dotson, radio Black that we have eyes on Golden Gate."

According to the scheme of maneuver, Second Platoon would now go firm while Lima 3/25 leapfrogged us to clear the next objective to the west. Daylight would fade by the time the reservists had finished, which meant we could plan on staying here for the night. After a long, hot day of clearing operations, the idea of dropping gear and resting swollen feet seemed most appealing. Dotson interrupted my reverie.

"Sir, Black wants us to clear trenches on the riverbank and have engineers sweep the bridge road for IEDs."

I nodded and told Dotson to get Hanson and Odie. The platoon's main body could go firm while small teams echeloned out to conduct cache sweeps and engineers probed the road. Seeking cover from the brassy heat while awaiting his return, I walked across the street and leaned against the stone wall where a large date palm provided some shade.

Normally, I wouldn't expose myself so casually, but with Marine units adjacent to us and a lack of enemy contact for the past three days, I felt reasonably confident that the insurgents were gone. In the background, tracs' hydraulic grinding marked Lima's progress toward the next objective as Sergeant Major materialized on the road and made straight for me. He was still in high humor.

"Sir! I thought I'd find you here. Colonel North is doing a show about the fight in Ubaydi. He's talked to Clemmey's boys, but he really needs to hear your perspective." He held up a square hand as I began to protest.

"Now, sir," he continued, "I know you don't want attention, but your Marines did well, and their story deserves to be told. The colonel is just down the road—I can be back with him in five minutes. What do you say?"

I relented, as he knew I would.

"Okay, Sergeant Major. But only for fifteen minutes. We still have trench clearing and cache sweeps to do." A part of me was secretly thrilled that I'd been involved in something notable enough to make national news. Sergeant Major grinned and charged off with the boundless energy of a drill instructor.

Settling back against the wall, I mentally ran through my orders to Staff Sergeant Hanson and Sergeant Odie. Our priority was the establishment of a firm base in one of the larger houses with a commanding view of the bridge. Then, we'd task a team to provide security for the engineers while—

I felt the concussion thump through my body before I heard the explosion.

In the deep silence that followed, I realized that all trac noise had ceased. Leaping to my feet, I turned northwest and spotted an immobilized AAV about a hundred yards away in a field. Scrub trees obscured my view of the trac's treads and roadwheels, but there was no doubt about what had happened.

Mine strike, probably a double stack.

Within moments, I heard distant shouts as running figures approached the stricken vehicle from several directions. There was no movement from the trac itself, except for black smoke billowing up in a rapidly expanding column against the pale sky.

I turned to a cluster of Marines standing nearby.

"Find Doc."

Doc made the order unnecessary by slipping out of a doorway and slinging his medical pack; then he broke into a trot toward the column of smoke. Dotson reappeared, handset pressed to his ear, brows knitted. He looked up.

"Sir, they need all corpsmen and combat lifesavers to help with Lima's casualties. Now."

His words were punctuated by a crackle of small arms rounds cooking off inside the stricken AAV, followed by a series of hollow thumps as heavier ordnance detonated in the troop compartment.

Did any of them get out?

I watched smoke boil up among a quickening cadence of ammo cook-offs. It was difficult to imagine anyone could survive that holocaust. The faces around me looked somber.

The call went out for combat lifesavers. Within a minute, several men with small, tan medical kits and rudimentary training as first responders were hustling after Doc. Rocking explosions drummed across the fields as mortar rounds, claymore mines, and grenades detonated in the raging inferno. I realized that my priority, now that we had sent what help we could to the reservists, was to tighten security in case insurgents decided to take advantage of the chaos.

"Go to 'Stand to,'" I commanded.

The order was repeated by troop leaders, who hustled off to coordinate the overlapping security vital to defense in an urban environment. Casting a last look at the funeral pyre in the field, I said a silent prayer for the injured and then prepared to inspect machine gun positions on the roof.

No one had to tell me the Oliver North interview was canceled.

———

Throughout that endless afternoon, medevac birds flared into the muddy field near the destroyed AAV, alighting briefly to receive burned men, then powering up and out with their precious cargo, bound for the shock trauma unit at Balad. Responsibility for the clear of Battalion Objective 6 shifted from the decimated reservists to Second Platoon. We packed gear and trekked over to the next hamlet while medevac helos clattered overhead. It was not until we went firm in the dull orange evening that the last helicopter lifted off, a slick body bag placed carefully on board by men pale with exhaustion and loss.

Doc Alcala and the combat lifesavers had rejoined us at the beginning of the clear.

The men's faces were drawn; they looked shaken. One, his cheeks streaked with soot, said simply, "I hope I never see anything like that again."

In all, Lima lost nine men with severe burns and six men whose families were about to hear the worst possible news.

And for what?

The thought came unbidden as I spread out a musty Korean blanket in the twilight and prepared to bed down. For the first time in the deployment, doubt crept from a hidden place. It was a place I refused to look. I couldn't believe our actions were fruitless.

There must be a bigger picture. Something we don't see at the ground level.

Total exhaustion is a powerful thought stopper. Pulling my poncho liner close, I fell asleep in moments.

———

MATADOR continued for three more days. We cleared more villages, destroyed more crops (in our efforts to avoid mines), and, during one memorable night, we spent hours scanning the Euphrates' black ribbon in search of a high value target named Abu Musab Al-Zarqawi. But there was no more fighting and, finally, having reached nearly to the Syrian border, we turned around early one morning and drove home.

No Marines remained behind in the farming villages that we'd cleared with such effort. No combat outpost marked a new chapter in the struggle for influence with the unfriendly residents of Ubaydi.

Despite the cost of nine dead Marines and dozens more wounded, we gave everything back to the enemy.

Later, secure in our desert base at Al Qa'im, we held a memorial service for the dead men and made plans for the next operation. Later still, reports trickled in from local contacts, confirming that Al Qaeda had flowed back into the abandoned towns, abducting or beheading anyone suspected of collaborating.

———

"Nate, I haven't heard from you in weeks. You didn't even ask how I'm doing." It was more than the poor connection over an MWR (morale, welfare, and recreation) phone that made my girlfriend's voice sound distant.

I'd sent her a brief email after MATADOR, referencing the operation and fumbling through the obligatory niceties. It didn't require women's intuition for her to realize something had changed. Now, as I sat hunched over a bench next to a

Marine who was busy investing a phone call with lies about his combat exploits, a great weariness descended at the idea of manufacturing emotion.

I felt nothing.

"Nate? Will you please say something?"

The bench was knocked together from scrap lumber and adorned with squads of sketched phalluses, the instinctive art of bored Marines. I rubbed my thumb against the grain, savoring its slight give in a world of cement and stone. Then my vocal chords made mechanical little movements and fired puffs of poison gas into the receiver.

"I don't feel anything. I'm sorry—I want to—but I don't." I paused miserably, grasping for a civil way to end the conversation.

Part of me cried out for the love, kindness, and sense of home that my girlfriend represented. But a more dominant part of me—the part that needed to lead Marines professionally during four more months in Iraq—required absolute, undivided attention to the mission. I could be at war or not. I was incapable of mentally shifting between the two.

"It's . . . bad over here." I stopped, surprised that I couldn't make myself talk about what had happened during MATADOR. The Marine next to me—who'd never left the base—didn't seem to have the same problem. His war stories continued with vigor.

"I can't do this while I'm here. I can't."

My girlfriend remained composed while wishing me well. Perhaps the voice she heard didn't sound like the man she once knew. Perhaps that made it easier for her.

I set the phone back in its cradle and gave my spot on the bench to an eager lance corporal.

Stepping into the night with a burning lump in my throat, one thought was ascendant.

Next time I go to war, I'll be single.

CHAPTER 25

Unknown Unknowns

Steve | 25 March 2002 | Cumberland, Maine

Nate emailed when I was home on spring break.

He'd been hurt by my response to him in November, he said, but he also realized that God was working differently in our lives, and he respected that.

"I'm concerned about some of the things that I'm hearing are transpiring at Faith Baptist right now," he wrote. "I don't like getting information secondhand or putting stock in rumors, so I'm asking you to explain to me what's going on. Although I don't correspond with you, Christine, or Mom and Dad very often, I still love you with all my heart and am concerned for your health: physically, spiritually, and emotionally."

What things had he heard? I wondered. And from whom?

I sat back in my chair and thought about all the weird things that had happened in our church while I'd been away at school. Allegations of sexual abuse committed by an ex–Sunday school teacher, criminal charges filed against him, and layers of demonic harassment, according to Wes. In the last few Sundays, my pastor had hinted that there were even worse things afoot, things that were beyond our wildest imagination.

Unknown unknowns.

It reminded me of a briefing I'd watched in February in which Defense Secretary Donald Rumsfeld talked about the possibility that Saddam Hussein was harboring terrorists and weapons of mass destruction in Iraq. Rumsfeld famously told reporters:

> Reports that say that something hasn't happened are always interesting to me, because as we know, there are known knowns; there are things we know we know. We also know there are known

unknowns; that is to say, we know there are some things we do not know. But there are also unknown unknowns—the ones we don't know we don't know. And if one looks throughout the history of our country and other free countries, it is the latter category that tends to be the difficult one.

His logic struck me as sound. Wes regularly shared horrible information with our church that we hadn't previously known existed and couldn't really prove. Stuff we didn't know we didn't know was always sure to ruin our day. Why should it be any different with a nation on its way to war?

Now I wondered what Nate knew about our church that I didn't.

I read on.

"If you like (I know how this works, anyway)," Nate wrote, "feel free to share this note with whomever you will. I am genuinely concerned and seeking God's guidance as to what my response should be regarding occurrences at Faith, whether they be positive or negative. I dislike having other people try to influence my opinion on issues, which is why I'd like to hear from you directly, so that I can make my own decisions and judgments."

For a moment, I considered replying directly to Nate's letter so that I could discover what he'd heard. How could I rebut what I didn't know? But then I decided to share the letter with Wes. Surely the man at the center of all the controversy in our church would be the best source to dispel any rumors.

But when I finished reading Nate's letter to Wes over the phone, Wes said simply, "Don't reply."

"You mean don't say anything about what's happening in our church?"

"No, don't reply at all," Wes said. "Pretend he never sent it. An email like that doesn't even deserve a response."

My long silence must have expressed doubt because Wes sounded frustrated. "Look Steve, we have been over this before. Your brother is in active rebellion against God and against God's anointed servant. If Nate wants to know what is happening at this church, he should not ask you—he should ask me."

"But whatever rumors he's heard must involve you as pastor," I said, surprised that Wes hadn't thought of this. "He's not going to believe anything you say."

"If he is serious about the truth, he will talk to me first about his sin. If you reply to him, you are disobeying God's servant. Is that clear?"

Wes's tone surprised me. Nate's questions seemed legitimate. Didn't he deserve a response for reaching out and trying to get our side of the story? Suddenly, I had a strong urge to argue with Wes, but I couldn't choke out any words. I wasn't sure I knew how to disagree.

Wes's voice was stern. "I said, 'Is that clear?'"

"Yes," I said softly.

"Yes what?"

"Yes, sir."

He had never asked me to say "sir" before.

After Wes hung up, I gazed out my bedroom window and prayed that the unknown unknowns of which Nate spoke were false.

But of course, they were all true.

July 2002 | Yarmouth, Maine

In May, the *Portland Press Herald*—the largest daily paper in the state of Maine—broke the story about our church.

By now I already knew the basics. A former Sunday School teacher who'd left our congregation the year before was accused of sexually assaulting an eleven-year-old boy in the church. The allegations came out during special counseling sessions with Wes. The boy's family had pressed charges and the man's wife had left him.

When police arrested the man, things got interesting.

Community members rallied to his side. Many ex-members of our church believed that the allegations were false. They thought they were trumped up charges created by Wes to punish the man for leaving our church. *The Portland Press Herald–Maine Sunday Telegram* did a front-page, above-the-fold story called "Pastor's Methods Set Off Concerns." Wes had created a suggestive climate in which everyone felt pressure to recover memories of supposed abuse, the reporter wrote. Now a good man faced prison because of these allegations.

A second article, by a different reporter, said that recovered memories could prove false and were often treated with both sympathy and skepticism by professional therapists and courts. It cited various experts who said that the theophostic technique itself was suspect and that in the wrong hands it could easily be abused. Even the district attorney doubted our story.

I had listened as Wes read the articles from the pulpit the week before, rebutting them line by line and word by word. I nodded as he made his defense. There was nothing new here, I thought. Just persecution by evil people who wanted to see God's good work in our church destroyed.

Channel 6 also ran an episode about us on the evening news. Jarringly, I saw Nate—recently returned from Marine Officer Candidates School—appear in an ex-church member's house. He wore a red-and-gold VMI T-shirt and his face looked tough and hard. He stared into the camera and said that Wes was the most manipulative and controlling person he'd ever met. For the first time in my life, I felt ashamed that I looked like Nate. I thought other church members might think that I was rebellious like he was.

For a while, the media exposure filled me with a thrilling sense of purpose. I believed I was being persecuted for righteousness' sake. But then the novelty wore off. Now I just wanted anonymity.

———

On a sweltering day in early July, I decided I needed an afternoon to cleanse my mind from the frenzied news reports. I was tired of thinking, tired of judging, and tired of fearing unknown unknowns.

Today, I just wanted to fly a kite.

On my drive north to Popham Beach in Phippsburg, I stopped at the grocery store in Yarmouth to cash my paycheck so I'd have money for parking. The girl at the service counter recognized me. "Hey!" she said, smiling. "Don't you work in the deli?"

I nodded. I'd picked up a few shifts while I was home from Taylor.

The girl had curly dark hair and freckles. Her smile warmed me and I responded to it with more than my usual defensiveness. I wanted her to like me. "I'm on summer break from college," I said, hoping to impress her.

"Which school?"

"Taylor University. It's a Christian liberal arts college in Indiana."

"I knew it!" she squealed. "I knew you were a Christian! I could just tell. Christians can always spot one another."

Too late, I anticipated her next question and my mind scrabbled to find a way around it.

"Where do you go to church?" she asked delightedly.

I tried to soften the blow: "I go to the most notorious church in the area."

She arched one of her eyebrows.

There was no way to avoid it. "I go to Faith Baptist Church in North Yarmouth."

The girl stepped back as if slapped. Her shock must have been terrible. On my way to the beach in shorts and sandals, sunglasses perched atop gelled hair, I probably didn't fit her image of what a "cult" member looked like.

"Oh!" she exclaimed, putting her hand to her chest. "I know a lot of people who've been hurt by that church."

Behind me, I could hear feet shuffling on the linoleum. A line was forming. My vision contracted; there was a thrumming in my ears.

"Well," I said, trying to sound sagacious, "the Book of Proverbs says that 'one man sounds right, until another comes forward and presents his case.'"

I felt pleased with myself. The Holy Spirit must have given me that bit of wisdom. "I'd encourage you to talk to current members to hear their side of the story," I said. "They might tell you that they've been hurt by some of the people who left."

The girl stared at me, emotions playing over her face like clouds over the surface of a lake.

I asked about my money.

"Right," she said. "Sorry." She slid the money across the counter and then quickly dropped her hands behind the desk to avoid touching me. All the light had gone from her face. "I'll be praying for you."

"Okay," I said, taking the small stack of bills. "You too."

Then I rushed out of the store.

I felt like a robber.

———

Throughout the summer, local papers continued to print articles about our church. Instead of making me feel odious, they only made me feel angry. When the district attorney dropped all charges against the ex–church member, I felt lost, as if once again God had abandoned me.

In mid-August, sweltering heat permeated the church sanctuary. We had no air conditioning except the windows. Wes finally allowed us to open them to catch a breeze.

Standing in front of forty-five remaining church members during the evening service, Mike sweated on the scarlet carpet as Wes plied him with questions. He was a young man who wanted to go to college. To do so, he needed to confess a life of misdeeds and affirm his gratefulness to Wes for counseling him onto the path of life.

Suddenly, tires squealed in the church parking lot and a female voice shouted, "You're a cult! You're a cult!" A male voice added, "You're a fucking cult!" Tires screeched again and the car raced away.

We sat stunned in our pews.

Mike paused in his confession and now Wes shook his head slowly, blinked, and said "proceed," as if nothing had happened.

My nerves frayed. Some local teens had just torn through our parking lot and screamed through the open windows. If someone could do that, I thought, then they could do something worse. They could burn down our church or, or . . . my mind faltered.

Or, they can shoot Wes.

The thought came unbidden. Yes, someone could shoot Wes and then he would be dead, and our church would be free, and I could see my brother again. For a split second, I turned the idea over in my head while Mike continued his confession.

What would I do if Wes was dead? What couldn't I do? Our church would disband, wouldn't it? Everyone knows that Wes alone holds us together. If he was dead, the church would dissolve.

Ka-chunk.

A mental barrier dropped, and I couldn't carry the thought further. But it was too late. I'd already thought it.

Someone could kill Wes. He was only a man, and someday he would die.

The thought was flaky pie crust in my mind. Through the rest of the night and for many weeks afterward I'd suddenly see the barest edge of the idea: what if today was the day Wes died?

Then I'd shove it down, shake my head, and ask God to forgive me. It was a sin to think of Wes dying. I prayed that Wes would live for many years and that God would bless us with his wisdom until I was an old man myself.

But the thought came back again, and again, and again.

———

The next Saturday, just before returning to school, I released the blade guard of the church push mower and let it sputter to a stop. Something had caught my eye as I edged near the road. I bent down and pushed aside some weeds in front of the mower.

Holy shit, I thought.

It was a ball of nails about the size of my fist, wired together, with the points facing out. I turned it over in my hand.

Twenty feet away, cars whizzed by on Route 9. I palmed the nail ball, then pulled the mower over toward the bushes near the church sign. I left the mower there and walked across the parking lot to the back of the church where I'd parked my car. Carefully, I placed the nail ball in the passenger seat. Then I covered it with my work gloves.

It could've been some random accident, I told myself. Maybe it fell off a truck or bounced out the back of a load of scrap. Or maybe it had some mechanical use I wasn't aware of.

Sure, that was it.

A nail ball used especially for—for what? Why would anyone wire together a bunch of nails and throw it on our church lawn? I remembered the truck screeching through our parking lot the previous Sunday and then I thought of the ball of nails and the passing traffic.

Why would anyone throw a ball of nails where they knew someone would mow? I looked down and the hair on my bare legs prickled.

I could think of only one reason.

CHAPTER 26

What Might Have Been

Nate | 18 June 2005 | Karabilah, Iraq

A week after Operation MATADOR, I was promoted to first lieutenant in a hurried ceremony attended by a handful of staff and officers. It's customary on such occasions for promotees to say a few words. Flanked by the battalion commander and Captain Ieva, I gravely surveyed the gathered leaders and dispensed pearls of wisdom accrued from my long career of two years.

"Always do right by your Marines. And question stupid orders."

My heart was in the right place, but my tact could have used some work. The captain's subsequent handshake and congratulation were curt.

Three weeks later, I once again led Second Platoon outside the wire on a named mission. Operation SPEAR was memorable for our use of mine-clearing line charges—each more than a hundred meters of rocket-projected C-4 explosive—to carve out safe passages through the IED-infested heart of Karabilah. The city had gained a reputation for wickedness when the battalion's mobile platoons were ambushed in its streets during MATADOR.

Darting over newly drifted piles of rubble on the second day of the assault, Second Platoon seized an Al Qaeda compound that yielded troves of intelligence and offered a rare, humanitarian moment. In the northeast corner of the compound, we liberated four terrified Iraqis who were discovered bound, blindfolded, gagged with packing tape, lying face down in their own filth. The men had been held for weeks, beaten repeatedly with rebar and fire hose, tortured hideously, and left to die by the fleeing insurgents on the first day of the operation.

The captives had sweltered for two days without food or water in the blazing heat, trembling blindly as explosions concussed their broken bodies—each man convinced the next bomb or tank round would snuff him out. While we clipped handcuffs off the scabbed and mutilated men, First Platoon was ambushed by a foreign fighter in a nearby house and Lance Corporal Crumpler was killed.

The death of another Marine affected the entire company. Combined with the discovery of an Al Qaeda torture chamber in the compound—complete with syringes of motor oil, a ceiling hook and bucket for electrocutions, and black painted windows muffled by wool blankets—we had no sympathy toward insurgents, living or dead.

The next day, a foreign correspondent rushed up to me on a debris-strewn street near the northern edge of town. I felt emotionally depleted, physically exhausted, and was dutifully planning an assault on the last uncleared pocket of buildings to our front.

The reporter was incensed. "Are you in charge of these men?" he asked belligerently, gesturing vaguely down the street.

"Some of them," I replied, not at all interested in entertaining a reporter when I had an attack to plan.

"I just saw them run over a dead body!" His tone was haughty and accusing.

I decided that I disliked him.

Peering past crumbled walls and the smudge of burnt-out vehicles, I couldn't see the crushed insurgent at whom he pointed. "It's a narrow street. Military movement has priority. I'm sure they didn't see it." I didn't really care if they had. And if they had, what did he want me to do about it?

"I saw them swerve to run over it! It was brutal and unnecessary!"

I stared at the man's thin face. Mine was impassive. Unmoving. It would have been difficult for him to report that I gave a shit.

"Huh," I grunted. Then I left him standing in the street, cleared of Al Qaeda fighters by the same Marines he condemned.

———

Many important lessons in war are learned from what might have been, rather than what actually occurs.

In mid-July, I led an early morning raid to kill or capture a high value target in Sa'dah, about ten miles north of our base. After navigating through streets lit blindingly by courtyard fluorescents, we dismounted at the dark edge of town and hit a tree-lined compound in an open field.

While Marines actioned the objective, Sergeant French—my trac commander—led a profane, grunting effort to cut a chain-link fence out from under our treads in time for us to return to base with six detainees. As men labored with the snarled equipment, I fretted in the TC hatch and watched green tracers float lazily into the western sky, pinpointing where local tribes were battling Al Qaeda in Karabilah and Husaybah.

I returned to base just as the stars began to pale, and walked wearily into the battalion operations center. Instantly, I was collared by the chain-smoking S-3 (Battalion Operations Officer) Major Day.

"Hey Smitty, I've got bad news." Major Day was one of my favorites; his bloodshot eyes and brotherly manner told a story of devotion to the men who executed his plans. The major never pulled punches. I waited for the hammer to fall.

"We got new intel, just as you left the objective. We had the wrong house. The right house," here Major Day pointed to imagery marked with red squares, "was actually right next to where you parked the tracs."

I couldn't believe it. "And nobody told us while we were there?"

Major Day was sympathetic. "We didn't know. Now we do." He looked at me blearily, in his perpetually sleep-deprived way. "You'll have to do it again tonight."

So, we did.

Captain Ieva, somewhat uncharacteristically, decided that it would be less prep simply to run the same team and scheme of maneuver and ordered a repeat of the previous night's operation. He backed up the departure from 0300 to midnight.

"Sir, I don't think we should take the same route," I argued halfheartedly and without success. I had to admit there were no obvious alternatives to the route we'd just taken. Most of it passed through open desert, while the city road was unavoidable and the most dangerous part anyway.

Ok, we'll execute dash two.

————

The night was moonless as we rolled through wasteland north of the base. Even the stars seemed muted. I raised a pair of PVS-7Bs to scan the flat terrain ahead. Seeing nothing, I switched off the useless optic and shoved it into my man purse. In gloom like this, an unaided eye was often more acute than expensive night vision goggles.

Glancing right, I saw Sergeant French in shadowed profile. He craned his neck as he relayed course corrections to the driver below. It was marvelous to watch the trackers navigate so confidently through the dark. Leaning back against vibrating steel, I tried to relax and waited for French to call out the next checkpoint. *Why did this mission feel off?*

The danger of running the identical maneuver two nights in a row was not that insurgents would be waiting for us. The danger was complacency.

I'd noted the subdued way men climbed into troop compartments. I'd heard their lack of banter, the flat energy as ramps lifted and bodies jumbled against each other for the forty-five-minute ride to the objective. This was old hat. We'd been five months in Iraq. Men who wearied of routine operations began to look forward to the end of our seven-month deployment.

My own thoughts turned toward home. Home was open water, swaying leaves, soft shadows dappled against green grass. Iraq was all angles and extremes, white light squeezing tears from aching eyes. I yearned for Maine, to breathe salt air and to leave the wasting desert behind. Perhaps at home I'd find some space to re-sharpen the mental edge that felt ground down by months of unrelenting responsibility.

"Sir, Checkpoint Two-Three coming up."

French's voice pitched low, as if to respect the silent desert.

Ahead, I made out the blur of a railroad bed, running west from the superphosphate plant toward Syria. The steel rails were perched twenty feet above the surrounding desert and were quite impassable, even for tracked vehicles. Checkpoint 23 was the packed-earth ramp that carried a single lane over the railway. I had made the passage a dozen times—most recently, last night.

We always dismounted engineers to proof the checkpoint for IEDs and mines. It was, after all, an obvious chokepoint for military traffic headed north from Camp Al Qa'im to targets near the Euphrates.

But we just cleared it. And we've never found anything.

Last night's operation had left me listless. I was ready to be finished with another futile raid.

Contributing to my reluctance was the fact that Second Platoon was due to rotate off "assault" status in less than twelve hours. The men could look forward to several weeks of base guard duty, regular meals, and complete safety. Guard was a lark. When we rotated back to mission status in August, the battalion would be three weeks away from its return to the States.

Let's just push through the checkpoint and get this done so we can go home.

French must've had substantially the same feeling, because the AAV barely slowed as we approached the ramp and our treads sank into the moon dust manufactured by scores of previous vehicles.

"Sergeant French," I said, "let's dismount engineers."

My inner conformist had triumphed. I was so steeped in Marine Corps doctrine that blowing through a chokepoint without following security procedures was impossible for me.

"Roger, sir."

The trac shuddered to a halt and two engineers climbed out through a hatch in the raised ramp. As they walked past, I noted that neither man had a metal detector or even night vision goggles. Corporal Baldwin, the senior engineer, looked up and called out cheerfully, but over the engine noise I couldn't decipher what he said. Not waiting for a response, he and "Cooter"—a tall, lanky West Virginian—drifted apart until each man straddled a tread mark laid down the previous night. Then, with heads bent, the engineers shuffled forward.

From my vantage above and behind the men, I couldn't make out anything in front of them. Even though the bleached dirt of the railway crossing showed faintly luminous in the night, it was impossible to discern more than a series of indistinct lumps and creeping shadows on the ground.

Can they even see anything?

Apparently, they could, because one of the men stopped, crouched down, and prodded the ground with a bayonet. The other engineer floated over, exchanged muttered advice, then dug his boot into the disturbed earth and gave it a good kick. I cringed, but there was no explosion and the men moved on.

Progress was slow but steady. From time to time an anomaly in the dirt was probed or kicked. Within five minutes the engineers had crested the top of the railway and were swallowed up by the night.

"Sergeant French, let's move forward to cover them on the other side."

The sergeant spoke briefly into his helmet mic. Instantly, the engine throbbed louder and we lurched up an invisible slope. I peered ahead, trying to regain a visual on the dismounted Marines. It was so dark; my fear was we might overtake them by accident before they could move out of the way. The thought added to the discomfort of being stuck at a chokepoint.

Only another minute or two and we'll be on our way.

I was so focused on the ground that I was shocked when two ghostly figures rose over the railroad tracks ahead. Their yelling was lost in the roar of the engines, but their waving arms were clear.

"Stop! Stop!! STOP!!" I shouted to French—unnecessarily, since the trac commander had already kicked his driver to a halt and was preparing to send us in reverse.

It took a minute to organize the other vehicles to back off the ramp. By the time we were all sorted, Corporal Baldwin and Cooter were back in the troop compartment passing word that they'd found an IED.

It had been buried in one of last night's tread marks.

———

We sat for an hour on the south side of the railway, set back a hundred yards in a cordon, waiting for a mobile assault unit to take over so we could continue the raid. Improvised explosive devices killed too many people for one of the bombs to be left unguarded, especially at night. During part of our time on the cordon, I mapped an alternate route to the west and briefed the new scheme of maneuver to my key leaders. But I couldn't help wondering what might have been.

What if my gut hadn't compelled us to stop? What if the engineers had gone through the motions instead of diligently exploring every suspicious rock and disturbed tread mark on a moonless night? What if the insurgents had done a slightly better job concealing their work?

Such questions led me back to Providence.

This was hardly my first brush with imminent death.

I should've been killed in Bani Dahir in April when I stupidly walked over a sandy mound on the outskirts of a cordon, only to discover that the mound was, in fact, an IED daisy-chained to a bomb being examined by EOD. Our interpreter had fired at the trigger man earlier that morning and driven him off, saving my life.

Or I could have died in a vehicle accident in early July when we'd flown to Al Asad Air Base to stage for a night raid with Reconnaissance Marines and light armored vehicles. We conducted planning and mission prep for three days while enjoying the generous amenities of Camp Chocolate Cake (as we scornfully termed it). Then, on a night with no illumination, we piled into seven-ton trucks and pretended that we had the training and optics to keep up with pro night operators like Recon and the LAVs. The starkest terror I ever felt in Iraq was during that pitch-black drive, sitting in the passenger seat of a seven-ton, squinting through grainy NVGs as a ravine rushed toward us at thirty miles per hour on the right side—my side—of the road. The driver flipped his optics up, then down, then back up again; shook his head helplessly; and put first one front tire, then the other, into loose dirt off the right shoulder. "Steer left. LEFT. GO LEFT! THERE'S A RAVINE!" I'd shouted, my throat hoarse with fear, as the turret gunner frantically kicked the driver's shoulder and screamed at him to get us back on the road before we all died. "I can't see!" the driver cried out plaintively. But somehow, he'd managed to turn the wheel just enough that our right front tire bounced over the head of the ravine. Back on the road, peering at a set of nearly invisible cat's-eye taillights ahead of us, I shivered with adrenaline and thanked God for deliverance. Ten minutes later, Third Platoon rolled a truck off a ramp while trying to traverse a railroad crossing. We spent the next hour evacuating nine mangled Marines.

It could have been us.

It could have, but it wasn't.

———

A mobile unit finally relieved us from the IED cordon; we passed beneath a railroad overpass farther west, eventually hitting our objective an hour later than planned. Except for our rotary wing air support dueling with an anti-aircraft weapon in eastern Karabilah, the raid proved uneventful. We returned to base at 0400.

Captain Ieva found me cleaning my carbine in the lieutenant hooch on his way back from the battalion combat operations center later that morning. He wasn't smiling.

"Lieutenant Smith, I thought you might like to know what EOD found when they cleared that IED at Checkpoint 23."

"Yes sir, I would."

"It was a 130mm projectile and 120mm projectile, tied together with det cord and placed on top of an Italian anti-tank mine." He looked at me meaningfully. "You owe the engineers a beer when we get home."

"Yes sir, I do."

Captain Ieva departed. I returned to Q-tipping dust from picatinny rails. In daylight, the thought of death avoided at a darkened railroad crossing was already theoretical, another near miss not worth dwelling on. Men cope with the vagaries of war in different ways. My way was to focus on the present, worry about the future, and let the past recede into oblivion.

It seemed like a good technique.

But when I returned to the States in early September 2005, I soon discovered that the past was not so easily contained.

CHAPTER 27
Radio War

Steve | 21 March 2003 | Taylor University, Upland, Indiana

I threw my fatigues on the bed, carefully arranged my boots and helmet, and grabbed my backpack from the chair.

The war was about to start, and I didn't want to miss it.

Double-timing to Kreg Salsbery's room, I could still remember my disappointment when our family television had broken and I'd missed the first Gulf War. Now the United States was about to invade Iraq and I could follow it all on television. I looked at my watch and picked up the pace. You could only see the destruction of a dictator a few times in your life.

That morning, people had stared as I marched to the dining commons in full uniform. President Bush had announced the deadline for Saddam Hussein to abdicate or else face a campaign of "shock and awe." Ironically, it was also the day I was scheduled to dress as General Douglas MacArthur for a presentation in history class. Cammied out and carrying a World War II steel helmet I'd borrowed from a friend, I felt more self-conscious than usual. It was a relief to finish the talk and return to my dorm to change.

Rushing into Kreg's room, I saw a couple of guys already clustered around the TV. They nodded and moved over to make room. CNN feeds showed Baghdad at night. Wolf Blitzer breathlessly explained that the American air campaign was expected to start any moment.

I unzipped my backpack and pulled out my history books. Nothing like getting a little reading done while watching the destruction of a foreign city. Mechanically, I unwrapped Hershey Kisses and popped them into my mouth. My eyes jumped back and forth from my book to the TV. One quadrant of the screen carried the greenish glow of night vision goggles, another had streetlights reflected from the Euphrates River; two other feeds alternated between keyed-up reporters and cityscapes.

Around me, guys talked and laughed as they finalized details for our coming spring break. As time passed and nothing blew up, they started to tune out. Outside, someone started a touch football game. Down the hall, a guitar strummed.

I tapped my pen against my cheek, then looked back at the CNN feed. Nothing but streetlights shimmering on black water and the outline of buildings in the green glow of NVGs. A reporter talked again about the reasons for war, then the feed changed to a previous briefing by Colin Powell that showed satellite images of what American intelligence officials claimed were movable chemical weapons labs.

It never occurred to me to doubt them. Saddam, I thought, had reaped what he'd sown. If any war had ever been just, then it was this one. I only hoped it would be over in a hundred hours like the last one. Before too many Americans got killed. Before Nate graduated from VMI in May and was commissioned into the Marines.

From outside the window, I heard the laughter of kids playing Frisbee. Then, in my peripheral vision, the screen flashed. Fire blossomed up and down the Euphrates River. I grinned like a schoolboy.

This was it.

Popping a Hershey Kiss into my mouth, I settled down to watch.

Thank God for TV.

———

22–26 March 2003 | Spring Break in Muncie, Indiana

Mark's family had no television.

Instead, I sat at the kitchen table in my roommate's house during spring break, tracing battle maps in the newspaper with the tip of a butter knife. American ground forces were flooding into Iraq and all I could do was listen to the clatter of heavy machine gun fire stuttering through the living room radio.

Mark's parents had left for work, but his mom had laid out breakfast on the kitchen table. Sunlight streamed into the room and fell on the white tablecloth. I sipped coffee and read the morning paper. The ground war covered the front page and spilled into other sections full of pictures. I put the paper aside and went into the living room to look for a TV to catch the war, but there was no TV.

I couldn't believe it.

For the second time in my life, America was fighting Iraq in a large-scale ground war, and I was missing it for lack of a television screen.

Mark's parents were sweet, salt-of-the-earth people, warm and hospitable. They were also God-fearing folk who'd decided that they would let no devil's box befoul their house.

To compensate, I spent hours curled up on the living room carpet, ear pressed firmly to the family radio as I ate toast and drank orange juice and coffee. For those few days, I was trapped in the 1940s, forced to follow a great war through sound waves and the morning paper. Just how my grandfather's family must have experienced World War II.

The AM news stations brought reports from embedded journalists and military experts. I heard the word "Nasiriyah," listened to the sound of mortars and heavy machine guns, and felt confused when reporters said that American soldiers had been killed and captured. I imagined blowing desert sand, plumes of smoke, snaking columns of tanks and armored vehicles, and plodding lines of soldiers and Marines.

After a few weeks, I thought—once Saddam had been captured, Al Qaeda had been defeated, and massive caches of WMDs were revealed to a skeptical world—there'd be nothing more to see. America would turn the country back to its people and walk away feeling a little taller, perhaps a little cleaner, like a Boy Scout helping an old lady across the street.

———

That summer, I went home and worked at a steel company in South Portland. In early August, Aunt Sally called to tell us that Gray had died. He'd passed away that morning, she said. There'd be a small memorial service and then he'd be buried in Eddy Cemetery, just a few hundred yards up the street from his home. The cemetery overlooked the Penobscot River. There were trees and flowers and in the evenings the breeze came up off the river and made the American flags snap. It was a beautiful place. Perhaps we'd like to go?

No, Mom and Dad told her. No, we didn't plan to go.

I went out behind the barn and stood among the aspen trees and listened to the leaves rustle in the wind. Gray's life was over, I thought, and I felt nothing. Where were all those happy times we'd spent together? What were they worth? The Indian spearhead, the fly fishermen, the purple-coated raspberries, and the World War II movies. What had it all amounted to in my life except poignant memories and the hangover of a dream gone horribly wrong?

Nate's military interest was a direct result of the stories and the legacy Gray had bequeathed, so there was that too. A solitary grave in Eddy Cemetery and perhaps the corresponding death of my brother in some godforsaken town in Iraq or Afghanistan. Yes, there was always that.

I spat on the ground.

Then I went to the shed, lifted an axe from its pegs, and cut down a tree.

The following week, I burned it.

CHAPTER 28
Ebb Tide

Nate | September 2005 | East Orland, Maine

The jet stream flung cirrus clouds like white caps across a sea-blue sky. Around me, not a breath of wind stirred the stands of fir, beech, and birch on the lower sections of Great Pond Mountain.

The day felt unseasonably warm. I stripped off my shirt as I walked, savoring the warm-cool-warm sensation of sun shadows stenciled on my bare shoulders by a canopy of hemlocks. Beneath my feet, clear water seeped out from patches of mossy earth and gilded the edges of scattered stones. Climbing higher, the forest thinned and skirted broad meadows of wild blueberries, their frost-burnt leaves spilling vermilion over granite ledges. The air smelled of pitch and warmed wood.

September was my favorite time of year in Maine. It was a month of comfortable transitions in which summer gave way to autumn in frosty mornings, and crisp evenings hinted at apple cider, wood smoke, and flaming maples to come. If philosophically I was an idealist, at heart I was a romantic traditionalist, reveling in nature's quiet beauty and the inherited sense of fulfillment embodied in the harvest.

Yet September was not without its heartache, marking as it did the close of another year absent my family. Eight lonely years slid into each other like a collapsible telescope, leaving me squinting back at the narrowing memories of youth. What I saw seemed bittersweet.

There was my father on this very trail, broad shouldered in a gray T-shirt, smelling like wintergreen, Skin Bracer aftershave, and sweat as he lifted me effortlessly to his shoulders and bounced me to the summit. And there was Steve, Smurf hat askew, dropping purple handfuls into green boxes amid fragrant bushes. Our sister, Christine, was there, too, happy in a safe place that rewarded quiet observation. Mom, her absence taken for granted by a mind too young to reckon with the effects of polio, would be waiting for us at camp with proud exclamations over our modest berry trove.

The pain of separation from the family I loved was usually numbed by activity, salved by relationships, or buried beneath my duties as a Marine. But after my return from Iraq in mid-September, the battalion had conducted a week of administrative duties, returned battle damaged gear, assigned officers and men to new units, and had then pushed me out on three weeks of leave.

Alone, inactive, and freed from responsibility, I drove home through a thousand miles of Eastern Seaboard that superficially resembled the land I'd left when I'd boarded a chartered plane to Iraq.

But things had changed.

I had changed.

Now, as I scrambled up lichen-crusted granite just below the mountain's summit, my soul sought space in which to unspool and process the cataclysmic events of the previous seven months. It wasn't a conscious thought, but rather a homing instinct that had brought me back to this place of captive boyhood memories.

Place is powerful. It blesses us with identity and grounds us in a chaotic world. It can also unmoor us from all we hold dear and mock every memory with a curse. In an unspoken way, I think I hoped that this mountain of gentle memories would sever the cords that bound me to a violent desert land.

The top of Great Pond Mountain, like every other mountain in Maine, was episodically crushed and gouged by glaciers over the ages. Ice sheets retreated twelve millennia ago, clutching car-sized boulders that settled indifferently on mountains and hillsides. Glaciers smoothed what was jagged and spirited away a substantial portion of the mountain's height, leaving it barely a thousand feet above sea level. I didn't mind the low elevation. It made for an easy climb and anyway, the rounded peak stood tall enough for me to look southeast over the green-black basin of Craig Pond, past a granite ridge and the shimmering surface of Alamoosook Lake, out toward the pale haze marking Penobscot Bay and the endless Atlantic.

It was quiet at the top.

The trail had been marked by a friendly hum of insects, but here a soft breeze advanced from the coast, breathing briny silence over crumbled rock and the pygmy tops of downslope trees. A waist-high block of granite beckoned, so I sat, one leg swinging, my palms pressed against the rough surface. Anchored to stone, I waited for release from my Babylonian captivity.

But Cyrus never came.

Far in front of me, a red-tailed hawk wheeled lazily, riding an updraft into the sun.

Distant traffic crawled soundlessly along Acadia Highway, windshields blinkering a message of haste and hurry. I wondered what stories rode wordlessly with all those anonymous drivers, what pain they left behind and what lay ahead.

Shifting forward, I dropped off the rock and began to jog toward the highest point on the summit. Stopping halfway, I turned, paused indecisively, then walked hurriedly back down the slope. Passing the block of granite, I descended to the forward edge of the slanting summit where it dropped into a scrubby mix of fir and aspen. Again, I stopped, a faint sense of confusion fogging my thoughts.

What I want isn't here.

This was the same serene mountain of my youth—unchanged, unbroken, unmoved. As a connection point with nature, it stood unmatched. But while my time on the mountain could make me happy, I realized that it couldn't give me peace. My subterranean sense of soulful wellbeing, of connection to a world of unlimited opportunity and universal security, was gone. In its place was restlessness, a ticking clock that never wound down.

I didn't linger at the summit. If the mountain couldn't give me what I wanted, it was just another object to be conquered and left behind.

I would seek my peace elsewhere.

November 2005 | Camp Lejeune, North Carolina

The new Kilo Company commander arrived late each morning in wrinkled utilities that somehow gave an impression of clothing rather than uniform. He hardly ever left his office. When duty required him to address assembled infantrymen, the Captain's disjointed comments were underwhelming and punctuated by jerky head movements and awkward fillers.

Staff Sergeant Thomas, platoon sergeant in the weapons platoon I inherited in October, was too professional to react to these strange homilies, but the set of his shoulders and flickering jaw muscles indicated endurance rather than inspiration.

At first, I felt embarrassed for the man who had nominally assumed command from Captain Ieva, so I made a point of demonstrating deference to him in front of the Marines, essentially staking him my hard-won credibility. I thought the Captain might need a little encouragement.

"Good morning, sir. Weapons Platoon is about to go for a run. Five miles, boots and utes (utilities). You're welcome to join us." Outside, a November dawn clung to pull up bars and made a drumhead of the ground beneath its fringe of dead grass. Inside, the company office smelled like the steam pipes clattering overhead.

It was a good morning to stare discomfort in the eye and tell it to fuck off.

I had encountered the commanding officer (CO) on my way to the barracks, where Staff Sergeant Thomas was taking platoon accountability and, undoubtedly, finding small discrepancies to fix before I arrived. The Captain needed to bolster his image. Sharing a hard run with the Marines was a way for him to do it. But instead of jumping at my offer, the man looked caught. He fumbled with a steaming thermos and made a blustering noise I found difficult to interpret. It occurred to me he might not be a gifted runner. I threw him a lifeline.

"It's ability level, and I always take the rabbits, so you could run with the middle pack—or," I added hastily, reading the CO's expression, "Staff Sergeant Thomas would be glad to have you run with his group." Like all athletes, Marines respect physicality, which makes infantry battalions not unlike institutionalized locker rooms. It was unthinkable that the Captain would demur when personally invited to a pain show.

"Uh . . . thanks Lieutenant Smith, but, uh, I have to get the Q2 training plan to the boss, ASAP. He'll tear me a new one if it's late." The excuse hung limply between us.

"Roger that, sir. There'll be another run."

The Captain's fear of the battalion commander (BC) was worse than his rejection of my invitation. I found the BC discomfiting—he was a short man of great personal courage but unpredictable temperament, given to screaming—but I'd never dream of letting it show to another officer, let alone a Marine of lower rank. Part of effective military leadership requires masking concern and evincing calm, regardless of the situation. It was unacceptable for a CO to show such naked weakness. Unsettled, I pushed out of the company hatch into the bracing cold and strode toward a huddle of Marines stretching under a vapor cloud in the grass.

After the run, I felt better, my confidence buoyed by endorphins and stoked by the joy that comes from pushing to the far side of suffering with good men. *He'll get better with time*, I decided, thinking back to my own learning curve when I first joined the battalion. *Just give him some time.*

———

Precious weeks slipped by during our pre-deployment training, but the Captain didn't seem to be growing into his role.

Perhaps he'd once been a competent platoon commander and now had got in over his head with a company. Or perhaps company command was second in priority to his family? Frankly, I didn't care about the reasons for his anxious incompetence. What I did care about was the fact that nearly two hundred officers and men depended on a calm, proficient commander to lead us through the looming savagery of Al Anbar Province. When it became clear that our captain was a dud, hard runs were no longer enough to dispel my unease. As December staggered into January, my embarrassment for the Captain grew fangs.

My reaction was inevitable.

Company command is unlike any other job in the Marine Corps. It's the ultimate test of tactics and leadership. Thus, company command is the wistful memory of generals and the envy of lieutenants. So outsized is the mantle of responsibility levied on Marine company commanders that they bear a nickname freighted with authority from the age of sail: Skipper. The title evokes images of lean men in salt-tarnished braid, hands steady on sword hilts as they prepare to lead boarding parties over the rail. There could hardly have been a greater contrast between that heroic image and the rumpled man with darting eyes who now stood in front of us at company formations.

In a sense, I viewed our hapless commander as a monstrous infidelity, a Marine Corps–issued breach of the sacred trust between leader and led. Every man in Kilo Company was prepared to give his life, if necessary, for country, corps, and his brothers in arms. But that willingness came with an expectation that death would be wagered judiciously. The fact that we had an incompetent commanding officer made our lives seem cheap. This feeling was strongest among combat veterans who knew the stakes, but even the greenest private could sense a disturbance in the force.

The Captain needed to go.

Unsurprisingly, the Marine Corps declined to seek my counsel in the matter. Behind closed doors and with discrete inference, older officers bearing sympathetic eyes but uncompromising loyalty to the Marine Corps reminded me whose job it was to make the Captain successful. His total incompetence was fairy-dusted away by a system hypersensitive to insubordination, as if admitting a single flaw in its framework could open a crack that could explode the entire structure.

What I had seen in Iraq made me more pragmatic than officers who'd cut their leadership teeth before the war. My highest loyalty was first to the mission, then to my Marines, and last to the Marine Corps. The corps was nothing but an idea anyway, comprised as it was of individuals knitted together by common culture and a shared purpose. How long would the idea survive if we sacrificed Marines on the altar of mindless conformity? My disenchantment was first conceived at the end of MATADOR, when we abandoned our gains to the enemy. But now it came to full term and was midwifed by Kilo Company's long slide into disarray during the winter and spring of 2006.

"Control what you can control," I muttered time and again when confronted by a particularly inept command decision or the lax standards of a new platoon commander. As our July deployment drew closer, I had the unsettling sense of an impending tragedy that I was powerless to stop. To regain a sense of control, I threw myself into the physical, mental, and tactical development of Weapon Platoon's half a hundred men, who would be attached to rifle platoons in Iraq.

"You will be a city on a hill," I informed the gathered mortar men, assault men, and machine gunners one brisk afternoon in late winter. Heads nodded earnestly, indicating that more than a few caught the reference. My fatherly pride in them was immense, hinged to their exceptionalism for volunteering for the infantry during a time of war and deepened by their daily commitment to excellence. They looked back guilelessly as I laid out my personal standard of performance.

"You will be the strongest, fastest, most proficient Marines in the company. When you show up to a rifle platoon, you will be a gift." I reminded them of the slow, red-faced gunners who'd struggled to crest Machine Gun Hill during RCAX (revised combined arms exercise) in Twentynine Palms before our previous deployment, delaying the entire company's scheme of maneuver. And I recalled to them the gunner who'd slumped in front of me from heat exhaustion during our assault into Ubaydi. "That will *never* happen again."

The men nodded grimly, meeting my gaze with an intensity that made my heart swell. Hard, unforgiving training was the only way I knew to prepare them for the great challenge that lay ahead.

———

A week or two after my impromptu speech, Staff Sergeant Thomas showed up bearing a red guidon emblazoned with a black "Voodoo Weapons, Co. K, 3/2".

I immediately pulled him aside in the company office.

"It looks great, Staff Sergeant, but you know we can't have that. Only companies are authorized guidons."

Thomas's brows arched; his brown eyes widened with mock innocence. "But First Sergeant okayed it, sir!" He knew me well enough to detect a glint of pride peeking out from behind my official disapproval. Seizing the opportunity, Thomas offered a compromise. "We'll keep it in the barracks and only bring it out for platoon PT. Goddam Popham and Old Man will take care of it." The two sergeants were Thomas's favorites.

I knew the pennant was a sign of disloyalty toward the Captain. It might as well have been stitched with a big "Fuck You."

As an officer, the right answer—the Marine Corps answer—was to order the guidon thrown away. But I had grown beyond simple black-and-white answers somewhere between Ubaydi and the day the Marine Corps issued me an incompetent company commander to take me to war. I loved what the guidon represented. If the guys were ashamed of their company, I was at least glad for the esprit shown for their platoon. Pride had pushed war elephants over the Pyrenees and raised Old Glory over Mount Suribachi.

Pride is what made men Marines.

"Okay. But never at company formations," I warned the gleeful platoon sergeant. As Thomas hurried off, I had a final, sobering thought.

In the future, pride might be the one lifeline these Marines will have to hold on to.

———

At night—every night—I drank.

In an off-base apartment that smelled faintly of ant spray and cheap carpet, I thought nothing of downing three or four tumblers of Black Velvet and Pepsi before falling into oblivion. As months passed, the ratio of mixer to alcohol grew slimmer, until my poolside companion in the spring was a Nalgene bottle brimming with a little ice, a lot of whiskey, and a splash of soda. "For color," I joked with Joe Clemmey, who'd moved over to Weapons Company in the fall but stuck with me as a roommate. "So people don't think I'm an alcoholic."

The whiskey provided effortless elimination of anxiety and was a quiet companion to my aching loneliness. I didn't drink to have a good time, and I rarely visited the noisy watering holes lining Western Boulevard and Highway 17. In uniform, I felt calm, confident, and in control, the world sorted and ordered in accordance with my silver bars and the US MARINES stitched diagonally above my left breast pocket. Out of uniform, I clung to my military identity like a security blanket but found its edges frayed, unable to shield me from a world in which I now moved as an outsider.

Without alcohol, it was difficult to focus and impossible to relax. Peace was unachievable, like a lost childhood memory of vibrant colors and heady smells. Occasionally I caught a glimpse of peace at the tail end of a church service, but the feeling never lasted beyond the parking lot.

It never occurred to me that I might have a problem.

I felt different after a tour in Iraq, but I chalked it up to perspective. During the work week I was up before dawn to lead the platoon in long runs, rigorous circuit training, or soul-crushing conditioning hikes, with nothing but a slight dehydration headache to remind me of the poor choices I'd made the night before. I was young and fit and, in 2006, it seemed the entire corps was slicked in booze and drinking wasn't a problem.

Until it was.

The drinking, the eroding discipline, and the proximity to war caught up with the battalion's staff and officers during a drunken Warrior Night in Twentynine Palms at the end of RCAX in late April. Intended to enhance camaraderie, the event quickly degenerated into a series of brazen insults flung at several unpopular captains by combat-hardened lieutenants who drowned decorum in a horned Viking helmet brimming with Budweiser. The evening officially concluded after several huge lieutenants tossed one diminutive captain bodily into a pool, but by that time civility had slipped its moorings and incidents of naked belligerence continued in and around the battalion's Quonset huts in the desert at Camp Wilson.

Tired and vaguely disappointed with the entire fiasco, I crawled into my sleeping bag before midnight and quickly fell asleep. I was soon awakened by shouts and a body crashing onto my legs. Jerking upright in the half-light, I watched groggily as our company XO—a former college football lineman—continued his drunken punishment of a mouthy lieutenant who'd struggled to lead my old platoon.

From two cots away, the CO jumped up in his PT shorts. "Stop! Stop it!"

But his shriek carried no weight and was ignored by the combatants.

Finally, First Sergeant and Staff Sergeant Moore intervened, physically separating the two battling officers as the Captain looked on, a perfect picture of forsaken authority.

———

From California, the battalion returned to Camp Lejeune and continued its training through mid-June before releasing us for three weeks of pre-deployment leave. Back home in Maine, I basked in the seaside summer like a man scheduled for open-heart surgery—possibly fatal, probably not, but casting common objects in sharp relief.

At camp in East Orland, I noticed with astounding clarity the green pond water curling off my paddle in brilliant quicksilver threads shot through with fire by a setting sun. Later, in the darkness before moonrise, the lake became an onyx carpet scattered with tiny diamonds and silent speeding satellites. In bed, with fingers laced behind my head and eyes staring up at the undersides of pine floorboards, I drifted off to sleep with the night breeze cool against my cheek and the mournful wail of a loon echoing across the pond like a hand stretching out from eternity.

The day before my scheduled drive back to North Carolina, I walked slowly through Portland's Old Port, stumbling on uneven cobblestones in the narrow streets while drinking in the salt air and familiar weathered brick. The day was an iconic Maine summer, seagulls circling and sunlight pouring down from a cornflower sky. Flocks of happy tourists swirled around me as I walked aimlessly down Fore Street, my only purpose to assimilate as much of the day as I could before leaving it all behind.

Something inside me believed that a man walking the streets of Portland in July was untouchable—especially so if he appreciated the storefronts with their coastal watercolors; the cry of gulls; and the scents of fish, tar, and warm brick. Such a man, I knew, might visit an exotic land and see sundry and diverse evils—but he himself would return home safe.

The idea was pure fantasy, but it sustained me.

CHAPTER 29
Wartime Conditions

Steve | Fall 2004 | Taylor University, Upland, Indiana

"Why can't you talk to your brother?" Phil asked as we ran the trails by Taylor Lake.

Phil was a sophomore from High Point, North Carolina. He always wore Carhartts and grinned easily. I'd joined him for several training runs as he prepared for a mini triathlon at Taylor. The pounding rhythm of our shoes past autumn trees reminded me of long runs with my brother.

The dislodged memory gained traction, and one afternoon I told Phil about Nate. I didn't know if my identical twin was deployed, I said, so I'd bookmarked a website that tracked coalition casualties in case Nate died and no one told me about it. Saying it out loud sounded pitiful and my gaze fell.

"Why don't you just give him a call?" Phil said. "I bet he'd love to hear from you. Maybe you could influence him in the right direction." The argument seemed so reasonable that it caught me off guard. I realized it would be difficult to explain church discipline to him.

We never called it "shunning." Instead, Wes said that we were inflicting church discipline on ex-members when we refused to talk with or acknowledge them. It was an act of love, he said, and designed to apply the maximum amount of productive pain to their lives to prick their conscience. And even if the guilty refused to repent, Wes said, church discipline benefited us.

"This life is a battleground, not a playground," he once told me. "You are living in wartime conditions as a soldier of Jesus Christ. So long as Nate lives in rebellion against God and against his anointed servant, your brother is the enemy. If you do not hate him with a perfect hatred, you cannot be saved."

It was no secret that I was Wes's spiritual scion, his protege, his chosen one to take over our church someday when he was gone. It wasn't enough for me to develop the mind of Christ. To be found worthy, I must strive with ever more devotion to cultivate the mind of Wes. And Wes found my brother repugnant.

The effect was that I'd shunned my brother and other supporting relatives for seven years. When I thought of it like that, it sounded like I was in a cult, so I tried to think of a different way to put it.

I fished for answers. "I can't have contact with him," I told Phil. "Nate has sinned against God's servant and against his parents. He needs to repent and turn back to God. If I reach out to him, it shows that I hate him. By refusing to see him, I show him severe mercy."

Phil remained silent. The only sound was the whisper of dead leaves underfoot and the distant horn from a soccer game. "Well," he said finally, "you must be worried about him. I'll pray for your whole family and especially for Nate, that God will bring him back safe and sound."

When Phil left to shower, I stayed by the lake wondering if it was as simple as making a phone call.

Could a phone call really change someone's life?

3 April 2005 | Van Wert, Ohio

The first call came at midnight.

After three days of dune camping on Shackleford Banks off the coast of Beaufort, North Carolina, several of us from the ten who came from the dorm traveled back to Van Wert, Ohio, en route to Indiana. We'd stayed the previous night at Phil's house in High Point, and now David, Ryan, and I were crashed at Ryan's house when his mother came sleepily to the bedroom door. "There's a phone call for you, Ryan. He says it's an emergency."

When Ryan returned, he was stricken. "That was Marc," he said. "Phil got hit by a car this afternoon. They're doing brain surgery to reduce swelling. If the swelling doesn't go down, he'll die."

His words made no sense.

Phil had risen early just that morning to cook us all breakfast. Humble, good-natured Phil. Phil with his acne problem and athleticism, his cheerful grin and quirky, literary humor. Phil who had been hit by a car while out for a run. Witnesses said he'd tried to evade a charging dog and stepped off the sidewalk into the path of a minivan.

Marc said that Phil's mother had been praying for the hysterical van driver while paramedics worked on her own bleeding son.

The three of us—Ryan, David, and I—prayed together and then fell asleep, exhausted with sorrow. God would work a miracle, we knew. Phil was going to live and we'd see him come bounding back to the dorm in a week with his goofy grin and beloved guitar and well-worn running shoes. We would surely see him again. This injury wouldn't kill him. Lazarus, come forth!

But Lazarus didn't come forth.

Instead, the phone rang again at 3:00 a.m.

Phil was dead.

In the morning, our grief was palpable. Our drive back to campus stretched long and lonely. Early spring light fell bleakly over rows of decapitated corn. Back in the dorm, we mourned together as a group of young men unacquainted with sudden death. We laughed as we remembered Phil and cried when we missed him and found solidarity in our shared suffering. The funeral was scheduled three days away in High Point. All of us would make the nine-hour journey together.

For the first time since Nate left home, I felt like I had brothers.

———

The next phone call was as unexpected as the first.

Wes discovered from my parents that Phil was dead, so he called to comfort me. A thousand miles away from my spiritual father, I sobbed on the phone and sought the serene assurance his confidence always gave.

I told him about the spring break trip and how Phil's gentle nature and kind heart had cheered us. Wes listened sympathetically and made clucking noises. I pictured him nodding reassuringly on the other end of the line, his brow furrowed with sorrow. "And now we're all going to drive to the funeral in North Carolina," I said, blowing my nose, "so please pray for traveling safety as we head down."

Dead air filled the line. Finally, Wes said, "You're driving to North Carolina for the funeral?"

"Yes," I said, sniffling. "We're heading down tomorrow in a caravan. Our hall director and assistant dean of students are going too, to make sure we're all safe."

"Steve, your priority there is academics," Wes said, his voice over the phone a mixture of kindness and sternness. "How long will this trip take?"

I didn't know. Three days. Maybe four. We wanted to spend time with Phil's family.

"God doesn't want you to go on this trip," Wes said, his voice rising like the blade of a guillotine. "It's the end of the semester and you have classes and tests. You are there at college to receive an education. God has helped you get a—what is it? A 3.97 so far? You're almost done. Don't let Satan get you off track. If you go on this trip, you'll dig an academic hole that you won't be able to climb out of."

His words were nonsense.

"Wes," I pleaded, "Phil was one of my best friends! I'll take classwork with me, I promise." I couldn't believe I had to justify myself. "The school already said that they'll make accommodations for any of us who are going to the funeral."

On the other end of the line, I could hear Wes stiffen. "God does not want you going to this funeral, is that clear?" he said. "'Obey your leaders and submit to their authority.' We've memorized that verse, haven't we? I am your spiritual father—you've said so yourself. You need to trust me, Steve. You need to trust the wisdom God has given me. And you need to obey me and the spiritual authority God has placed over you."

I whimpered but wouldn't agree.

Wes's voice grew stern. "Remember that the church has given you a scholarship every semester to help support your education. That's a total of sixteen thousand dollars over four years at Taylor. You wouldn't be there without our financial support. And you couldn't possibly repay it."

I knew that he was right.

And I hated him for it.

"But Steve," Wes continued, "that scholarship comes with conditions. It is dependent on you taking your classes seriously. If you go to Phil's funeral, then you are placing a dead friend over the purposes God has for you there at college. And that's not in your best interest, is it?"

I made a snuffling noise that Wes rightly interpreted as defeat.

Hatred for Wes's cruelty paled in comparison to my own self-loathing. I realized that any reasonable person would slam the phone down and never speak to Wes again—no matter the cost. But I was not a person of reason. I was a saint of blind faith. And I believed the price to pay for ignoring Wes was eternal damnation. I was living out the bitter principles of "worm theology," a sour Calvinistic nettle that vilified self and forsook the pleasures of earth. That attending my friend's funeral now fell among those godforsaken joys appalled me. I had nothing left to say.

As always, my silence begot compliance.

"I know that you are hurting," Wes said. Now that I'd caved, his tone softened like melting butter. "But you are there on assignment, and Phil's funeral is not part of your coursework. Like it says in 2 Timothy 2:4, 'no one serving as a soldier gets involved in civilian affairs, he wants to please his commanding officer.' You are in wartime conditions. Phil's funeral is a civilian affair."

From one thousand miles away, I could almost hear him smile.

"And I am your commanding officer."

CHAPTER 30
Unhinged

Nate | 3 August 2006 | Camp Habbaniyah, Al Anbar Province, Iraq

A half-moon stood pale against an orange sky. I was running steadily down a wide boulevard on the northern edge of Camp Habbaniyah. It was hot, but dry and bearable. With sundown, daytime temperatures had dropped twenty degrees to the low nineties. Palm and eucalyptus lining the road gave off a pungent smell that pleasantly reminded me of sage in California's high desert.

To my left, a scraggly fence of razor wire and roofing tin ran along the base perimeter. It was an insignificant barrier that barely obscured the shanty town of local workers beyond. The Iraqi Army had captured a suicide bomber in the shanty and it was rumored that several muj snipers were casing US positions from its jumble of improvised shelters.

Technically, I was still on base, but as I put distance between myself and the battalion area, I couldn't shake the feeling that I was being watched. A Beretta stuffed into a pocket on my Camelbak jounced comfortingly, but would prove of little practical value if an Al Qaeda cell decided to snatch a lone American out on his evening run. I dismissed the temptation to turn back to the populated areas. This was only my third run since arriving in Habbaniyah. I needed it to clear my head.

As the moon rose higher, the sky darkened. Bats flitted like tiny fighter planes through the night. It was quiet, the only sound a cadence of footfalls, steady breathing, and the distant, intermittent throbbing of a medium machine gun.

———

The deployment had begun poorly.

On July 18, the day after we arrived at the former British armored cavalry and airbase between Ramadi and Fallujah, the battalion had unexpectedly ordered levies from the line companies to meet base guard, detention facility, mess, and advisor duties. I couldn't understand why an already lean infantry company was forced to give up trained, motivated men to scoop scrambled eggs for seven months.

When I informed Sergeant Collare and Staff Sergeant Champlin that they were being sent to a military transition team with the Iraqi Army north of the Euphrates, I felt sick to my stomach. Advisor duty would eventually turn into the war's main effort, but at this juncture we darkly referred to it as "the Eastern Front." Both men took the news philosophically, grabbed their gear, and departed.

The hits kept coming.

Sergeant Popham, the most respected non-commissioned officer in Weapons, was snatched by Third Platoon the following day to act as platoon sergeant. It was effectively a promotion for him, and I knew it was the right decision for the company, but it meant Weapons Platoon was left with only one sergeant. Thomas and I pulled the Marines together and spoke reassuringly about our confidence in their training and ability. I believed what I said, but in my heart, it still felt like everything we'd worked to build in the months before the deployment was being ripped apart.

The next night, completely dark as only a desert or mid-ocean night can be, a tank ran over the front of a Humvee while Marines operated blacked-out vehicles on the base airfield. Somehow, no one was injured in the incident, but it sent a jolt of reality through us all. More reality followed the next day when First Sergeant and Lieutenant Marc Bullock cornered me under the cammie netting stretched across the entrance to the company berthing area. They looked grim.

Marc was direct. "Champlin got hit this morning on his second patrol with the IA."

My stomach knotted. First Sergeant's face was a stoic, brooding mask. I asked the necessary questions mechanically, already sheltered behind the synthetic calm that protected me from despair. "How bad? Is he alive?"

"He is for now. He was on a 'left seat—right seat' patrol. The advisors were gathered at the back of the formation as it was about to reenter friendly lines. The muj packed an oxygen tank full of explosives and waited until the IA went by before triggering it. They were targeting the Americans. A Marine captain was killed and another Staff Sergeant badly wounded." He paused. "Champlin's going to lose his legs."

There wasn't anything to be done. Champlin was already at the shock trauma facility in Balad, with a follow-on flight to Germany as soon as he was stabilized. I broke the news to the platoon that evening and watched young, strong faces etch with lines of grief.

No one expected to lose a guy before we'd finished unpacking.

The next several weeks confirmed my low opinion of the Captain. I observed his erratic decision-making, his habit of handing off company-level mission planning to lieutenants, his disappearing acts.

Less expected was the amateurish mission planning coming from the battalion's staff officers. They were decent men, but inexperienced in counterinsurgency warfare. And I had to watch it all silently in my capacity as intelligence representative and FiST (fire support team) leader for Kilo.

After sitting mutely on the sidelines for two days, listening to staff officers who'd never been to Iraq work through an upcoming operation like it was a tactical wargame, my patience broke. Words coming out of their mouths possibly meant death to men I knew well. Seething, I listened as three captains spent the better part of an hour arguing about whether commander's intent allowed Marines to harden firm bases in the AO, only to conclude eventually that it did not. They looked pleased with themselves, as if they had scored well on a tricky test.

I erupted.

"How is this even a discussion, gentlemen? Of course, we can harden temporary bases as required to protect our Marines. If the Two-shop (military intelligence) reports accurate muj mortar teams and snipers, why would we leave Marines in unhardened positions to get whacked?" My anger gave each word an edge and seemed to stun the captains into silence. I relied on a Marine Corps culture that placed preeminence on truth spoken from experience to cover what was otherwise naked impertinence.

Off to one side, the battalion executive officer, an extraordinarily capable major, who happened to be a VMI alumnus, stared at me with compressed lips under a salt-and-pepper crew cut. Whether he was suppressing a smile or readying a rebuke was unclear. I didn't care. The inexperience and indecisiveness of the battalion operations staff seemed criminal.

After ten seconds of uncomfortable silence, the S-3 (operations officer) changed the subject and planning continued. I sat glowering self-righteously.

When the session finally broke up in late afternoon, Rob Sipe, our battalion gunner, a warrant officer, pulled me aside. "Hey Nate, you need to tone it down." Rob cut off my objection with a wave of his hand. "Everyone on the ops staff knows you've been here, and they haven't. So why don't you find a tactful way to add value, rather than blowing up and getting a reputation as the disgruntled lieutenant?" Gunner Sipe was a man I deeply respected; his blunt words had their intended effect.

"Yeah, you're right," I admitted. Nevertheless, I still hated the feeling that the world had been tilted from its proper axis. The staff who had never been to war were making dangerous plans that the rest of us would have to manage and execute. It felt like I had two enemies: one outside the wire and one inside it.

Rob must've known what I was thinking because he clapped me on the shoulder and winked conspiratorially. "Besides, do you think the XO is going to let this plan fly? Wait until tomorrow. Hearts will be broken."

He was right.

At the final planning session, the XO allowed an enthusiastic captain to brief the concept of operations, then interrupted to smack down the "hammer and anvil" scheme of maneuver as completely irrelevant to our war. The plan was changed. I left the room feeling grateful for the major's intervention, but uncomfortable that he'd had to get involved at all.

That was the night that I laced up my running shoes and sweated out my frustration along the base perimeter.

The next day a tanker was killed while conducting counter-IED operations on Route Michigan, the main supply route running east to west on the south side of Habbaniyah. That evening, an army Humvee rolled over on base when the driver rounded a turn at high speed, killing the turret gunner who had taunted him to drive faster. Neither casualty was from our battalion, but the drumbeat of death reverberated around us in a way I'd never seen in Al Qa'im.

———

The war took common things and corrupted them.

Soap—unbranded, unscented, plain old soap—was used by insurgents to manufacture napalm, which they added to IEDs in hopes of incinerating men in armored vehicles who survived initial bomb blasts. I discovered this tidbit when Staff Sergeant Thomas brought over two bearded NCIS (Naval Criminal Investigative Service) agents from the Naval Special Warfare house to brief Kilo staff and officers on sensitive site exploitation.

The agents glided in casually after lunch, wearing cargo pants and button-down shirts. Pistols peeked out like afterthoughts from paddled holsters in their waistbands. I saw a few raised eyebrows from Marines accustomed to exacting standards of military grooming. But the agents radiated a calm professionalism and easy confidence that was undoubtedly part of the reflected glow from working every night with Navy SEALs on direct action missions throughout the AO.

Packed into a room that stank of feet and stale sweat, NCOs and officers in their early twenties poised colored pens over green notepads and spit Copenhagen into plastic bottles. Youthful faces showed tension lines, the mark of serious men at the beginning of many months of care.

"Good afternoon, Marines!" the senior agent barked from the front of the room, scanning the faces around him with a friendly smile.

From my position in a shadowed corner, I was glad to hear a hearty response from the crowd of leaders.

After a moment, the bearded agent nodded, apparently satisfied with what he saw, and continued, "We're not supposed to be here. NSW owns us and they don't like sharing intel with other units." Here he cocked his head in the direction of the dusty building across the square with its blacked-out windows, security cameras, and foot traffic of what looked like professional athletes in non-regulation uniforms. "So do us a favor," he said drily, "and don't tell dad we're here."

There was general laughter, the ice was broken, and the two agents proceeded to deliver a comprehensive summary of enemy tactics, techniques, and procedures in our area of operations, at a level of detail that was entirely absent from our own battalion briefs. Marines furiously scribbled notes as the agents gave expert advice about how to exploit a target in a way that would ensure bad guys went to jail. They spoke for an hour, then stuck around to answer questions from a half-dozen Marines eager for more specifics.

Eventually, the room cleared as First and Second Platoons prepared to stage for a cordon and search on a suspected IED maker near the "Dirty Mosque," so-named not for its state of disrepair, but because of the insurgent activity conducted within its shadow. I thanked the agents for their insights as Thomas and I walked them to the front of our building.

The senior agent stopped and turned to us before they stepped out into blistering heat.

"NSW does great work. They're out there almost every night, direct-actioning Al Qaeda. We're there to help gather evidence and ensure the detentions stick." Here his voice vibrated with unconcealed anger. "But they can also be prima donnas who don't want to do any non-sexy stuff, like search for a lower-level bomb maker. It's fine if they don't want to do it, but it's total bullshit for them to withhold actionable intel from your battalion that might save a Marine's life or legs." After agreeing we were all on the same side, the agents committed to pass to Thomas any intel the SEALs didn't want to action that might be useful in our efforts to rid the AO of bomb makers.

Their collaboration couldn't have come at a better time.

First and Second Platoons departed friendly lines at 1600 and hit the suspected IED maker at 1700. Initially, the Marines thought they had a dry hole. Nothing suspicious stood out, and the head of household adamantly denied any knowledge of insurgent activity. Lieutenant Gaffney was about to order his men to mount up when a Marine poking in a trash-littered corner of the courtyard found a burlap bag full of hundreds of bars of soap. Then he found another bag. And another. Six in all.

Smelling blood, the Marines conducted a new, exhaustive search of the property. At its conclusion, they had uncovered dozens of tape players and circuit boards, four propane tanks, and one propane tank filled with explosives and wired with an initiation device. The head of household was detained, and his guilty brother was grabbed by a mobile patrol at a nearby gas station.

Marc and I were in front of the company area to greet the platoons when they rolled back in, just before dark.

Because two platoons had been involved, the Captain had gone along nominally to lead the mission. Now he exited his vehicle helmetless, raised his arms and yelled, "Touchdown!"

Marc, ever the professional, responded with a series of questions to distract the Captain so he wouldn't further embarrass himself.

In minutes, the Captain was gone, headed to battalion headquarters to "brief the boss." Marc and I tracked down Lieutenant Gaffney in his hooch to ask how the mission had gone down.

Gaffney, a bespectacled, deeply religious man of quiet temperament, was uncharacteristically livid. "Know what he did? He sat in his vehicle on the cordon while we cleared the house. Refused to get out. Said we were sitting ducks." Gaffney paused to push glasses back up the bridge of his nose. "One of the Marines reported he saw movement on a rooftop. Not great, but not an emergency either. The Captain wigged out. He jumped out of his Humvee and ran down the middle of the street, shaking his fist at the rooftops and screaming, 'You want to shoot me? Shoot me! Shoot me, motherfuckers!'"

I winced, thinking of all the enlisted Marines who'd witnessed the Captain's meltdown.

Gaffney laughed mirthlessly. "Oh, it gets better. Sergeant Schwartz eventually convinced the Captain to get back in his vehicle. About that time, we reported the IED-making material at the target house. So, what does the Captain do? He orders Marines around him to raid the 'Dirty Mosque' and detain anyone they find. Oh yes," Gaffney continued, appreciating our shocked expressions, "he gave an order that directly violated Division ROE (rules of engagement) about Americans not entering mosques without prior approval."

Marc recovered, but his eyes were huge. "Please tell me you didn't raid a mosque. The whole town will turn against us."

Gaffney sat back in a folding chair and sighed. He looked weary. "Of course not," he said quietly. "Staff Sergeant Moore headed them off before they got to the gate. He told the guys to ignore the order and return to the cordon."

"What did the Captain say?" I already knew the answer.

Gaffney laughed. "What do you think? He pretended it never happened. Stayed buttoned up in his Humvee until we left and did an end zone dance when we got back."

The three of us were silent for a moment.

Just how fucked are we for the next six months?

The handful of missions Kilo Company had conducted so far had been discrete stabs into local towns, lasting just a few hours. Soon, we knew, the company would pack combat loads and leave the comfort of Habbaniyah to clear and hold firm bases in the deadly river towns on the road to Ramadi. If the Captain couldn't keep it together for three hours outside the wire, what would happen to him after three days? Or three months?

What would happen to us?

CHAPTER 31

Bury the Dead

Steve | May 2005 | Taylor University, Upland, Indiana

In early May, Marines conducted a major clearing operation along the Euphrates River near Al Qa'im in Al Anbar Province. They called it MATADOR.

I sat riveted as reporters from the *Washington Post* rode along with Marines in amphibious assault vehicles (AAVs) and heard bullets pinging off the sides while RPGs exploded nearby.

Nate's company was spearheading the operation.

I stayed up late to watch news reports.

Early the next morning, I jogged to the dining commons for breakfast. The *Post* had a front-page picture of a burning AAV billowing thick clouds of smoke. Around me, other kids jostled in line for pancakes and grits, but I stood frozen in front of the newsstand.

Was Nate trapped in that burning trac?

Skipping class that morning, a punishable offense if discovered by Wes, I spent the next four hours trying to learn which Marines had occupied the burning vehicle. By noon, I had some relief. It was a reserve unit out of Ohio that had been hit, not Nate's company from Camp Lejeune. Most of a squad was dead, but it wasn't Nate. I kept looking for information about the operation. A British paper quoted my brother. Other reporters noted the frequent medevacs traversing the area of operations. The news felt gut-wrenching, but at least it wasn't Nate's unit.

Then I saw a casualty list that claimed a Marine from Kilo Company 3/2 had been killed in action during MATADOR. Other Marines were wounded. I waited, sick, until the Marine's name and hometown appeared on the list.

Lawrence Philippon from West Hartford, Connecticut.

I read it as *Not Nate*.

That's how I classified all information coming out of Iraq in the spring of 2005.

It was either Nate or not Nate.

Nothing else mattered.

Summer 2005 | Biddeford, Maine

Returning to Maine after graduation, I got a job as assistant to the dean of students at an osteopathic medical school in Biddeford. Situated with a stunning view of the Saco River, the school had once been the site of a Native American village.

Every lunch I spent walking along pebbled shores, slapping mosquitoes on wooded trails, or wedging myself into sea caves near Biddeford Pool. In October, when a Nor'easter roared in with horizontal rain and twenty-foot waves, I donned my greatcoat and walked along the bluff near a lighthouse, feeling spray pelt my body like fistfuls of gravel. Having lived so long in the cornfields of Indiana, I couldn't get enough of the sea.

Wes was also thrilled that I was home. He put me into a specialized program of translating the book of Acts from the original Greek, listening to hundreds of church tapes, and serving as his personal assistant. The schedule kept me occupied even on my forty-five-minute commute. It was a tactic that Wes said was designed to keep me out of trouble until I went to seminary.

27 October 2006 | Biddeford, Maine

Late in October 2006, just hours before a major event to honor the first-year students' completion of Gross Anatomy, the associate dean called the office from her home. Her husband was recovering from open-heart surgery, she said, and she couldn't leave his side.

"Can you give my speech tonight?"

My stomach tightened. I was no public speaker. "Where did you leave the draft?" I said, steeling myself.

"There isn't one."

"Pardon?"

"There isn't one. But I know you'll think of something."

The ceremony began in two hours.

I broke into a cold sweat.

An hour later, sitting in front of my computer, I still had nothing on my screen. Trying to write a formal congratulatory speech, something I thought a proper administrator might say, proved a disaster. Nothing came to mind. Instead, my vision contracted, and a loud thrumming filled my ears.

I can't do this, I thought, banging my keyboard against the desk. *I can't do this and it's not fair!*

Yes, you can, came a quiet voice. *I'll help you. But you'll have to work fast.*

A thought came to mind. I typed quickly for an hour, read the draft, then printed it off and sprinted over to the multipurpose room on the other side of campus without a chance to practice.

Taking a chair in the front row, I gulped reflexively as more students filled the room. Then came the professors in jeans and flannels, followed by a clot of college administrators and clinicians in suits, ties, and power dresses. I couldn't stop my knees from bouncing. To avoid talking with anyone, I kept looking at my speech, trying to will it into something meaningful.

The dean of the college rose first and told a few off-color jokes. I loosened my tie and took a deep breath.

Someone was saying ". . . and now, Steve Smith will deliver the keynote address."

Keynote address? I thought. *I didn't know this was the keynote address.*

There was a polite smattering of applause.

I stumbled onto the stage, then over to the podium. Hot lights scorched my view. Dimly, I could see a standing-room-only crowd.

"Are there any paramedics in the room?" I asked. A few students raised their hands. "Good. I'll see you later." There were a few chuckles. I began to read.

A gust of laughter surprised me. I glanced up. Students in the front row were grinning and poking each other. Was my nose bleeding? I swiped a hand across my face, but it came away clean. Why were the students laughing? I read further and the laughter grew. Dumbly, I realized that they were laughing at all the right parts. Students jabbed each other and gave knowing looks. I continued.

Laughter and claps rippled out in widening circles. I gripped the podium and read desperately until, at last, I came to blank paper, mumbled "thank you," and bolted from the stage.

A loud noise erupted as I returned to my seat. Around me, students were cheering and clapping and suddenly they were standing and shouting . . . .

And why are they doing that?

It didn't make any sense. I took my glass of sparkling cider and downed it.

Jake, a former all-American decathlete from Buffalo and now student body president, approached the lectern. "I was supposed to say a few words," he said. "But how do you follow something like that? I'm glad that the dean was able to make a few fart jokes before things really got good."

Then he walked off the stage.

Someone patted my shoulder. Someone else brought me another drink and this time it wasn't sparkling cider. I downed it in one burning gulp.

Dr. Cross, the famously crusty Gross Anatomy professor, walked over to my seat. He stuck out his hand. "I've been here since the first year we opened this school with cadavers on sawhorses," he said. "I've never heard a speech like that. This is my last year here. Thanks for letting me leave on a high note."

I mumbled something idiotic, grabbed my overcoat, stumbled down the aisle, out into the lobby, and then out into the night. Above me, stars blinked and my hot face felt gloriously chilled.

I looked up at the sky.

"Thank you," I whispered over and over. "Thank you so much."

9 November 2006 | Cumberland, Maine

Two weeks later, Wes sat stiffly in our living room, in the blue-and-white fabric armchair by the window, my father's chair, and opened his Bible.

"It has come to my attention," Wes said, "that you have taken the liberty of reading emails from Nate, and that Carol has a picture of him in this house. You are holding the Lord in contempt. He is very displeased."

We sat in silence, waiting for lightning.

Wes opened his Bible to a page marked by a small piece of paper. He was about to read. His thick lips parted and his prominent Adam's apple worked convulsively. Then he paused, inclined his head ever so slightly, and said, "Doug, could you please open your Bible to 1 Samuel 2?"

Dad glanced up earnestly. "About Eli's wicked sons?"

"This isn't a game," Wes snapped. "You don't get points for knowing what's in the chapter. Just turn there."

Dad flinched. His face flattened into a mask and he thumbed the pages of his Bible until he reached the passage.

"Please start reading in verse 27," Wes said.

We all knew the passage.

I had it almost memorized.

It was a pronouncement of judgment against the house of Eli, the high priest of Israel in the days just before King Saul and King David. Eli's sons, who were also priests, had cheated the people, despoiled the sacrifices at the Tabernacle, and committed sexual immorality. The stench of their actions had ascended to heaven.

Dad cleared his throat. When he read, the words fell like hammer blows. Then he reached the central passage: "'Why do you honor your sons more than me?' Therefore, the Lord, the God of Israel, declares: 'I promised that members of your family would minister before me forever.' But now the Lord declares: 'Far be it from me! Those who honor me I will honor, but those who despise me will be disdained.'" The chapter concluded with a prophecy about the death of Eli's sons in battle.

"That's enough," Wes said. He closed his Bible with a soft *whump*. The breeze from its pages carried the scent of his Aqua Velva aftershave. Wes looked first at my mother. "Carol, why did you print off a picture of Nate when you know that he is in rebellion against God and against God's anointed servant?"

My mother plucked at her denim jumper, eyes downcast, her hands frightened little birds. Then she looked directly at Wes, her chin thrust up, eyes defiant. She seemed to gather herself like a wave about to break and wailed, "Because I *love* him!"

Her cry tore at old scabs inside of me. We didn't speak of my brother. When he left our church, we shunned him as "one who had gone out from us because he was not one of us." To us, he was dead.

But my mother's shriek broke some inner wall of ice and made me admit to myself that I still loved him. Of course, I did. I couldn't get through a day without thinking about him, without whispering a prayer for his safety. That's why I collected small artifacts that reminded me of him, why my heart leaped when I heard that Aunt Sally had pages and pages of his emails, why at lunchtime I stood on the shore of the Atlantic and looked out across the waves wondering how many miles separated me from Iraq.

I loved Nate.

Deeply, helplessly, I loved him.

How could I not?

Wes's face darkened. The last grains of patience had run through his glass. "Carol, do you not realize that a woman somewhere will have to give birth to the antichrist?" He leaned forward and pointed a long finger at Mom. "How do you know that you are not that woman?"

My mother chewed her lower lip and said nothing. The ticking of the clock seemed loud. I watched the birds flutter in her lap.

Wes looked at my father who sat hunched and silent in his wooden chair. Then Wes looked over at me. I was his chosen one, his scion, the future seminary student who would carry on his legacy among God's tiny remnant of elect people. He had groomed me to succeed him, counseled me in his office, bent me to his will. I had proved my devotion by cutting ties with Nate, by refusing to attend Phil's funeral. And all of this I had welcomed as a clay pot must welcome the heat of the kiln, welcomed it as I waited for enough suffering to translate my soul to heaven.

Wes looked at me now. I saw a slight softening in his eyes. "Steve, I have to say that I'm surprised at you. *You* of all people. Surely, you realize that you have treated the Lord with contempt? Will you continue to defy the living God?"

The burden that Wes placed upon me was unbearable. It was the judgment of God, the dark wine of his fury. The only way to remove it was by renouncing my sin. Today was the day to expose everything, to remove my brother's Christ-hating image from my soul once and for all. If I confessed my sins, I would be saved.

Wes held up the picture of Nate.

I thought Nate looked handsome in his Marine officer's uniform with his tan, smiling face. Nate didn't *look* like the antichrist, I thought.

He looked exactly like me.

Ka-chunk. The old mental barrier crashed down. It was the rule of law, the enlightenment of submission. If I suffered enough, then I would be saved.

Wes sat looking at me—me!—instead of at my parents. I realized dimly that he needed me to repent. That somehow my submission made him complete. Perhaps if I forsook Nate one more time, if I sunk to one more level of abasement and death to self, I would finally win Wes's ultimate approval and the favor of God.

I cried out my confession, trying to sound as brokenhearted as possible: "I repent! I repent! Lord have mercy on me, I repent!" Then I put down my head and sobbed.

This was my Final Solution.

Through my cries, Wes said to my parents, "You see what the Lord's work in a man's life can produce? Look at your son as an example of true confession and a humble, penitent heart." Then I heard him say tenderly, "Steve, the Lord is so pleased with your repentance. He forgives you and so do I. You may go upstairs while I deal with your parents."

I fled to my bedroom and lay for hours on the cold linoleum floor. Then I got up, wiped away my tears, and ransacked my journals for bits of my brother's life that I had secreted away over the years. Pictures of Nate's promotion ceremony to first lieutenant that I'd found online, news articles from Marine operations in Iraq, and Nate's emails . . . pages and pages of emails.

Feeling like Achan, I went to my bookcase and pulled from its shelves a large collection of military histories, novels, and DVDs. I stacked the books on the floor until they reached waist-height, a leaning tower of sin. I stared at it in revulsion, horrified by my own carnality.

Finally, I took down from its shelf the flint spearhead that I had found along the banks of the Penobscot River so many years before. I turned it over in my hands, felt its cold heaviness, then dropped it onto the stack as the last vestige of my grandfather's influence. Gray, whose own military service had so inflamed both Nate and me.

Later that night, long after Wes had left and my parents were gone to bed, I took the whole forsaken pile outside and dumped it in the trash. It nearly filled a garbage bag. I stood looking at its jumbled contents as if it were my own brother lying in his casket. As if I had buried his memory, flagless and forsaken, in the folds of black plastic.

Then I padded upstairs and prayed for obliterating sleep.

PART III
THE PLACES I HAVE BEEN

I have been welcomed home many times, but I have never come all the way back from the places I have been.

Benjamin Busch, *Dust to Dust*

CHAPTER 32
Beyond RUBICON

Nate | 23 August 2006 | East Husaybah, Al Anbar Province, Iraq

We entered the house quickly, crunching over broken glass on our way to the stairs. The Iraqi family was anonymous and I brushed indifferently past a glaring old man. My foot was on the first step to the roof when a flash of color in an adjacent room checked me mid-stride.

Startled, I glimpsed a beautiful girl in her early twenties, staring at me with coffee-colored eyes. My heart stopped. For a breathless moment, I contemplated the dusky figure draped in maroon and pale blue, so out of place in a room of shattered windows and stinking men.

Her gaze dropped to my chest, where I cradled an M4 loosely in gloved hands. Flushing, I wanted to explain, to tell her that I was sorry, that the carbine wasn't meant for *her*. But of course, it was. It was meant for all of them. Despite being smitten by the girl's unexpected beauty, an impassable chasm of culture and circumstance stretched between us. Regaining composure, I stomped up the stairs to catch up with the command group.

Emerging onto a blazing rooftop, I noted the Captain pacing erratically, as was his habit when unsure or scared. The practice struck me as unmanly and irritating. In this instance, the Captain couldn't raise platoon commanders on the radio. Cursing, he swayed like a diviner to gain better reception, then fiddled helplessly with knobs on his handheld.

Eventually, the 81mm mortar forward observer, a streetwise corporal with a reputation for competence, cast me a pleading look before surrendering his larger radio to the Captain. The exchange was pointless. I suspected platoon commanders could hear the Captain but had ordered radio operators to ignore his worthless and sometimes dangerous orders.

Annoyed that I was stuck with the Captain, I made my way to the opposite side of the roof and leaned over a waist-high wall. Ten feet below, a fragrant garden sent vines creeping around melons; enormous sunflowers beamed at the early morning sun. The blue-shadowed trellis was soft and silent compared to the rooftop's hard glare.

My head hurt and a sweat-stained flak bit into my neck and shoulders. Hunching forward to shift some of the armor's weight onto the crumbling wall, I noticed a sudden movement below. It was the girl. Bare feet gliding, she began to sweep polished concrete between house and garden.

Something in the moment caught and I was seized by an intense longing to stop, to throw off my weapon and armor and responsibility, and once again be a young man in a world away from war. The garden, the flowers, and the girl were intoxicating. Where a year of enemy action had failed to pierce my martial resolve, a pretty girl with a palm-frond whisk stopped me in my tracks.

For a few moments, I did not feel like an invader in an alien land. The girl's quiet grace swelled my heart with memories of youth and beauty and peace.

The girl must have sensed she was being watched because she suddenly straightened and looked up. For several heartbeats, our eyes met and her features softened into an odd little half-smile. In that instant I was home. Then she shyly dropped her gaze and disappeared into the house.

Far off, a pair of helicopter gunships stalked wickedly through the morning haze. The clanking roar of armored vehicles throbbed from a nearby road. Exhaling, I pushed away from the wall and turned back to the command group.

The operation had just begun.

———

Operation RUBICON was a clear of farm towns, fields, and riverbank extending from a broad, upward curve in the Euphrates, south to Route Michigan. At the end of the operation, Kilo Company would scatter three rifle platoons across the area to fortify firm bases and deny the enemy freedom of movement.

According to intelligence estimates, the area was one of the worst stretches in the thirty miles between Ramadi and Fallujah. Previously, the army kept Route Michigan free from IEDs by parking tanks and Bradleys (armored fighting vehicles) within eyesight of each other to form a picket line along the main supply route between the largest cities in western Iraq. It was an effective tactic but didn't contribute to a broader strategy, focused as it was on minimizing the symptom rather than rooting out the cause of violence. An enemy with freedom of movement outside Route Michigan's ribbon of cratered asphalt was an enemy with initiative. Seizing the initiative meant putting men on the ground where the enemy lived, where he worked, and where he plotted attacks.

As RUBICON progressed, suffocating temperatures above 110 degrees Fahrenheit forced weary men in seventy pounds of kit to move with measured economy. The advance was further slowed by exploitation of dozens of weapons and explosive caches that wreaked havoc on the battalion's timeline.

Halted in a target house well short of our planned phase line on the first night of the operation, I rolled out a foam sleeping pad in the dark and contemplated our surprising lack of enemy contact. Nothing but a few rounds had snapped over our heads, compared to heavy fighting along the river that resulted in several recon and riverine craft casualties.

The enemy, it appeared, preferred to vacate an area about to be flooded with infantrymen and, instead, nibble around the edges, using terrain to offset our staggering advantage in firepower. It wasn't a technique that would win impressive victories, but it just might bleed us to death.

———

By August 26, RUBICON was complete and Kilo began to fortify firm bases. The operation's cost included seven men wounded and one killed, a half-dozen concussions from bomb blasts, several heat casualties, and three blown-up vehicles. The enemy had peppered us with small arms fire, mortars, and rockets. But their most effective weapon was the IED.

Now, with firm bases strung across several kilometers of towns and farming villages, our daily supply convoys and mounted patrols had to navigate unpaved roads lined with drainage ditches and intersected by culverts—all prime locations for IEDs. A handful of wreckage-strewn chokepoints over a dirty canal were the only means to access our area of operations from Route Michigan.

Insurgents lost no time filtering back into the area and turning their fury against us.

Entries in my platoon commander notebook documented a dramatic rise in enemy activity and friendly casualties over the next two weeks. One incident stood out for its gruesome pathos:

> Sun, 3 Sept–Kilo Mobile struck a mine . . . . The mine was a double-stack enhanced w/an IED and detonated directly under the 4th Humvee. Most Marines were dismounted, but the Humvee disintegrated. The driver was thrown into the canal, where he was found an hour later, missing an arm and leg. The gunner was found underneath the turret in a ditch . . . . Both KIA instantly. Marc and 1st Sgt/Gunny took control of the scene; the (Captain) was there, but useless.

This terse report cannot possibly convey the descent into darkness that Kilo experienced during those two weeks. In our area, which in cooler weather and lighter clothing could have been comfortably walked from end to end in thirty minutes, the inimitable pressure-push and *thump* of IED and mine attacks sent quick reaction forces (QRF) scrambling thirteen times. Marines were attacked more than twenty times by small arms, mortars, RPGs, and snipers. A dozen armored vehicles were damaged or destroyed, sixteen Marines and soldiers were wounded, and four were killed.

We were in a fight with an aggressive enemy who refused to concede. As we sweated through patrols, filled sandbags on rooftop strong points, and waited for the next *thump* and frantic radio call, it was difficult to see how the battalion could sustain this casualty rate for five more months.

On average, we were losing two men, killed or wounded, every day.

———

Despite extraordinary violence in the ville, hardly anyone wanted to go back to the battalion's forward operating base (FOB) at Camp Habbaniyah. Men feared they'd get blown up on the way and preferred companionship with their buddies in the fight. When Marines were forced to return to base, on a supply run or for a mandatory forty-eight-hour break from combat, it wasn't uncommon for staff non-commissioned officers to kick them out of the chow hall because of torn and bloodied cammies, or to rage at dirty faces and crumpled covers. Wartime purveyors of peacetime standards garnered infantrymen's universal disdain and were forever memorialized as "fobbits."

I was ordered back to base in mid-September to discuss fire support issues with the battalion staff. Catching a ride with an evening convoy, I arrived at the company berthing area long after dark. Feeling luxurious, I savored a long shower, changed my utilities for the first time in three weeks, then fell onto a cot for a dreamless sleep.

The next morning, I walked a half-mile, past lines of dusty eucalyptus, to the battalion combat operations center. The subject of the meeting was Kilo's Third Platoon. They were operating out of a small base in the northwest corner of our area and had engaged in four brutal firefights during the past week. In each fight, the battalion failed to provide timely fire support, sometimes taking ninety minutes to deliver steel on target.

In one instance, a Marine on the roof of a water treatment plant on the bank of the Euphrates had lost his leg to an enemy mortar round. Making a bad situation worse, army Paladins (self-propelled artillery) then mistakenly dropped a half-dozen high-explosive shells around the Marine position instead of on the enemy eight hundred yards across the river. During another gun battle, Marines ran out of ammunition and water and had to retreat under fire. Explosions and the roar of automatic weapons lent urgency to their repeated calls for fire support. It never came.

There was plenty of blame to share. Marines on the ground hadn't always followed proper targeting procedures and often failed to appreciate the extraordinary pressure faced by battalion staff officers to avoid civilian casualties. On the other hand, staff officers seemed to distrust front line leaders, and had issued maps that carefully labeled hundreds of buildings within our area but none of the buildings outside of it.

The result was that Marines looking for a fight along the western edge of our mapped area had no way to identify targets several hundred yards farther west. Marines under fire were forced to revert to compass azimuths and estimate distances to targets, while bomber pilots at twenty thousand feet and staff officers six miles away tried to pick out the right building from a dozen others. Bombing the wrong house would destroy our efforts to gain local support in the fight against Al Qaeda.

The meeting lasted two hours and was productive, insofar as we all agreed to get back to fighting the enemy rather than each other. The battalion executive officer promised to send a Marine pilot as a forward air controller (FAC) the next time we were likely to get into a fight.

———

"Hey Smitty, I need to take a shit."

"Bert" was sweating, half-reclined next to me in an awkward jumble of antennas and new field gear. The sun had begun its morning climb into a washed-out sky. We were sprawled in a dry irrigation ditch two kilometers northeast of Third Platoon's patrol base, on the eastern edge of a cultivated peninsula that jutted into the slithering belly of the Euphrates. Thirty meters to our north, a reinforced squad from Third Platoon occupied the only building in sight. Several Marines showed conspicuously on its roof as the morning brightened.

I didn't like any of this.

Glancing six hundred yards across the river at a knot of small houses, I searched for movement in windows or between dark clumps of bushes. Nothing. I looked back at Bert. Tall and thin with a long jaw, it was easy to trace the FAC's callsign to its Sesame Street origin. You had to give our pilots credit. Not only did they sound cool on the radio, they were also *funny*.

Bert was in obvious discomfort.

"Go ahead, sir," I said. "We've been here so long, it's a guarantee that as soon as you drop trou we'll get contact. Maybe it'll get things moving."

Corporal Torocco, my 81mm mortar forward observer (FO), grinned from his position several feet down the ditch. We liked having the pilot along, partially because of his eagerness to be in the field with the infantry, but mostly because of the guaranteed air support that he represented. To be honest, it was also good for morale to see a fobbit slide over the lip of the ditch and start a grunting, struggling attempt to take a tactical shit.

"Hey, sir. Is Third doing *jumping jacks* on the roof?"

Torocco's question brought me back to our mission. After meeting with the battalion staff to discuss fire support the previous week, it was decided that a Third Platoon patrol would once again "go fishing for muj," as Sergeant Popham fondly termed it. This time, the squad was bolstered with snipers, an FAC, 60mm mortars, me, and Torocco, who, besides controlling 81mm mortars, could also direct fire from the Paladins at Camp Habbaniyah.

We'd set a trap for insurgents, who couldn't seem to resist using terrain to achieve standoff to engage our patrols. Adding to our desirability as a target, insurgents knew from captured American maps that the area north of the river was US Army territory, which meant Marines south of the river were prohibited from firing across it until we coordinated with the army. That division-level coordination took time, which the insurgents used to full advantage for hit-and-run attacks. Lieutenant Jones, the Third Platoon commander, believed a patrol here would prove irresistible to any muj lolling north of the river.

I was less enthusiastic about the plan. I didn't believe insurgents would fall for it, and I didn't like Marines exposed on the roof. Several talented enemy snipers operated in the Ramadi/Fallujah corridor, including one who was reputedly a former Olympian on the Iraqi national rifle team. It might have been him who had drilled Lieutenant Jones through the shoulder two weeks before, when the Third Platoon commander impatiently mounted a rooftop wall to look for the enemy.

The bullet missed bone, Jones coolly called in his own medevac, and he was back in the saddle after a few days' recovery at Taqaddum's Surgical Shock Trauma unit. Nevertheless, it felt wrong for Marines to frolic on a rooftop. I glanced toward Third's position and then back at the FO.

"Looks like it," I replied impassively.

It wouldn't help if the corporal knew how I truly felt. Torocco looked at me searchingly, then broke into a grin when a string of curses scorched the air. It sounded like Bert, hidden from view on the west side of the ditch, was in heavy contact.

I eyeballed the far side of the river again. Still no movement. My radio crackled.

"Green, this is Blue. Popping red smoke, over."

Jones, impatient for action, had decided that calisthenics weren't enough to entice the enemy. Since I was in a support role, the radio call was only a courtesy to ensure my element wasn't surprised by the grenade. Several nearby mortar men looked quizzical. Third wasn't really going to highlight their position with a smoke grenade, were they?

They were.

I'd gotten as far as, "Roger Blue, that might not . . ." when a wisp of red smoke curled up from the roof. Faint laughter echoed across the field. I grimaced and raised my carbine to use its four-power optic to scan across the river. With surprising clarity, I caught black shadows flitting through a palm grove a microsecond before two shots cracked out. A moment later, the call came from Third's radio operator.

"Black, this is Green. Reaper just whacked two muj in black masks who were setting up to take a shot, over."

It was on.

A pair of medium machine guns opened fire from the rooftop, the sound growing in duration and volume as gunners found their range. Jones was on the radio with the company command post, working belated coordination to fire something bigger than small arms into army country, while I gave instructions to Torocco and our mortar men.

I nearly jumped out of the ditch when a body slid down behind me.

Whipping around, I saw Bert pulling on his Kevlar with a grin. He was triumphant. "I did it!"

I smiled. "Congratulations, sir. We need air."

"Right." Instantly, the FAC's face hardened into a calculating mask as he keyed his handset to engage aircraft overhead. I was impressed by Bert's sangfroid in his first firefight. Upon reflection, it made sense. Pilots risk death each time they leave the ground, so maintaining calm in any circumstance is a prerequisite for the job.

With Bert coordinating air and Torocco working mortars, I scribbled a hasty fire support plan onto my battle board, the Lumocolor arrows and military shorthand forming a tiny symphony of death on plexiglass. Mortars and machine guns would fix the enemy, then shut down for sixty seconds to allow rocket and gun passes by helicopter gunships, followed by several more minutes of mortars and machine guns.

I quickly briefed the plan and set a time on target, then rocked with anticipation while the gunfight hammered along for several minutes.

At the designated time, the plan unfolded in a towering display of concussion, noise, and light. Mortars crunched down on rooftops and shredded vegetation in hurricane bursts, while tracers stitched red patterns across windows, doors, and shadowy fighting positions. Bert slipped in Cobras and Hueys just as the mortars and machine guns fell silent. The gunships thumped past mere yards above our heads, their rockets ripping into palm groves and buildings with staccato thuds and miniguns hosing down enemy positions with an infernal *brrrrrrrrrrr* that sent streams of shell casings tumbling to the dust around us.

As the gunships thundered away, a string of rounds crackled defiantly from a wreath of brown smoke and drifting dust that clung to a shattered house across the river. I shook my head in grudging respect for the courage of the invisible assailant, then turned to the FAC.

"Sir, can you make that house go away?"

He could. A five-hundred-pound JDAM hurtled from the sky with the sound of a freight train in a tunnel. My mouth slightly open to guard against concussion, I watched with satisfaction as a tubular gray cloud mushroomed out of the house along the bomb's path. Jagged bits of concrete tumbled end over end before smashing into nearby date palms and rooftops.

The firing stopped.

Intelligence reports later concluded that four enemy fighters had been killed and two more were wounded in Third Platoon's riverside trap.

It was about time.

Despite all our casualties, they were the first enemy we'd killed in nearly two and a half months in country.

CHAPTER 33

Prostitutes and Tax Collectors

Steve | 2008 | North Yarmouth, Maine

I pulled into the church parking lot before our Good Friday service. Snow piles rose almost to the eaves of the church. Forecasters said it was the snowiest Maine winter on record. Despite this, Wes refused to allow plows to push snow onto the church lawn. He said he didn't want them to gouge the grass. Ice and snow backed up until the lot shrank to half its normal size. There was only enough space for each car in our church family.

Exactly.

For this reason, Wes had asked me to arrive early and serve as traffic director for the special service. "Don't let anyone get past you," he said. "Position each vehicle precisely. We have just enough room if everyone carpools." He didn't say what to do if there was a visitor, but guests were uncommon; we rarely took them into account.

In the church lot, Wes's Buick sat in its first spot by the driveway. Also in the lot was an orange-and-white rental van parked in the rear corner, taking up two spots. No one sat in the cab. I'd seen a similar van when I mowed the church lawn the previous summer. I wondered now who'd left it there again.

Inside the church, Wes's office door stood open.

I walked over to his desk.

"Hello Steve," he said, without looking up. "Are you ready to direct traffic?"

"I think so."

His head shot up. "'Think so?' Don't let anyone get past you. Those are your orders."

I nodded. "But there's a van in the lot. It's blocking a couple of spaces."

Wes frowned. "A van?" He swiveled in his chair and looked out the window. As he did, I saw a blue Jeep pull into the lot. It parked at the opposite end of the lot from the van. A young woman in tight jeans climbed out, grabbed a brown bag from her seat, then closed the door, shook out her blonde hair, and walked casually over to the van.

"Uh oh," said Wes. "I've seen this sort of thing before." He stood and peered through the window.

I stepped sideways so I could see around him. The woman knocked on the glass of the van's front passenger window, waited a moment, then opened the door and climbed in.

Wes turned quickly toward me. "You need to go outside immediately and tell those people to leave!"

His urgency surprised me. Wes rarely displayed haste, especially at church where he was in complete control. "Okay," I said. "I know we need the spots."

"It's not just that," Wes said. "She's a prostitute."

My mind skittered.

A prostitute? How does Wes know?

The word landed between us like a sputtering red firecracker. Prostitute! A sick thrill scurried up my spine.

"I'll watch from the window," Wes said. "You better move fast."

Better move fast? Why?

Oh . . . *that*. Yes, I had better move very, *very* fast. Suddenly, I felt like a small schoolboy. I wrung my gray Glasgow cap in my hands as my face went warm. I turned to Wes. "So, uh, do you just want me to go knock on the door? I mean, just go right up to it and—"

"Yes," Wes said. "Hurry."

I threw open the church door and slipped on the icy steps. Wes wouldn't let us use sand on them lest dirt get tracked into his spotless sanctuary. I had to grab the railing to catch myself.

A prostitute!

My heart hammered in my chest. Just knock on the van door, Wes had said. Easy enough for him to say.

And it's not my problem what's happening in the van. Just do what you're told.

But what if . . . ? I wondered. *And then what?*

I stumbled across the slippery lot.

Don't think about it. Wes is watching you. You must do it.

Approaching the van, I looked to see if it was shaking on its axles. It wasn't. *Thank God.* I reached the van door and saw the woman sitting in the front seat. It looked like she was eating her lunch. My legs buckled with relief. A Latino man with a mustache and goatee now sat on the driver's side. His face was heavily pitted with acne scars.

I knocked on the glass; the woman turned and smiled. She was very pretty. She rolled down the window. "Yes?"

"Uh, hi," I said, feeling foolish, like a freshman interrupting a popular girl in the cafeteria. "We're about to have our Good Friday service and we need all the parking spots in this lot. Would you possibly be able to move your vehicles for the next few hours?"

The woman turned to look at the man. He shrugged. She turned back to me. "Sure," she said. "No problem."

I heaved a huge sigh. Then, without thinking, I said, "But you can come to the service too. There's plenty of room—everyone's welcome."

Oh crap! Why did I invite them? There're not enough parking spaces and besides, Wes will never allow a prostitute inside his church.

The woman smiled. "Thanks hon, but I think we'd better go."

The man stared at me impassively.

"Okay!" I said, a little too loudly. "Thanks so much!" Then I turned and rushed off. As I crossed the church parking lot, I saw Wes standing in his office window, arms folded, lips pressed tightly together, nodding his approval.

During the three-hour service that followed, my thoughts returned again and again to that scene played out in the church parking lot. It took some effort to pull myself back to the bloody message about Jesus dying for prostitutes and tax collectors.

———

In April, Wes stood in the church parking lot and held up two objects: a cigarette butt and a small pebble.

"Who is responsible for this?" Wes asked quietly, looking from man to man.

The group of us stared studiously at the objects, avoiding Wes's withering gaze.

Our annual "Men's Work Day" was wrapping up and the men had just finished push-brooming the one-acre lot. Most had blisters forming on their hands. All were sweating.

Wes had come outside to inspect our work. In the hot sun his creased Dockers, pressed shirt, and shined shoes seemed a miracle of propriety. He glanced around the semicircle. Hangdog looks greeted him. "I said, 'Who is responsible for this?'"

No one moved.

Wes inclined his head toward a tall man in the group. "Doug, *you* are responsible. As leader of the push-broom crew it was your responsibility to ensure that this parking lot looked spotless. You failed to properly oversee at least one careless worker. The Lord wants you to know that he cares as much about this church parking lot as he does about your soul."

Doug shuffled his feet. "I'm sorry, Wes, I did my best."

Wes looked slowly at each man in turn. We were all guilty, every one of us. Then he put the offending objects into his trouser pocket. "Your best wasn't good enough," he said. "Next time work as unto the Lord."

As Wes walked stiffly toward the church, I felt fear fluttering in my chest. It wasn't his words that scared me. They fit perfectly within the terrifying image of a perfectionistic God I had already come to expect. What rattled me was Wes's posture. The years of late-night counseling and demon-chasing had taken their toll. For the first time, I noticed that his once-powerful shoulders were slumped. I also noticed that he was limping. He looked like a wax statue left too long in the sun.

He looked like a god about to fall.

CHAPTER 34

Hours of Darkness

Nate | 10 October 2006 | Camp Habbaniyah, Al Anbar Province, Iraq

"Lieutenant Smith, do you know why you're here?"

Major Leonard's question was businesslike without being brusque. He'd been a great leader for so many years that he knew the exact intonation to hint at fraternity without giving up an inch of authority.

This was a man I trusted absolutely and with whom I could be candid. Internally, I was disoriented by loss and foreboding, but outside I remained in complete control. Crying wouldn't make anything better.

"No, sir. But I assume I'm being fired and sent to a MiTT (military transition team)." I paused, then added the second worst thing I could think of.

"Or maybe my mother or father has died."

———

A week prior I'd been standing watch in the Kilo Company command post when the battalion commander's mobile unit had unexpectedly radioed in and reported that they'd be at our location in twenty minutes. The Captain, seated nearby reading a magazine, jumped up in panic.

"Shit! The jump is coming?" The corporal on radio watch confirmed that it was.

"Shit!" the Captain repeated, frantically running pale hands through thinning hair. "How long do we have?"

Without waiting for an answer, he turned to me and declared, "I'm going to inspect Third Platoon's position. Get Mobile ready." I nodded to Staff Sergeant Thomas, who disgustedly exited the room to rouse gunners and drivers from their video games and naps.

The Captain fled to his hooch and returned in five minutes, buckling on his Kevlar.

"You have it, Lieutenant Smith. Let the Colonel know I'm out with Third and that I don't expect to be back before twenty-hundred."

"Roger, sir," I responded with rigid professionalism as the Captain disappeared through a sandbagged entryway. Outside, a heavy door slammed, then four up-armored Humvees crunched out of the courtyard in a familiar refrain of revving engines and squealing brakes. I raised an eyebrow at my platoon sergeant.

"Goddam, he was in a hurry not to be here," Thomas said with a laugh. The corporal grinned, then thought better of it when he saw my lips compress.

"Yes, he was," I agreed. Turning to the corporal, "Get ready to call Warpig in case Voodoo Mobile gets hit." Then I added, "And tell Blue that Black is on his way to their pos."

The corporal bent to his work while I exchanged a quizzical look with Staff Sergeant Thomas. Something was up.

In a few minutes, the jump called to request permission to enter friendly lines. I stood expectantly by the radio, waiting for a shouted report from Voodoo Mobile that would signal an IED or mine strike. I hadn't heard vehicles outside, so the Colonel surprised me when he strode alone into the CP and stopped at the door, measuring the room's three occupants with a glance. He didn't remove ballistic glasses or helmet.

"Good afternoon . . ." I began.

He cut me off.

"Where's your boss?" The Colonel didn't look angry, and the question was pleasant enough. I decided to answer without elaboration.

"He's out inspecting Third Platoon's position, sir."

In a flash, the battalion commander was across the room and planted inches from me. Head thrust up, flecking spittle, he unleashed: "What the *fuck* are you doing? Huh? Why the fuck aren't you delivering chow to your Marines? *Why*, Lieutenant?" He went on, veins pulsing in his neck.

I barely heard him. My mind reeled from a weird mix of fight-like adrenaline and mortification at being reamed in front of enlisted Marines. I stood silent until it registered what the Colonel was saying. This was about . . . *food?*

Vaguely, I recalled a battalion mandate that we deliver one hot meal per day to every Marine in our area of operations. The order stemmed from a congressional inquiry, which had originated when a Third Platoon Marine wrote home that he was wearing filthy cammies, sweltering without air conditioning, and eating

MREs at every meal. In short, he described life as a combat Marine.

The letter writer's horrified mother contacted her congressman about the terrible conditions inflicted upon her son. Congressman DoGood, who couldn't care less about a lance corporal's lunch in Iraq, did care about votes in the next election. His staff prodded the Marine Corps to deliver special amenities to its far-flung flock.

The order seemed stupid. Third Platoon operated at the far edge of our area, accessible only by roads saturated with mines and IEDs. We lost a vehicle nearly every time we drove to their position. Mandating a daily convoy just to deliver cold food was almost murder by fiat.

Now I understood the Captain's sudden flight. It had been his decision not to deliver hot chow, but I had the responsibility to offer an explanation to the raging Colonel, whose tirade finally seemed to be winding down.

"Answer me, asshole! What the *fuck* are you doing?"

I suppressed my emotions and began a calm explanation of our position. "If you'll step over here, sir, I can show you the history of mine strikes on the routes to . . ."

The Colonel tried to cut me off with a profane attack on my manhood. I ignored him and continued. For a few moments, his piercing diatribe threatened to overwhelm my steady delivery. At one point, I thought he was about to punch me. Then he stopped yelling.

Surprised, I turned from the map and saw an expression of disgust wither the Colonel's features. Spinning on his heel, he strode to the door and paused. "Fucking faggots." Then he left.

The radio watch looked windblown. Staff Sergeant Thomas trembled. "No one talks to me like that," he choked out through lips white with rage. "I'll kill that motherfucker."

I was sympathetic. "I get it, Staff Sergeant. But what we need to do is forget any of that just happened." We had Marines outside the firm base on dangerous roads who relied on our focus and professionalism. The corporal nodded and sank down on his bench, treasuring up this story for another time. Thomas guided me to the back of the room and leaned in.

"Goddam, sir. I thought that little bastard was gonna coldcock you. He didn't like being stood up to."

"No, he didn't," I agreed.

My actions would likely have consequences. I certainly hadn't intended insubordination and felt that I had a duty to brief the Colonel about his disobeyed order. But now I felt uncomfortably vulnerable. The Colonel had a reputation for punishing men by sending them to military transition teams with the Iraqi Army.

———

One evening, a few days after the Colonel's visit, I was dropped at Third's position to accompany a patrol leaving the next morning to seek enemy contact. Night gathered in the corners of a high-ceilinged room while I plotted pre-planned targets with several filthy mortar men. The squeak of alcohol pen against plexiglass was interrupted when a corporal approached, his face a study of courteous curiosity.

"Sir, Black needs you back at the CP right away." There was no explanation for the Captain's unprecedented demand.

A night patrol to escort me back to the company command post?

The next morning's operation would proceed without a fire support team leader.

We left within the hour, a staggered line of young Marines treading carefully through darkened palm groves and ragged pastures. I walked between two fire teams, fretting at the unknown force that had the power to pluck me from the fight.

Had Mom or Dad been killed in a car accident? Steve or Christine? They hadn't been listed as next of kin since my emancipation, but I reasoned that the death of a close family member might wend its way through official channels. Or maybe I was being relieved of command. The timing seemed odd, but perhaps the Colonel had stewed for a few days before making the call to remove an irritant. I felt dislocated and self-consciously aware that every man around me was in danger only because of me.

For the first time, *I* was the mission.

Tracks and cart paths glowed faintly between dark thickets under a watery moon. From time to time, we took a knee, faced outboard, and peered into the night while a hole was opened in a fence to our front.

"We never go through the same breach twice, sir," a faceless shadow whispered during one pause. "They always seed them with IEDs. You can hear mules hit them during the day. Poor fuckers." He snorted. "But great mine clearers."

On Canal Road, we picked up the pace, making up for time lost in the fields. Route Michigan slumbered invisibly to our right, its presence suggested across the canal by an expansion of the night. It felt spooky to glide past overlapping craters at the Blue Mosque intersection, where five men had been torn apart in the past month. Our boots sent jagged pieces of Humvee clinking through the dust.

Well past midnight, we stumbled into the courtyard of the company CP. I thanked the patrol leader for a safe passage and took him with me to the radio room, expecting that the Captain would tell me what was going on. Instead, a sleepy radio watch confirmed that the battalion had recalled me without further explanation. I'd leave with a resupply run in the morning.

———

Major Leonard's eyebrows arched. "Fired?" He leaned forward. "Why'd you think that?" He brushed aside my explanation about speaking truth to power and moved on. I tucked away this insight into the battalion commander's personality. He respected fighters.

"The Colonel knows you're the most experienced lieutenant without a platoon. Yes, I know," he quickly interjected, as I began to protest, "you have a weapons platoon, but they're attached out and will be fine without you." I swallowed at the news that the men I loved were no longer mine. The major continued without pause.

"He admires your leadership and wants you to take care of an issue in India Company."

Major Leonard briefly outlined the scandalous details of a platoon that had mutinied on its weak commander in the battalion's most dangerous area of operations.

"The squad leaders and lieutenant have been removed. You will take command."

I felt off-balance. On the one hand, a great weight felt lifted from my shoulders; my fate was no longer hinged to Kilo's incompetent Captain.

Maybe I'll survive the war.

On the other hand, my heart burned as I silently mourned the band of brothers I'd just lost. Nevertheless, as I stood at parade rest in front of this trustworthy executive officer, a glimmer of enthusiasm flickered in my brain.

I'll have a platoon again, not just sitting by a radio while events happen around me. I can make a difference.

A thought occurred.

"Sir, who's leading the platoon now?"

"The India Company commander is." Major Leonard stood up and came from behind his desk. Squeezing my hand and then clapping me on the shoulder, his eyes held a mixture of sympathy and kindness.

"Let's go see the boss."

———

The meeting with the Colonel was a formality, in which he complimented me on my leadership and wished me good luck. The interview lasted two minutes and ended with a firm handshake. I might disagree with the old man's style, but at least he was direct and gave me every indication of confidence in my ability to handle a challenge. I left his office feeling like the air had been cleared.

The next afternoon, I met my new CO. Of middle height, with sandy hair and piercing eyes, the captain flashed a tight grin that bespoke fatalism rather than warmth.

"Coming from Kilo, I see." His voice was a fast drawl.

"Yes sir. From Weapons Platoon." The captain's eyes indicated his mind had already leapt past this introduction and moved on.

"Glad to have you. The platoon is a mess, their living quarters are all fucked up. It's a highway overpass, so quality of life is pretty fucking terrible. Lieutenant Adams watched videos with his Marines, got buddy-buddy with them." The captain paused. I waited, recognizing the implied challenge. His *fucks* were gritted out through clenched teeth. I heard them not as vulgarity, but rather tiny pops of release. He continued abruptly.

"I took them on a patrol yesterday and we had a Marine fucking shot in the stomach. Went out again this morning and another one got hit in the arm. There's a sniper who knows what the fuck he's doing and IEDs everywhere."

As the captain launched into a harangue about the Colonel's unrealistic expectations for India in this murderous area of operations, I mentally shifted gears from expectant subordinate to seasoned professional. The man wanted someone to make his problems go away, not a junior officer to manage. I waited for him to wind down.

"Understood, sir. I'll take care of it." The words implied a confidence I didn't yet feel but knew that I had to fake to manage the situation.

The captain's relief was palpable. He became immediately gregarious, offered me a chew, and informed me that we'd depart friendly lines at 1900. My face must've registered surprise at such a late departure, because the captain grew suddenly sober.

"We only stop at the bridge during hours of darkness."

———

A single chemlight cast an orange pallor against the semicircle of faces surrounding me. It was otherwise pitch black. The fortified highway overpass spanned Route Michigan and led to the only Euphrates bridge in our area of operations. The terrain was so critical to coalition movement and local economics that the battalion had erected dirt-filled Hesco barriers on the overpass, parked a platoon on it, and christened it Observation Post 611.

Normally, I gauged my message and delivery based on nonverbal cues from my audience, but in this ghostly group no emotion, no reaction was visible. Staff Sergeant Iturrino, my new platoon sergeant, stood to my left beside a plywood table spread with maps and heaped with confiscated AK-47s and G3s. He cleared his throat and growled.

"Listen up, First Platoon. This is Lieutenant Smith, our new platoon commander." There was no response. Iturrino turned in the dark and muttered, "They're all yours, sir."

I took one step forward, stopped, and scanned faces masked by the night.

What would I want to hear, if I was one of them? If I'd lost two brothers in the past two days to stupid daytime patrols, and three squad leaders for standing up to incompetence?

With my calmest, most confident voice, I began to speak.

"Good evening, Marines. Most of you don't know me. I got tossed from a Humvee as it drove by and have no idea who you are either. But based on how fast that convoy got out of here, I suspect this is probably the worst place in the whole AO."

There was a stir among the men, a flicker of appreciation.

Good, you've got pride.

I decided to establish my bona fides without threatening their competence or dwelling on the fact that they'd mutinied.

"I'm coming from Kilo Weapons, a few klicks west of here. Last pump I was in Ubaydi during MATADOR." I paused, again trying to gauge the response. It was important that they understood I was experienced, without being arrogant.

"I don't know shit about your AO. *You* are the experts. But I do know we aren't doing any more daytime patrols." Heads began to nod. "We'll move when it's dark, go firm, and then observe and interdict. It doesn't make any sense to move during the day and get Marines shot." More nods. It isn't difficult to gain acceptance from Marines. Just tell them you trust them, and that common sense will prevail.

"Staff Sergeant tells me there's a patrol going out in the morning. I won't be with it. You all know what you're doing. I'll be here getting up to speed with Staff Sergeant and the other NCOs. Eventually I'll go out with you, but for now," here I turned my head in exaggerated fashion to the right and left, taking in the tattered uniforms and faces burnt and thinned by weeks of unrelenting operations in the brutal heat, "I expect you'll be just fine without me."

There were a few relieved grins as Marines recognized a departure from the company commander's methods. Time to wrap up; my purpose had been achieved.

"Over the next few days, I'll make changes but there will be reasons for everything that I do. I'm glad to be here." I nodded to a muscular Marine who exuded quiet competence and stepped back from the map table. "Go ahead with your patrol brief, Sergeant Singh."

Later, after passing my initial guidance and priorities of work to Iturrino, I lay on a dusty cot, hands clasped behind my head, and gazed through torn cammie netting at stars winking in a great canopy. Wisps of cloud smudged the view from time to time. To my left, an occasional low murmur marked an elevated machine gun position, its ballistic glass spiderwebbed and part of its sandbagged roof collapsed from an RPG hit earlier in the week.

A great loneliness seized me, rooted in my separation from the men I'd left behind and in the responsibility that lay ahead on this fire-swept bridge.

Will I be good enough for them? When it matters, will I have what it takes?

CHAPTER 35

Three Reasons

Steve | 2008 | Dallas, Texas

"Give me three reasons why I should believe in Jesus Christ, and I'll give you a hundred dollars."

Startled, I looked up from my book. It was the day before Thanksgiving. I sat reading theology beneath a sweet gum tree near the seminary library.

An unsmiling man stood over me. He wore heavy black boots, new jeans, an untucked shirt, and a black peacoat too warm for the mild Dallas afternoon. A tan Kangol ball cap covered his bald head. His lips were thick, and he had fleshy ears and colorless eyes narrowed with fat.

He held up three pudgy fingers. "Three reasons. A hundred dollars."

Three months into my first semester at seminary, I felt more like a spiritual failure with every passing day. Other students spoke happily of evangelizing the homeless or preaching at nursing homes. Not me. I was taking Greek and learning Hebrew; in my few moments of leisure I listened to Wes's church tapes or reviewed Bible verses while walking the campus at night by myself.

Now, as I looked at the fat man, I wondered if God was giving me an opportunity to act like a real Christian and share the gospel with an unbeliever. I closed my book and laid it aside.

"Three reasons why you should believe in Jesus Christ?" My brain struggled through its fog. "Well, he's the Son of God, he died for your sins and the sins of the whole world, and he daily lives to intercede for those who trust him."

The man squinted. Then he reached into his pocket, pulled out his wallet, and forked two fingers into his billfold.

I held up my hand. "I don't want your money. I don't need any money." That was a lie. I'd run out of cash before the semester ended. Wes had disallowed me from working so that I could focus exclusively on mastering Greek and Hebrew. Privately I questioned such logic, but I knew that doubting Wes was a sin and so I agreed. Now, as my bank account dwindled, I tried to put my hope in God.

The man arched his eyebrows and gestured again with his wallet.

I shook my head. "I don't want your money."

His fleshy face creased into a thin smile. Then he looked around the empty campus. "Hey, can we talk some more about Jesus? I was just going to Jack in the Box to get coffee. Wanna come?"

I got up, shouldered my bag, and stuck out my hand. "Sure. I'm Steve."

He shook my hand. "I'm Josh."

———

At Jack in the Box, we sat in a crummy little window table while cars sped past. Customers entered and left. But all I felt or heard for the next hour were the questions Josh asked. He drilled me with such knowledge of the Bible that it made me wonder if he was a fallen minister.

"Does God love everyone in the world?" Josh said. "Does he love homeless people too? If God loves homeless people, how come the church doesn't?"

I shrugged.

He leaned forward in his seat and whispered conspiratorially. "I visited twenty churches. Twenty! Sometimes I walked into a church dressed like a bum and sat in the back pew just to see what people would do. And you know what happened? Of course, you know. They treated me like a tax collector. Wouldn't even speak to me. And so, what did I do? I went home, cleaned up, put on a suit, and went back to the same churches. No one recognized me, but what did they do? They came up and welcomed me and asked me to come back the next Sunday."

He tipped back in his chair, pulled his hat lower over his eyes. "And I never went back."

I felt hot with shame, like I was the one who'd done this.

Josh smiled a frigid smile. "What about you? Are you all about money? How much money do you have? Are you wealthy?" He asked his questions so quickly that they piled on top of each other before I could speak. I wanted to convince him that I was different, that I was genuine. I said that I had just enough money to pay my tuition and rent for the month of December.

Josh seemed surprised. "So, after next week, you basically have no money?"

"That's right."

He looked at my pants. "Your jeans have holes in them."

I felt embarrassed. I couldn't afford new clothes. "Maybe I'll get a new pair for Christmas."

Josh stared out the window for a few minutes, then he turned abruptly and said, "Is Jesus your number one?"

"Yes."

Josh gave me a piercing look. Then he purred, "Don't lie to me, son. Just be straight with me. There's nothing I hate worse than hypocrisy. If Jesus isn't your number one, just tell me and I won't think twice about it. I just want to know if you're genuine or not. Can you look me straight in the face and tell me that Jesus is your number one?"

I nodded.

"If a man walked into this Jack in the Box with a gun and said that he would kill anyone who was a Christian," Josh said, "would you stand up and say, 'Jesus is my number one'?"

I squirmed in my seat, but said, "Yes. I think I would."

"Just tell me the honest truth and I won't bother you again," Josh said gently. I felt there was nothing I would hold back, nothing I *could* hold back, from his gaze. His eyes pierced me. I knew there was nothing about me that he didn't already know. He was a priest, and I was his acolyte. I felt myself growing lighter and lighter, my heart swelled, and a buzzing filled my ears while inside me bubbled a nervous joy. Classes, relationships, cares and sorrows, all were forgotten in the rush of this test. I would do anything to prove my devotion to Jesus, I thought. If Jesus hadn't been my number one before this, then he would be now. Now and forever. Until the end of all worlds. Amen.

Josh looked at me kindly. I could see that he was true. "Is Jesus really your number one?" he said. "If he's not, tell me so we can be square. I won't think badly of you. I just want to know the truth."

It was the way he said it again, the way he seemed to see right through me, that made me invite him to my apartment for a slice of fresh-baked pumpkin pie. The whole time, he plied me with questions, kept asking for reassurance that I was a genuine Christian. When my roommate came out of his bedroom, Josh quickly turned away and smiled at me. "How 'bout I treat you to lunch at McDonald's?" he said. "We can talk more about our lives and about Jesus. I think I'm just about ready to decide for Christ."

At McDonald's, Josh gave me six dollars to buy a Southwest salad for me and a small coffee with cream and sugar for him. As I ordered, Josh went outside to sit. The sun broke through a scud of clouds and the afternoon warmed considerably. Josh still wore his peacoat and hat. I felt happy and daring.

"What's your favorite Bible verse?" Josh asked. I told him. Then in a fit of manic disclosure I told him that I loved it so much I used its numbers for most of my passwords.

Josh leaned forward and his eyes glinted with interest. "You use it for your passwords?"

I nodded, feeling proud of my vulnerability. Now Josh would surely decide for Christ. He could see that I was holding nothing back. It was then that I noticed his wedding ring. It was an unusual snake-like coil with interlocking engravings.

"Are you married?" I asked.

He looked at me sideways and grimaced. "Was. She ran off with a preacher."

I felt terrible.

"Don't worry about it," Josh said. "I think I'm finally ready to make a decision for Christ. There's only one thing I need to put the icing on the cake. What's the most precious thing that you own?"

I reached into my backpack and took out my Bible.

"Can I borrow it for half an hour?" Josh said. "I want to read the book of Job."

I handed it over.

Josh thumbed through its pages, then laid the book aside. "Can I see your wallet?" he asked.

I put it on the table.

He placed his fat wallet next to mine. Then he pulled out my two debit cards. "Can I hold onto these while I read your Bible?" he asked. "I'll bring them back to your apartment in half an hour and then we can have pumpkin pie. This is the last test that will prove to me that Jesus is your number one."

I thought that sounded like a good idea.

Josh smiled. "I'll put these cards right here in the book of Job—chapter 2—and meet you at your apartment in half an hour."

Job chapter 2, I recalled, was the place where Job lost everything.

In a daze, I stood up from the table and slowly walked the two blocks back to campus. Part of me felt high from the conversation and part of me felt afraid. *I should go back*, I thought. But then I remembered the look in Josh's eye when he said that he only needed to find one genuine Christian to convince him that Jesus was true.

If I go back, then Josh is damned. Jesus came to save prostitutes and tax collectors. Who am I to put a stumbling block in front of Josh?

It was the most compelling argument I could think of.

It sounded far less persuasive two hours later when I called the police.

CHAPTER 36

The Bridge

Nate | 13 October 2006 | Observation Post 611, Sadiqiyah, Iraq

My radio crackled with a crisp notification from the recon patrol leader. "Evil One, this is Evil Two. We're kickoff in vicinity of Grey Goose and Michigan, over."

"Roger, Evil Two, copy all. One-three is firm at Sierra-eight-six. Break. No other friendlies outside six-one-one, over."

Seated on an upended ration case in the bridge's cluttered radio room, I marked a road intersection five hundred meters due west. Then I stepped out beneath tattered netting and into checkered sunlight. A Marine in the machine gun position ten yards away called out visual updates on the patrol until it disappeared into a warren of narrow alleys and mud brick homes on the south side of Route Michigan.

A daylight patrol in our sector made me uncomfortable. Somewhere out there lurked a muj sniper who'd connected with two out of his three targets in the past seventy-two hours. I drifted from post to post, ostensibly to ensure that Marines knew the direction of the friendly patrol, but really to check on their readiness. Satisfied, I made my way to a pull-up bar tucked behind stacked Hesco barriers and worked the tension out of my muscles.

The stuttering roar of gunfire and a series of resounding explosions in the middle-distance broke my second set of pull-ups. I covered ten paces to the radio shack, my chest tightening and heart surging with the adrenaline that always accompanied enemy contact.

Sergeant Singh ordered Marines to "stand to" battle positions, his hastily donned flak open, a carbine swinging from one hand. Rounds crackled overhead and were answered by a rattling burst from the M240. Multiple gunfights raged around us.

The Marine at the radio frowned as I approached, a handset to each ear. "Sir, two-three (the reconnaissance patrol) took contact and has one urgent surgical (casualty). Sniper shot hit a recon Marine in the back, under his SAPI (small-arms protective insert). Small arms and RPGs from multiple directions."

"Which one is Company Tac (tactical channel)?" I grabbed the handset and jammed it to my ear, trying to piece together an idea of the situation from the reports flooding the net. Since I didn't own the other patrol, my job was to figure out how to support the medevac that was being arranged, while controlling my units on the bridge and in town.

The radio watch broke in on my racing thoughts. "Sir, one-three (our security patrol) just took fire. They returned it, but don't have a BDA (battle damage assessment). No friendly casualties."

I nodded and continued to listen to the company tactical network. Shouts and gunshots echoed as Marines fired at muzzle flashes in the ville. Four of the company's units had been hit at the same time. Even the Iraqi Army position across the river was engaged. Five separate attacks had been coordinated with perfect timing to a single shot against a moving patrol.

Not since MATADOR in 2005 had I been in a fight with a proficient enemy who'd risk taking on an entire company of Marines. But unlike my situation in Ubaydi, now I was understrength and unable to maneuver. One of my squads was under attack in town, one was under attack on the bridge, and one still manned a position at the company firm base several kilometers away. I could scrape together a single fire team on the bridge as a quick reaction force, but I wasn't about to lead four men into the chaos swelling around us. Things took on a dreamlike quality, where events tumbled together without clear sense of progression.

Minutes stretch out slackly in the heat, time shuffling its feet to gunshot percussion. Snap, snap, snap. Darting eyes search for targets and fail to find one. A quarter of an hour passes. Out of sight, the recon casualty is gingerly loaded into an armored Humvee. Engines roar and whine underneath the bridge as the medevac convoy blurs past on its way to Taqaddum.

The Marine dies.

The town quieted as gunfire eased and then ceased. In the breathless stillness that followed, a dark green Opal sedan nosed out of a side road near where the Marine was shot. The driver seemed to hesitate, then gunned the vehicle across Route Michigan and swung onto the dusty ramp that ran past our position and led to the Euphrates bridge.

Someone barked out a warning. "Watch that car!"

At the machine gun position, the gunner traversed toward the sedan, while next to him a corporal raised his rifle to fire warning shots. In a tomb-like town, the

Opal's aggressive movement was the height of suspicion. Whether car bomb or getaway vehicle, we all sensed that the car's occupants were dirty.

Crack. A tracer flashed into an embankment ten yards in front of the oncoming vehicle. It stopped.

"Sir, I'm gonna go snap (search) that Opal." Sergeant Singh dropped down from the machine gun position; his announcement caught me off guard.

I felt satisfied merely stopping the car. Singh's plan to venture out from behind concrete and ballistic glass to walk exposed on a raised highway ramp toward a possible car bomb, a few hundred yards from where a sniper had just killed another Marine, seemed suicidal.

Nevertheless, I trusted Singh's instincts. "Roger, we'll provide overwatch. Who do you want to take?"

With the die cast, the sergeant didn't waste any time. "No one, sir."

With profound respect and a hint of envy at his courage, I watched as Singh leaped over a Jersey barrier and began the long walk to the battered green car.

As it happened, the Opal was empty of weapons or contraband, even though its male occupants leered maddeningly during the sergeant's detailed search. They knew that we knew they were insurgents. They also knew that without any evidence to prove a connection to the attack, Singh would have to let them go. He released them after several minutes and returned to the bridge unscathed. The vehicle turned around and tore off in a cloud of dust.

This action, and a half-dozen others more impressive than it, were included in Singh's Bronze Star recommendation that I submitted at the end of our tour. Singh never got the medal. An awards board decided that the sergeant had "just done his job" and knocked it down to a Navy Achievement Medal.

It was one of my only regrets of the war.

———

The next four weeks were the cruelest of my fourteen months in Iraq, a gauntlet of exhaustion, loneliness, and violence that tested the depth of my endurance, courage, and leadership.

At their end, I stopped talking to God and wrote off the Marine Corps as a career.

It all began because we had to move.

In the early hours of October 18, an engineer unit began construction of a new observation post five hundred meters west of us, on the north side of Route Michigan. The division had conceded to local demands for a demilitarization of the bridge by planning observation posts to the east and west. Once these posts were established, the bridge would open to civilian traffic. Because of the sniper threat, engineers worked at night and left before dawn, their gear stacked inside a square of partially filled Hesco barriers.

The town reacted poorly to the temporary Hesco base.

For several hours after first light, our patrols warned off locals stealing US government property from the unguarded site. By midmorning, petty thievery had escalated to vandalism and suspicious activity. I radioed for a mobile unit to string razor wire and post warning signs around the new position, thereby eliminating casual access and helping to establish hostile intent for any locals who breached the wire.

It took the mobile unit over an hour to arrive. In the interim, I peered through my rifle optic at a swirl of activity in the machine shops and store fronts near the construction site. The situation seemed a microcosm of our entire deployment, holding the requirement to thwart insurgent activity in tension with the reality that most Iraqis just wanted to go about their lives. Marines operated at the center of a Venn diagram, where innocents and insurgents blended. Which activity was harmless? Which was hostile? From a distance, it was almost impossible to discern.

The spotter for a sniper team that had joined us the previous day called out: "Sir, we've got a group of MAMs gathering behind the Hescos. Look pretty shady."

Shit.

We theorized that insurgents blended into groups of civilians to mask IED emplacement along the road. There might be a perfectly innocent reason for a group of MAMs to skulk on the unobserved side of the construction site, but I wasn't going to stake Marine lives on it. I turned to the radio watch. "What's Evil Mobile's ETA?"

"Five minutes, sir."

If I was going to err, it would be on the side of protecting Marines. I gave my decision to the snipers. "Kill anyone who drops anything at the site or who tampers with the Hescos. I'm assuming probable IED emplacement."

"Roger, sir."

The sniper team leader, call sign "Reaper," squinted through his spotting scope to find a target, while his partner lifted his cheek from the camouflaged stock of an M40A3 sniper rifle, drew a deep breath, and leaned back into the weapon.

Discomfort chewed at the edges of my conscience. This was how innocents died.

To my relief, India Mobile arrived and dismounted several Marines before Reaper could engage. Half a kilometer away, shouting mouths formed black dots in an angry Morse code. Locals cleared out as gloved Marines wrestled bales of concertina wire into position.

The dismounted men moved with urgency. They knew their arrival had started a race against the clock. The race would end either when they jumped back in their vehicles or when the enemy sniper finished stalking and sent a round down range. None of us doubted the muj sniper was out there. Like air, he was always present, always unseen, and only noticed when acting against an object.

My eyes darted from windows, to shadows, to wilting vegetation.

Where would I be if I was setting up a shot?

The race was won. Marines drove in the final engineer stake and clambered into Humvees. On the bridge, we sighed a collective exhale of relief.

But before India Mobile managed to depart, the battalion commander's jump suddenly roared under the bridge and squealed to a halt next to the newly laid wire. The BC's entourage included journalists and a civil affairs officer. Doors popped open and a handful of men began to walk casually around the vehicles, pointing at the construction site and snapping photos. Their relaxed manner was insane. The principle was basic: unconcealed movement invites sniper fire.

It was over in sixty seconds.

A single gunshot cracked and CAG 6, the major in charge of civil affairs, collapsed with a bullet through his face. I gave unnecessary orders to Marines already searching for the gunman and watched sympathetically as small figures huddled around the officer's crumpled body. In the time it took to rack a round, aim, exhale, and squeeze the trigger, a second gunshot rang out and spun goggles off the helmet of a jump Marine pulling security.

"Why the fuck don't they pop smoke and get the fuck out of there?" someone asked.

Why dismount Marines in the open with a known sniper threat? Why weren't we consulted about the visit to the construction site? Why?

The jump quickly recovered its dismounts, loaded its casualty, and roared off. The major miraculously survived.

We never found the sniper.

———

Construction of the new posts and preparation for the demilitarization of the bridge piled additional work on our exhausted and understrength platoon. The engineers took only a few days to fill Hescos, build watchtowers, and complete the shells of the two new positions. When they left, all the finishing work to make the posts defensible and livable fell on us. Meanwhile, our primary mission to secure Route Michigan hadn't changed.

The strain began to tell. Squads rotated off all-day security patrols and headed immediately to one of the new construction sites in the dark. There, they filled and stacked thousands of sandbags, strung wire obstacles, built blast walls and rocket platforms, and completed dozens of other projects to ready the posts. Well past midnight, nearly sleepwalking men returned to the bridge and fell into cots or rotated into guard positions to relieve men scheduled for the next patrol.

We were always tired, always dirty, always behind.

A bout of dysentery rippled through the platoon, striking down man after man. Like most of the Marines, I tossed defiled underclothes onto a burn pit and went naked beneath trousers stiffened to cardboard by weeks of grime and sweat. Sick men shivered behind machine guns and hobbled out on patrols so that sicker men could snatch a few extra hours of rest.

It was a horrible, beautiful time.

Enemy activity continued relentlessly. The insurgent sniper shot a patrolling Kilo Company Marine through the throat. A few days later, he shot an India Company Marine between the eyes. We found or detonated IEDs nearly every day.

I felt worn out and frustrated. Our presence had done nothing to reduce enemy activity. I was under-resourced to secure Route Michigan, under-resourced to build observation posts, and under-resourced to engage in civil affairs. Yet my challenge was the same challenge for all Marines in western Iraq; so rather than nursing resentment at the powers that be, I blamed myself for everything that affected my men.

As the lone officer on the bridge, I had no friends with whom to consult or from whom to gain support. What I did have were books. Some I'd brought in my sea bag, others I'd given to friends and family before deployment, requesting that they send me a new book every few weeks.

One dusty afternoon in between duties, I found the companion I craved in T. E. Lawrence. *Seven Pillars of Wisdom* became my Iraqi bible, its sweeping narrative giving context to the desert war, Arabs, and the insecurities that I faced. I read it off and on for weeks.

In early November, I put down the book and looked up at an achingly beautiful night. A waning autumn moon glowed like quicksilver against a blue-black sky. Smoky clouds flung themselves at the brilliant disc before sliding on to spread moon shadows across the desert wastes. Here and there, sparkling points of light glittered like icy diamonds against a hundred million years of space.

It was a night of stark beauty and infinite possibility. Gazing up at the sky, I forgot about the war. All the world was hushed beneath the silent sweep of the heavens. God felt unimaginably remote and inexplicably near. History seemed laid out to me like the glowing expanse of sky.

Who am I?

How many millions of faceless men had died over millennia of savage wars in these same ancient sands? I heard the marching feet of the conquering armies: Egyptians, Assyrians, Babylonians, Persians, Greeks, Romans; and later, Moslems, Turks, French, British—and Americans. The clash of metal and the cries of the dying seemed to echo through the night. Their blood coursed beneath my feet, seeping through the white sand, into the Euphrates.

The river was my part of the war. Just out of sight from where I stood, beyond a fringe of ghostly palm trees and graceful rushes, its silvery surface glided between silent banks. Since the Garden of Eden, the Euphrates had watered this land and its people.

It will continue to do so until the end of time—until the final battle fought on these worn sands chokes its depths with the slain multitudes of mankind.

Armageddon was the conclusion of history, the final chapter in the violent litany of this land.

So, where am I? What chapter am I fighting?

The introduction was clear to me, as was the conclusion. But the present was as fleeting and ethereal as the moonlit clouds.

A distant explosion drifted on a cool breath of night air. It brought me back to the present. Inside a nearby bunker, a radio hissed and a Marine responded anonymously in a low, clipped tone. The rare beauty of the night was ruined. Duty and responsibility beckoned. Always, they beckoned. Shoving my hands into my pockets, I stole one last, lingering glance at the timeless wheel of the stars. It's enough to live in the present if one can occasionally glimpse eternity.

Turning quickly on my heel, I ducked beneath a canvas covering and went back to the war.

CHAPTER 37

Shackleton

Steve | 2009 | North Yarmouth, Maine

Under the purple flicker of fluorescents Wes looked terrible.

He'd asked me to join him and the two deacons, Peter and Randall, to work on our church budget while I was home on Christmas break.

Sitting across from Wes in one of the dim Sunday school classrooms, I was shocked by his emaciation. Wes had once played football for an undefeated Philadelphia team and had been recruited to play at Princeton. At church softball games, he could smash home runs well into his sixties. But today his cheek bones protruded, his eyes darted brightly from above dark circles, and his movements seemed slow and deliberate. His skin, always pale, now glowed bluish green.

After the two-hour meeting, Wes shuffled papers in front of him, carefully aligned them with his fingertips, then said quietly, "I've never asked this before, but I'd like you men to lay hands on me and pray for me. I really need your prayers."

The earth might as well have opened its mouth to receive us.

I'd never seen Wes vulnerable.

We gathered around, the three of us, and placed our hands on Wes's shoulders. I smelled his Aqua Velva aftershave. Beneath his starched shirt, his shoulders were thin and bony.

"I haven't gotten much sleep over the past year," Wes admitted softly. "I just keep getting weaker and weaker. I thought I hit bottom three months ago, but the Lord keeps taking me deeper and telling me that his grace is sufficient. I don't know how I can go on."

For over a year, Wes had been counseling with himself almost nonstop. The previous decade of theophostic counseling with other church members eventually led Wes to conclude that the man most afflicted in our congregation was himself, and that from his birth he'd been the special victim of a great, Satanic conspiracy.

Once Wes realized that he alone was the primary target of Lucifer, a new problem confronted him: who was qualified to offer him counsel? This was because the wisest man he had ever known was himself. To Wes, the answer seemed obvious: he would perform his own counseling. He would use his wife as a sort of medium between himself and the Lord, asking her questions and waiting for her to receive answers from God.

Within weeks of starting his own counseling, Wes had plunged into a brambly shadow world populated by wraiths of recovered memories and ghosts of demons. He spent up to forty hours a week in self-arranged sessions. All other church responsibilities fell by the wayside. If any of us had suffered, then Wes had suffered more. His memories of alleged abuse were legion.

Lest we feel excluded, every Sunday evening Wes spent an hour and a half sharing graphic details from his previous week's sessions. He entitled the sermons "It Was Fitting: A Personal Testimony," and assured us that God wanted us to know what had happened in our pastor's life so that we could empathize with him and glorify God as we saw the Lord heal and sanctify him.

While all of us had grown inured to tales of normal abuse—years of immersion desensitized us—Wes's stories took us to places dark and deep. He believed that nearly every man in his life had abused him at the behest of Satan, including famous seminary professors. His troubles with SI (sacroiliac) joint pain—ostensibly the result of foolishly carrying a heavy table down to the church basement by himself one day—suddenly he blamed on body memories related to childhood abuse. He was targeted by Satan because of his own holiness, he said. The demonic realm knew how special Wes was—he shone in this present darkness—and covens of warlocks executed sexual judgment on him every night in the hopes of derailing him from his sanctified mission.

But there was more.

Wes stood in front of the church Sunday after Sunday, describing in lurid detail his unwilling participation in orgies outside of Philadelphia when he was a young man. He recovered memories of being driven to house parties by Satanists, of busty classmates, who later starred as B-movie actresses, seducing him. I fidgeted uncomfortably in my seat as Wes described sex with these women in excruciating detail, yet with an undercurrent of twisted pleasure. In front of me, several fourth and fifth graders sat stoically, their entire childhoods saturated with perverted sexual content from the pulpit.

But there was more.

Wes spoke of Satanists calling him out of his house at night to go to wicked rites, of men entering his house by walking through walls when every door and window was locked. One night, he looked out at the small congregation sweating in the sanctuary and told us that he had been forced to have sex with certain women in our own church, as recently as last week. That Satanists had arranged meetings between him and the wives of church members to bring God's name into disrepute. My spine stiffened with horror as I watched these unwitting women weep in the pews, their husbands helpless with agony. Objectively, there was no evidence that any of this had happened—only the clear-eyed assurance from Wes that it was so.

"The Lord is refining me through these painful times so that we might go deeper as a church," Wes said one Sunday evening. "We have gone as far as I can take you, but the Lord has even deeper things for us, things that we never would have believed even a few months ago."

An involuntary shudder passed through me.

What can possibly be blacker than the darkness we've already suffered?

Instead of a church committed to the work and power of God, we were a community stricken by demons. It was all we talked about, all we dreamed about in our darkest nightmares. If you defined a church by what it focused on, an objective observer would call us a synagogue of Satan.

So, I was unprepared for what greeted me when I returned the following summer.

———

"How many of you are afraid of me?" Wes asked.

In the broiling upstairs sound booth, where I was recording his sermon, I craned my neck to see how many hands went up from what was left of our tiny congregation.

"It's all right. Please be honest. How many of you are afraid of me?"

Alone in the balcony, I raised my hand. I peered over the guardrail. I didn't need to count. It was unanimous.

Wes looked around and sighed. "I am very sorry," he said. "I don't want you to be afraid of me. That's not how it's supposed to be."

During the rest of the sermon, Wes shared his own struggles and mistakes. It was an unprecedented liturgy of public confession. Since Wes had come to our church in 1984, he'd stood before us claiming to represent the voice and face of God Almighty. If someone pointed out an error in Wes's life or doctrine, they were considered a rebel. Now almost every negative thought I'd ever entertained about Wes came pouring out of his own mouth in a calm monologue of remorse. It seemed miraculous. The light pouring into our sanctuary glistened like ice melting from a frozen world.

"Growing up, I was not in touch with my emotions," Wes said sadly. "I was repressed, so I was obsessive-compulsive. I tried to channel my energies into objective things that I could measure and control. I desperately wanted my kids to have a better life than I did. I wanted them to be healthier in their inner life. I didn't want them to struggle, like I did."

From my bird's-eye view, I saw Wes's three adult children nod and dab their eyes.

"I genuinely desired God's blessing in our lives. And because of this inner drive, flowing from my own sense of inadequacy and deprivation, I was overly motivated as a Christian father. I was always something of an overachiever. I had unrealistic expectations for my kids. I was overly strict. I was a taskmaster."

A thrill shot through me. "Taskmaster" was exactly how I viewed God, because Wes represented him. I'd written false profiles of God for an assignment at seminary; nearly every portrait read like a description of Wes Harris.

Wes continued. "I had a mechanical orientation to the Christian life. I saw it in terms of self-discipline, doing what God wants you to do, resisting temptation, being a good person, ministering to others, witnessing to the lost. At times, my obsessive orientation caused me to overcorrect my children. Overcorrection makes life more difficult for children. It hampers their growth as individuals. It gives them a sense of not being able to achieve, of not being able to satisfy their father. It makes them anxious and depressed."

I continued to nod. Everything Wes was saying about his parenting style was true about him as pastor.

Wes motioned for me to pause the tape. Then he hung his head and blew his nose with a clean, white handkerchief. After wiping his eyes and adjusting his glasses, Wes raised an index finger and motioned for me to resume taping.

"We need to encourage each other more." He looked out at the assembled congregation. "But a dutiful orientation to life, plus our underlying anxiety, tends to make us more prone to correcting and overreacting rather than being relaxed and encouraging. Anxiety causes us to be overprotective. We think we are just having appropriate concern for whomever we are trying to control, especially if they are very significant to us emotionally. If things get out of our control, we become more anxious and try to impose order on our world. We try to become the god of our own little world so that everything feels okay."

Something inside me exploded.

There it is!

Wes had just admitted it. He'd tried to control the church and everyone in it because of his own obsessions and anxiety. In a flash, I recalled dozens of ways that Wes's obsessiveness and perfectionism had harmed me over the years. I knew without asking that everyone else in the congregation could scroll through their own lists of abuse. It was a crucial moment. I thought that Wes might step down from his pastoral role right then and there.

Instead, Wes sighed deeply and said, "I'm asking God to help free me from my bondage and perfectionism, things which have placed unfair demands on you. Please pray that God will help me to be kinder and gentler with all of you so that you do not need to be afraid of me. I'm asking God for another twenty-five years of biblical ministry. God is faithful, and he will do it."

I walked out of the service feeling disoriented. Wes had admitted to the very things that my brother had once accused him of: obsessiveness, manipulation, and control. The spotless image I'd had of Wes lay shipwrecked and unsalvageable. But, in its place, there spread out an awful unknown. Like a member of Ernest Shackleton's crew, I walked reluctantly away from the ruin of my ship, frozen in Antarctic ice. I had no idea if venturing into the trackless waste would improve my chances for survival.

Nevertheless, once home I stood at my bedroom window and noticed how blue the sky was, how green the grass.

I couldn't stop smiling.

———

Throughout the summer, Wes continued to act more gracefully toward all of us. He preached about the kindness of God. He overlooked transgressions and mistakes that previously would have brought his harsh condemnation. He told jokes, laughed at himself, and reminded us often that God was pleased with us.

It was our own period of glasnost, a miraculous season of openness and warmth that found crocuses raising delicate heads after twenty-five years of spiritual winter.

So, it was with newfound joy that I returned to Dallas in August.

And it was in that same spirit of hope that I made a grave mistake.

———

"What have you done?" Wes said, and his voice over the phone sounded more sober than I'd ever heard it. My heart shrank, but I still hoped that the whole thing could be redeemed, that somehow everything would turn out okay.

Ashley was a bright, pretty girl who wanted to become a missionary. In my group of friends at seminary, she was the sparkling center. To me, she also seemed like the only girl who might possibly receive Wes's approval. I felt swept along by our friendship and wrote page after page about her in my journal. A part of me that I'd long kept locked away came blinking into the light.

When Ashley's father came to town, I met him at a local coffee shop and asked about dating his daughter. Then I shared my feelings with Ashley. Telling her I needed some time to figure a clear course forward, I set myself to devising a plan that would enable me to introduce our relationship to my pastor without him shutting things down.

It seems stupid now. But at the time, I truly believed that with the new focus on grace and openness in our church, marriage to an outsider would be back on the table.

Tragically, my next step was to tell my parents.

Word filtered back to Wes.

It only took him a minute to pick up the phone.

"And you did all of this without consulting your pastor?" Wes asked. "What on earth led you to do that?"

I told him that I thought the Holy Spirit had guided me.

"In something as important as this?" Wes said incredulously. "Rather than talking with your spiritual father, your pastor who knows you better than anyone and who has direct access to the will of God?"

"Yes," I said quietly. "I was trying to follow the dating guidelines you laid out for me last August before I went to seminary."

"I never gave guidelines about dating," Wes said.

But he had. I'd written them down on a 3x5 card in his office while he watched. The card now sat on my desk in front of me. "Yes, you did," I said. "You gave me criteria to look for in a woman. You said that a girl would need to fulfill most of those criteria for me to consider her a marriage prospect. I believe that Ashley meets those requirements."

Wes snorted. "We never talked about that."

"But we did. I have the card you told me to write—"

"Don't lecture me!" Wes snapped. "Satan has deceived you. Now you are trying to justify yourself. But there is only one thing to do here. You need to cut things off with Ashley."

"But that would be cruel!" I protested. "At least we should remain friends and I can tell her that I don't have the green light now to pursue a relationship."

"This is not an argument," Wes said coldly. "You can choose either to obey or disobey. If you choose to disobey, then you will have to come home because I will revoke your scholarship money. You are privileged to be at seminary. It is a privilege that can be rescinded."

It was the same heartless blackmail he'd used to keep me from Phil's funeral. "But why?" I pleaded. "What have I done? What has Ashley done? We're not even in a relationship yet."

"Satan is at work!" Wes cried. "He has influenced you and gotten you off track. You are there to study God's Word and prepare for a life of full-time Christian ministry, not to get a wife. I think you are being influenced by the same Satanists who tormented me at seminary."

I said nothing. I couldn't think of anything to say. How could one argue against mists and wraiths? More important, even though I'd heard Wes's confessions of fallibility, I still wasn't prepared to knock him from his citadel of divine power.

In my mind, Wes still spoke for God.

"Don't do anything," Wes said. "I'll check with the Lord and get back to you tomorrow. In the meantime, don't talk to Ashley. At all."

That afternoon, I skipped class and lay on my bed feeling sick to my stomach. I thought about leaving the church, striking out on my own as Nate did. But at this point I had too much invested. I'd already spent a lifetime trying to convince myself and everyone else that God was at work in our church, that Wes was a godly man who had access to the will of God. I'd already shunned Nate and my relatives for over thirteen years. I'd said no to other relationships and I'd cut off other people. Did it really make a difference if I cut off yet another relationship?

It does.

Ashley had done nothing wrong except to act kindly toward me—and to enter Wes's orbit of destruction. She had no idea what was about to happen and no reason to suspect anything.

Closing the door to my bedroom, I got down on my knees and stayed there for the next six hours. When I finally climbed into bed in the wee hours of the morning, I still couldn't sleep. I was about to hurt a girl I admired. I couldn't see a gentle way around it. I wasn't brave enough to leave the church. It was still easier to believe that Wes was right than to recognize that everything I'd ever believed was wrong.

I couldn't forsake everything, could I?

Or can I?

———

At noon, Wes called. He told me I was to cut things off with Ashley. His voice came hard and fast. I realized he was reading from a paper. "Do not invite her to your room and do not go to hers," he said. "Ask her to meet you in some public place and then explain that you disobeyed your spiritual authority and that it is not God's will for you to date. Tell her that because of your disobedience, you must end things with her completely. It will be easier that way for both of you. It is God's severe mercy."

I made small noises of assent.

"Are you writing this down?" Wes asked.

"No."

"Write it down so there can be no confusion." He repeated his orders.

I wrote them down.

"Read what you have written."

I read it.

"And one more thing," he said. "You must do this in five minutes or less. I don't want Satan getting you off track explaining all kinds of things to Ashley or trying to defend yourself or make her feel better. The devil is in the details. You have nothing to apologize for. It is Satan who has deceived you. If Ashley is truly following the Lord, she will respect your request and not press for details."

"Five minutes?" I choked. "What can I possibly say in five minutes? That will only crush her and cause her to ask more questions."

"Read what is on your card," Wes said.

I read it.

"That only took two minutes. You still have three minutes to elaborate."

I started to dry heave.

"Steve, you have gotten yourself into this mess," Wes said coldly. "It is my job to get you out. This is how God is delivering you."

There was a pause. I heard a female voice in the background. Then Wes said, "Hold on a minute." Thirty seconds later, Wes came back on the line. "My wife said that five minutes might be a little too harsh. I checked with the Lord. He said to give you ten minutes."

Ten minutes. What grace.

Wes said, "Call me just as you're leaving to meet with Ashley and call me as soon as you finish. If it's longer than ten minutes, Satan has influenced you. I am going to keep you accountable."

I couldn't believe it.

Wes is going to time my breakup?

After I got off the phone with Wes, I composed myself and called Ashley. The sound of her voice made me feel sick with shame. An hour later, we met in the common lounge area on my floor, and I told her what Wes had dictated to me. She sat stunned. My heart broke for her. When it was over, I felt like a butcher.

Choking back my emotions, I walked to my room and called Wes.

His voice came over the phone flooded with warmth. "Oh good, Steve," he said. "God really helped you. Now, you must avoid all contact with Ashley."

A cold wind blew through my soul. "But Ashley is the center of our entire group of friends," I said. "I have no friends who aren't friends with her."

"Then I guess you will need to look for new friends," Wes said. He said it as if he were suggesting I try a new dish soap.

After Wes hung up, I sat on my bed and looked out the window. The sun still shone through the live oaks, but I didn't feel it.

All these years, Wes had been the one to hurt people, reject them, excommunicate them, call them evil.

I'd followed him. I'd obeyed him. I'd shunned my brother and most of my relatives.

But today, for the first time, I'd been the agent of harm.

For no reason.

You did this. Not Wes. Not Nate. Not God. You.

I got up, went into the bathroom, and washed my face.

I hadn't eaten in two days.

I looked at myself in the mirror and was shocked by what I saw.

Under the purple fluorescents, a terrible mask with hollow eyes looked back at me.

In the flickering light, I looked exactly like Wes.

CHAPTER 38
The Evil One

Nate | 9 November 2006 | Sadiqiyah, Al Anbar Province, Iraq

Under a blue autumn sky, the bridge that had been barred from local use for two years was finally reopened.

Instantly, a human wave of shouting children boiled out from storefronts and alleyways, tearing at the remaining wire obstacles, engineer stakes, and military road signs of our former outpost in a frenzy of looting. Interspersed throughout the throng of children were knots of swarthy men.

Marines in our new observation post half a kilometer away stood next to a grenade launcher, peering through clouds of dust. MAMs lingered suspiciously beneath the partially obscured span.

As quickly as the melee started it was over. The last small boy disappeared into a filthy house dragging a military road sign that warned residents not to stop near the bridge or they'd be shot. All was quiet, except for a trickle of civilian traffic enjoying its newfound freedom.

Later that morning, I bummed a ride with another platoon to drive under the bridge and set a blocking position to the west. Shadows beneath the bridge drifted gray with moondust. Here and there, a torn sandbag delivered its contents back to the desert. Though this had been our home just a few days ago, the area felt foreign and seemed to crawl with evil.

We set the blocking position. Within minutes, we had to trade places with a vehicle on the far side of the bridge. As it drove toward us, the oncoming Humvee trailed a cloud of dust. Just as it broke out from the shadow of the overpass, a familiar concussion thumped through me and the oncoming vehicle disappeared in a sheet of flame and brown smoke. The explosion seemed soundless. For a heartbeat—two—blood pulsed in my ears. Then the Humvee emerged from the smoke in slow motion, damaged but drivable.

The blast seemed to jar loose a moral inhibitor in my brain.

Returning to the observation post, I radioed for a sniper team. My instructions to them were clear. Since insurgents took our Western morality for granted and concealed their hostile actions with innocent trappings, any IED emplacement activity around the bridge, regardless of the age or gender of the person involved, was to be engaged. I would risk no more Marines based on an inherited moral quagmire.

Under cover of darkness, the snipers inserted into a house with good observation of the bridge. Early the next morning, I was rattled out of unimportant thoughts by a gunshot to the north. Rushing to the radio, I caught the sniper team leader's matter-of-fact report.

"Evil One, this is Reaper. Engaged a target ten meters south of six-one-one bridge. Break. Target fell behind embankment. BDA (battle damage assessment) is enemy KIA, over."

"Roger, Reaper, this is Evil One. What was the target doing, over?"

Did we just kill a civilian?

Reaper allayed my concern. "Uh . . . target dropped a black bag underneath the bridge, over."

I felt relieved. But I needed more information for my report to the company. "Roger. Need a description of the target, over."

There was a slight pause on the other end of the radio, as if the operator was conferring with his colleagues. "Evil One, this is Reaper. It was a kid. Gray shirt, black pants. Probably seven or eight, over."

Horror.

This was the brutal consequence of my orders.

With effort, I suppressed my reaction, chastised myself for the lapse of self-control, and recalled the now compromised sniper team. When they returned to post, I callously joked that the kid only counted as half a kill.

Partly it was a brusque comment intended to validate the Marines and spare them any anguish about taking the life of a child. But partly it was to further deaden me to any semblance of normal emotions. By force of effort, I'd come to the point where I had less emotional turmoil about the death of a child than I did when I authorized Marines to shoot wild dogs around our position. At least the dogs were innocent.

And yet, a seething anger struck at the foundation of my sense of goodness, hope, and faith. I blamed God for putting me in a place where every decision seemed evil.

Alone with my laptop that night, I poured out my soul as a way to deafen the silence of heaven.

What has happened to me? I wrote, the words coming in a hot rush.

I fear that this war has cost me my soul. Not because of the violence that I have witnessed: for violence deadens but does not destroy. Nor for a loss of innocence: my innocence vanished years ago apart from any field of battle. But my soul flinches and withdraws from the evil that I am forced to embrace for the sake of my Marines. Every good and noble trait within me is a weakness. Kindness, compassion, gentleness, generosity—each of these has been exploited for the benefit of the enemy. Over the course of weeks and months, I have gradually suppressed my better instincts: buried them beneath layers of cold, dark calculation and mechanical decisions.

Because I have not the predator's nature, I must stifle my naturally pacific disposition with forced cruelty. Things that once meant something to me in a former life now factor only as parts of an equation, calculated without emotion to produce the greatest good to my platoon. Women and children, the infirm or the elderly—what are these, but artificial indications of weakness classified by a Judeo-Christian ethic? Women are not weak but strong, if they can exploit our Western sensibilities and prohibitions to successfully smuggle weapons. Unquestioning, misdirected eight-year-olds make superb IED emplacers.

The impossibly wide ethical spectrum in the United States has narrowed into a line of razor sharpness in the stinking filth of Iraq. On one side of the line is life and on the other side is death. Black and white. Right is life and death is wrong.

The greatest good is that which keeps the greatest number of my Marines alive and still accomplishes the mission. Every infantry Marine instinctively knows about this iron law of combat. Every grunt strives desperately to keep himself and his buddies squarely in the thin margin of light and life.

Darkness surrounds us. It stalks each patrol; it whispers in the eddying smoke from each explosion; it laughs with the snap of a sniper's bullet. What would happen if a shade of gray was introduced between black and white in this monochromatic world? Gray is darker than light. Murky, unresolved questions about right and wrong would blend the lines between life and death: confuse, trip up, and snare the Marines. Gray would abruptly lead to black. Equivocation is as deadly as the darkness, but with added mental torment.

I have seen the mental anguish inflicted upon young Marines by their leaders' refusal to sweep away the gray haze of moral relativity and replace it with arbitrary black and white. Eighteen-year-olds were never intended to be arbiters of life and death—to make them so is intolerably cruel. Further, I have seen Marines excoriated and hung out to dry by their lead-

ers for making instantaneous decisions between right and wrong in combat, when afterward the rear echelon officers inserted an armchair filter of gray. I have looked into the hollow eyes of boys who have realized, in a glaring instant of awful truth, that they have taken an innocent life and their world will never be the same.

My responsibility as an officer is to ruthlessly eliminate any shades of gray from entering the black-and-white world of my Marines. But even savage, war-torn Iraq is not a black-and-white world: God created shades and shadows, temperature and degree. The only possible way to eliminate the gray is by artificial decree—by forcing a man to believe that the gray that he sees is really black or white. How is this done in a rifle platoon in combat? It is done by me—the officer—who embodies the sanction or censure of the US government to my men.

What relief—when a Marine is in doubt—to obey a lawful order that cuts direct to the heart of any situation, regardless of how ambiguous or uncertain the situation may be. The balance of black and white remains and with it the Marine's mental stability and moral certainty is safeguarded.

But at what cost to the officer?

It dehumanizes me, strips me of feeling, emotion, and isolates me from the rest of my men who operate placidly in worlds of stark contrast. To save my Marines, I must sacrifice my conscience.

I live in a shadow world of gray. As events or situations transpire in the haze of combat, I instantly judge, catalog, and relegate to black or white each potential threat or each possible good. How arrogant. For a man to take the intricate world as created by God and parcel it into artificial realms of right and wrong must surely compromise his morality. To keep my men moral, I consciously become immoral. Does God understand and will He forgive me?

I don't know.

I don't think so.

I don't feel like I can be forgiven for some of the decisions that I have made over here.

November 2006 | Camp Habbaniyah, Al Anbar Province, Iraq

The battalion supply shop was tucked away in a sleepy corner of Camp Habbaniyah. Apparently, it was unknown to the Marines I questioned for directions as I left the chow hall. Back at base for less than twenty-four hours, I preferred to return to my hooch to sleep, but this was more important.

Eventually I found the supply shop on my own and pushed my way inside through a neatly painted door. Despite fluorescents buzzing overhead, it took a few seconds for my eyes to adjust from the dazzling daylight outside. In those dim moments, my impression was of a blur of shelves and binders, several desks, and two Marines rising uncertainly from office chairs in front of me.

"Can I help you?" said a gruff voice.

Surprised, I glanced down at my collar to check that my rank hadn't fallen off. The speaker was tilted back in his chair behind a cluttered desk in the alcove to my right. I turned to face him. Like the other Marines in the room, he wore a skivvy shirt instead of a uniform top. Huge biceps reflected good chow and copious gym time. Glancing at a blouse draped over his backrest, I noted double rockers beneath black chevrons.

"Yeah, Gunny, you can. Why don't you start by getting off your ass when you're talking to me?"

The gunny's expression flashed from faint insolence to fury, then hardened into lines of obstinance.

Never one to let customs and courtesies pass by the wayside, I was even less inclined to overlook a breach of discipline from an arrogant war voyeur when I'd just returned from combat ops in the ville. Out of the corner of my eye, I saw the two junior Marines stiffen to attention.

Grudgingly, the gunny slid out of his chair and got to his feet. From his trouser pocket glinted the clip of a brand-new Benchmade knife.

I ran my eyes over the other Marines, noting that they also sported new Benchmade knives. I turned to the smoldering staff NCO. "Gunny, the Colonel mentioned in August that the whole battalion was getting issued Benchmades and Oakleys. It's November. I've got guys whose personal knives are dull or broken, and their eye pro is so scratched they can barely see on patrol. When are we getting the new gear?"

The gunny's eyes glinted. "Sir, you'll get the gear when there is enough for everyone in the battalion. Until then, you'll have to make do with what you have."

"That's bullshit," I said. "The Colonel's orders were clear: units outside the wire get priority. Yet every pogue staff NCO at the chow hall is wearing new Oakleys, and everyone in supply has a new Benchmade. When the fuck are you going to do your job and take care of the Marines in the fight?"

I considered it undignified for an officer to raise his voice, but in this case my sense of injustice ratcheted up the volume.

"We're testing them," Gunny replied with a smirk.

"Testing them? What the fuck is . . ."

Suddenly, daylight flooded the room. A shadow darkened the door. Turning, I saw the supply officer, a fellow lieutenant, breeze in, pull off his new Oakleys, then stop when he saw me squared up with his supply sergeant.

"Hey man," he ventured meekly. "What's up? Can I help you with something?" A Benchmade knife peeked out from his pocket.

I cast one last glance around the air-conditioned office.

"No, I don't think you can."

I turned and walked out.

15 December 2006 | Camp Habbaniyah, Al Anbar Province, Iraq

After a month of grinding operations outside the wire, I returned to base once more for an operational briefing. Stepping from the chow hall into dreary December twilight, I jammed on my crumpled cover and barely acknowledged the greeting of a Marine smoking next to the door. Distracted by problems personal and professional, I almost brushed by the small knot of men gathered to one side; evidently, they were waiting for me.

They were all members of my old weapons platoon in Kilo, which I'd been forced to give up in October. They had noticed me eating inside with my new company commander and had courteously waited to approach me until after dinner. Much happens in two months of combat. We spent the next few minutes catching up.

As we talked, I noticed one young Marine with a green foam plug sticking out of his right ear. He was a short, pale boy with close-cropped hair and piercing blue eyes. I remembered him as a quiet, intense machine gunner who'd done well in several vicious engagements in August and September. I asked him what was wrong with his ear.

"Well, sir," he began earnestly, "the membrane got pushed back when Warpig Charlie hit a mine on Jack Road. See, I was in the turret two hundred yards away and the concussion just must've hit me the wrong way, sir."

"It's the second time it's happened, sir," a big, good-looking corporal chimed in. "The first was back a couple months ago, so his ear is pretty fucked up. You may have to talk louder for him to hear everything."

I looked searchingly at the injured Marine. His wide-eyed innocence was heartbreaking.

"Well, what did the docs say, Perry? When will it be back to normal?" The gray light was fading, and I had to peer intently at Perry's pale silhouette to catch his facial expressions.

"Well, sir, they said that right now I've lost ninety percent of my hearing, but that when the membrane heals, I might get 30-50 percent back." He dropped his gaze and spoke in a barely audible whisper. "You see, sir, it's been a hard deployment for me. My dad died three months ago." He hesitated for a moment. I shifted uncomfortably.

"I went home for his funeral," he continued. "Four days later, my fiancée left me. She said she had no feelings for me anymore, since she hadn't seen my face or talked to me in so long." The last part was said without a trace of bitterness, just young hurt and bewilderment.

"I'm sorry, Perry. Sorry that you had to go through that." What else was I supposed to say? That his dad was in a better place and that a selfish girl didn't deserve someone as brave and forthright as him anyway? The darkness deepened around us. His next words sounded hollow.

"Right when I got back, Hertzberg got killed. Then Sergeant Z a few weeks later . . . ." His voice trailed off.

The cluster of Marines stood in sympathetic silence as Perry wrestled with his emotions. Abruptly, he raised his head and said firmly, "But I'm just gonna do my best until we go home, sir. I'll make it through." His squared jaw and gleaming eyes left me no doubt that he would.

I've never been good at responding to shared emotions, particularly with Marines. I never wanted them to see how much I cared. Perry's story left me with a lump in my throat.

Commenting thickly on the darkness and an invented timeline, I hurriedly shook hands with the Marines and strode away.

I hadn't gone ten steps before a swishing of boots through gravel announced someone hurrying to catch up. I turned. Perry's ghostly figure was framed against the inky blackness.

"Sir," he said before I could open my mouth, "I just wanted to thank you for—for everything, sir. You and Staff Sergeant Thomas taught me so much and—and I wanted you to know, sir, that Kilo put me up for two meritorious corporal boards already. And it's because of you and everything you did for me, sir."

I stared fondly at his nervous, upturned face. In my chest, for no reason that I could put into words, I felt what fathers feel when their sons tell them that they love them.

"No, Perry. It wasn't because of me," I said. "It was because of you, and who you are. Are they putting you up for the next board?"

"Oh yes, sir! I didn't have the test scores last time, but now I do. I'm sure I'll get it this time!" His eagerness was contagious, and I grinned despite the stinging in my eyes.

"Well, that's great, Perry. You deserve it." I grabbed his hand and gripped it hard. "Let me know when the promotion is. I'd like to be there."

Perry's face brightened into a huge grin. For a moment, dead fathers, lost brothers, and stupid girls were forgotten.

"Oh, would you sir? I'd like that!" His grip was surprisingly strong. I held it for a moment, then let him go.

"I'll see you then, Perry. Be safe."

"You too, sir. See you in January!" He turned and was swallowed by the night.

I stood in the dirty gravel and creeping darkness and stared at nothing.

But I thought for a long time.

February 2007 | Cumberland, Maine

"What's it like over there?"

Framed by a carousel of beef jerky and plastic towers of Maine State lottery scratchers, the Mobil gas attendant flipped up a bill holder and expertly whipped several wrinkled notes out of the cash register without looking away from me. The man's gelled hair and heavy cologne struck me as ambitious for a small-town gas station. Behind him, hazy plate glass revealed dirty parking lot snow graying in February twilight.

I felt hot beneath the gas station blowers.

Perhaps my haircut gives me away.

Or maybe it was my stiff posture, smooth jaw, and my reflexive use of "sir" in a region that eschews class. Maybe it was something else.

It doesn't matter.

The attendant correctly identified a serviceman on leave and seized the chance to add color commentary to headlines proclaiming the "Al Anbar Awakening." Slush slid from my boots and puddled on brown tile.

Disdain welled up inside me.

What is what like? Iraq? The desert? Being dirty and deprived and despised for months on end? Or what's it like to fight? To fear? To kill? To die?

What's it like?

Eight Weeks Earlier | Sadaqiyah, Al Anbar Province, Iraq

It's like shards of sunlight stabbing down from an azure sky, crashing against helmeted heads and blinking, blinded eyes.

"What a beautiful day, huh? Two days after Christmas and—"

It's the rending crash of an explosion, the sooty scent of dust and degraded TNT.

"What's that?!"

"IED! That was a fucking IED!"

"Who'd it hit? Marines? Our Marines? Where?" *Oh, fuck!* Thinking it so they don't see you lose control.

Your throat chokes out calm commands past a plug of huge fear. Quick off the roof, down through the pungent house, out into sunlight and the deadly street.

"Hurry up, follow me. Spread out. Where are they?" Breathing in short, shallow gasps. Holding your breath before you speak, containing the fear, calming the tone, appearing in control.

"Where'd they go? Here?" You peer down an alley littered with shredded paper and a pile of scattered rags.

"Keep moving! Get in that courtyard. Yes, that one. I don't care, break it down!" A gate crashes off screeching hinges.

"They're not here."

Wait.

A Marine scoops up a shattered, US government-issue rifle from against the far wall.

"Sir! Look what we found." You stare at the abandoned weapon, knowing what it means. This will be bad.

Too far.

"We went too far."

Back to the alley and the tattered rags that aren't rags but a shattered body.

You blink to make sure.

Maybe he's just knocked out.

But you already know. Fear and despair flood icily into your chest. Two blasted craters smoke eerily next to the broken lump heaped against a cinder block wall.

He's all alone.

You need to go to him.

But you're too scared to run toward death. You twist your neck looking for a Marine to order into the alley in your place.

I don't want to go. I don't want to go. I don't want to.

But who else will?

Go, you fucking coward!

You go.

"Get over here, Doc. Help me out." You say the words quietly, unemotionally, like ordering a pizza. He will remember it afterward and remark to the platoon about your calm under pressure. Only you know the truth. Your forced calm is a coping mechanism, a way to mask your horror. And it is your job.

The Marine is chalk white beneath a film of scorched dust. Scarlet rivulets seep from his ears and nose, and gurgle from gray lips. Sightless eyes stare into dirt.

You don't know what to do.

Doc glances hopelessly at the Marine's mangled legs and moves on to a gaping wound in his abdomen. Next to his bleeding head, you pluck pathetically at the strap of a shredded assault pack.

"Try to keep him awake, sir."

Cradling the Marine's helmet in your lap, you brush tufts of damaged Kevlar like ballistic broccoli sprouting from shrapnel seeds. Avoiding the waxen skin beneath the armor, you murmur meaningless words to the silent form.

"Come on buddy, you're gonna be fine. Stay awake, buddy. We'll have you out of here in no time." The words are acid. You are lying to a corpse who was a boy whose name you can't even remember now.

"Come on Billy, you'll be alright." Doc knows his name.

You repeat it while glancing guiltily at the corpsman. He's too busy assessing wounds to notice your desecration.

Seconds slide by. Small eternities. A pressure settles behind your eyes. You need to think, to figure something out. But fragments of thought slip past. *A decision.* You need to decide. But the urge to lie down and quit is almost unbearable.

Click.

And that's it. With no explanation, a mental mechanism snaps into place and achingly deliberate decisions form.

"What can you do, Doc?" Something needs to happen. Someone needs to do something.

The nineteen-year-old corpsman looks up. Stamped upon his boyish face are torment and despair. "I—I can't help him, sir. I . . . ." His voice trails off into a helpless shrug.

"Calm down, Doc. Do *something* for him. Pick an area and start working. You can do it." You look at him encouragingly, though you feel like throwing up.

Doc pulls out a pressure bandage and bends dutifully to the greatest trauma.

Turning to a Marine hovering nearby, you deliver quick, calm orders. The casualty is already buried in your mind. "Go set up security at that intersection. Stay behind cover so you don't get shot. One casualty is enough for today."

The Marine nods, glances at his fallen friend, and rushes off.

Gentling Billy's head to the ground, you rise, snatch up your carbine, and stride toward a house at the end of the alley where Marines gather in an aimless knot. "Where's your doc? Get him out here to help! Let's go!"

You repeat the order twice before a senior corpsman pushes past. This is the squad that was hit by the IED and they're in shock. The squad leader stares vacantly over your shoulder at the sailor bending close to his bleeding friend. You grab his bicep and turn him to face you before a flicker of recognition crosses his stricken face.

"Corporal V, listen to me. Let the docs work on him. I need you to provide overwatch from this side so that we don't get hit again before the QRF (quick reaction force) arrives."

The order is unnecessary. Other Marines have already taken up key positions. But it gives the stunned men simple tasks to direct them away from an awful fixation. First responders wrap crash victims in blankets to treat for shock. In combat, you wrap traumatized men in the comfort of tasks made simple by training.

It works.

As Marines take up crouching security positions, you turn back to the alley.

"He's gone, sir." The senior corpsman's voice is choked.

Gazing down at Doc's twisted face, you're fascinated by the morphine cap wavering in his mouth like a blue plastic cigarette.

"He just–. There was too much trauma. We couldn't do anything to help."

You can tell the doc is trying to convince himself more than he is trying to inform you.

"I–. He didn't feel a thing, sir. He was dead when we got here."

A pause.

You force yourself to look at the dead Marine's face.

Framed by wisps of dusty brown hair, it shines white through black grime and crimson smudges. A child's face. And you think involuntarily of how much his mother must have loved her little boy.

How would she feel if she was here right now?

If she could see her son broken from the blast of three artillery shells, sprawled in the center of a sad little circle of kneeling corpsmen and silent Marines.

How would she feel?

"Get him in a body bag," you say.

And you walk away.

———

What's it like?

"I guess it's like anywhere," I said. "Good days and bad days. Maybe more bad than good."

The attendant hesitated, disappointment tugging at the corners of his mouth, before grudgingly dropping change into my outstretched hand. I pocketed it without comment and headed for the exit.

"Okay. Well, thank you for your service."

"Glad to," I mumbled and stiff-armed the door. Its push bar was shined to silver where a legion of hands had gone before. Outside, the cold smells of dirt and diesel.

What's it like?

230

Don't ask.

Don't ask, because you don't want to know what it's like to have part of your soul buried in Tennessee.

CHAPTER 39
Ninety-Five Theses

Steve | 2009-2010 | Dallas, Texas, and North Yarmouth, Maine

For the next three months, I could barely drag myself to class. As week followed week in a gray slide of academic drudgery and friendlessness, I waited for Wes to follow up with me.

His phone call never came.

After all the years of excruciating involvement and perfectionistic demands, it was Wes's silence that produced a crack of light.

Why would Wes leave me to my own devices if he really believed that I'm being attacked in Dallas by Satanists? And why, after all that happened, does Wes not call to see how I am doing?

Rather, Wes didn't believe the things he told us from the pulpit, or he didn't really care about his sheep.

For almost two years now, he'd focused on his own life to the exclusion of anything else. But our congregation was in a shambles. Depression ran rampant. Didn't Wes see it? If he couldn't see it, he was a blind guide.

And if he does see it but has decided to ignore it, that makes him something worse.

Indulging this line of thought, I wrote a small list of questions to ask Wes when I returned home for Christmas break.

For me, they were breathtakingly insolent.

And the first question was, "Since our worldview seems harsh and unlivable, how then can it be true?"

———

In Wes's hot kitchen, I sat watching chickadees flit from branch to branch in

Sweetser's Apple Orchard behind his house. Winter light gasped into pitch darkness. In my pocket, I felt the crinkle of the index card on which I'd written my five questions of dissent, my own Ninety-Five Theses.

I still retained a shred of hope that Wes might somehow satisfactorily answer my questions. But it seemed more likely that the list would ignite his fury. After that, I would have to decide if I could and would stay in my family and in my church. I hadn't yet decided if I would renounce my own renunciation. I was no Luther. But I was also no longer the same young man who'd rolled over with every kick for the past twenty-five years.

I tried to gauge my emotions.

All I feel is anger.

But I needn't have worried. For two hours, Wes and I sat across from each other as he talked of his own life over the past three months. He seemed to have forgotten all about Ashley and the Dallas Satanists. Instead, he shared story after story about his own alleged abuse, how difficult life was for him, and how much he had suffered.

My skin prickled with sweat. I stuck my hand in my pocket and clutched the damning card. Could I just break in on Wes and tell him to shut up? Tell him that I had a list of grievances that he *must* address?

Yes, I could.

I opened my mouth—and then I remembered the day Nate left home thirteen years before. I remembered how my mother had sobbed. I remembered the wracking cries of my father alone in his downstairs office, the splinters of pain that lodged in our chests and made it difficult to breathe for the next five years.

Yes, I could.

But I wouldn't. Not today. Not in this house. Not with this man. There had to be a better way, a way that would preserve my family and perhaps even transform Wes into a truly good man.

Isn't that God's way? To reconcile and restore and redeem?

I didn't yet understand that sometimes God's love braids a whip of cords and overturns tables.

Wes waved his hand. I'd been daydreaming. "Did you hear what I said?" he asked.

"Sorry, I was thinking about something else." My face turned hot.

Wes gave me a disapproving glance. "I said, 'Do you know what your only problem was this past semester?'"

I shook my head.

That you made me stop speaking with a girl I wanted to date? That I lost all of my friends? That, apparently, Satanists are wrecking my life in Dallas? That I'm sinking further and further into a swamp of depression? Please, tell me, Wes. What was my only problem this past semester?

Wes smiled benignly. "Your only problem over the past three months was that you didn't call me more."

I felt stunned by his hubris.

Rest assured, I thought, *if there's one thing I'll do this semester, it's to never call you again.*

Later, backing my car out of Wes's icy driveway, I glanced up at the picture window full of warm light. Wes limped through the orange living room and waved goodbye. Stooped, framed with light, he was a shadow of the powerful man who'd arrived in Maine exactly twenty-five Decembers before.

Around me, lights glowed on the trees and stars crackled overhead. For all my life I'd wanted to live in the gauzy assurance of a Christmas card. Now the little parsonage lay cozy and warm beneath the cold sky. I wished for a moment that it really could've been Bethlehem's stable and that the man in the window really could have been my savior.

I didn't know that it was the last time I'd ever see him.

———

"What's wrong?" Teresa asked.

She stared at me from the passenger seat. A light rain pattered on the roof. Early evening shoppers bustled in and out of the Corner Bakery on Preston Road in Dallas. We'd come here for a quick dinner but now we sat in the car with our stomachs growling, trying to figure out life. Trying to figure out us.

Since Thanksgiving, I'd formed a new group of friends at seminary. The person I valued most was a Taiwanese-American girl named Teresa. She was lovely and smart. I thought that she was wonderful. Now I sat gazing at the steering wheel, numb with fear.

"Steve, what's wrong? You said you couldn't date me, but you didn't say why. You have to say something."

I said nothing.

Teresa sighed. She'd been patient with me, but I could tell that we were on the verge of collapse. I'd told her we couldn't date, but I had no valid reason. God seemed to be bringing us together. We had the same interests, the same vision for ministry, and we were in love.

But dating would be wrong, I thought. So very, very wrong.

And Wes will kill it.

Teresa looked at me and frowned. "Can you at least tell me what you are feeling right now?"

I felt nothing. My feelings were like weird, tropical fish swimming behind thick plates of glass. I could see them, but could not touch them.

"I feel numb," I whispered. Something bad was about to happen.

"Numb? Why are you shaking?"

My hands trembled on the steering wheel.

Something bad, something bad, something bad is about to happen.

"Because I'm afraid."

Teresa nodded. "What are you afraid of?"

This is wrong. I mustn't go here. I mustn't speak about the problem to another person.

I remembered my unexamined index card of grievances, torn and thrown into a trash can after my Christmas meeting with Wes. Rain drummed on the roof. We waited for a long time.

Finally, I cleared my throat and said, "I'm afraid of Wes."

"You're afraid of Wes? But honey, he's your pastor. You shouldn't be afraid of your pastor."

I knew what she said was true.

But what I'd said was true too.

I am so afraid of him.

My fingers shook. A hot line of sweat ran down my back.

Teresa reached over, put her hand on top of mine. "Honey, you shouldn't be afraid of your pastor. If that's the primary feeling you have when you think of him, that's wrong."

Wrong?

"Yes, wrong."

And it was at that moment that I realized that it had been wrong from the beginning.

———

Two weeks later, Teresa and I were dating.

It was an act of total opposition toward Wes. I also knew that I had to confront Wes about his abuses and to expand my index card of questions into a clear testament of reformation. Still, after everything, I hoped to be an internal reformer. I hoped that somehow our church might be preserved. But if not, I knew that I would have to leave our church just as Nate had done so many years before. This revelation, exotic in its audacity for a conformist like me, was still foreign enough that I preferred to place it at remove.

I'll cross that bridge when I get there.

I sat alone in a study room. Books and papers spread across the table. It was well past midnight. I was supposed to be working on a Greek exegetical paper. Instead, I pulled up a new Word document and typed: *Dear Wes,*

What came then wasn't so much composition as dictation. For years, my mind had stored away its own secret files of abuse, indexed and illustrated, waiting for this moment. The thoughts came one after another in a rapid but orderly progression; they were like the liberated POWs I'd seen in black-and-white footage from some of my grandfather's World War II documentaries, walking emaciated but unbroken past barbed wire.

I knew that Wes would excommunicate me for such a letter, but I still hoped that somehow he wouldn't. I still hoped that, instead, he'd receive my letter humbly in his present state of weakness and that it might prove a watershed in the life of our church. I hoped that Wes might acknowledge his abuses and either step aside or rapidly institute a comprehensive series of changes that would involve a plurality of elders and would end the twenty-five years of winter at Faith Baptist.

But I knew the truth. Unless a miracle occurred, my parents were about to lose another son.

It came as a relief when Dad called a few days later. "Wes is in the hospital," he said over a bad connection. "He's really weak."

"Who's taking care of the church?" I asked.

"Peter and Randall. They'll take turns delivering Sunday sermons until Wes feels well enough to return home."

He must not return home.

The thought came crashing into my brain and shattered all mental barriers about Wes's removal from church office.

He must never *return to that pulpit.*

But all I said was, "Okay. I'll be praying for him."

Spies were everywhere.

When I got off the phone, all I could think about was this:

I must tell Peter and Randall what I've written.

They were one step ahead of me.

That Sunday, the two deacons called a special church meeting to explain their concerns about Wes's leadership style. It was a public gathering unprecedented in the life of our church. But there were some in the congregation who doubted, some who thought that Wes just needed a bit of rest.

Screw that. A few more years of Wes and we'll all be dead.

On March 14, Teresa and I drove down to Houston for spring break. At her parents' house, I sat up well past midnight retooling my letter to Wes. I redrafted it as a five-page letter to Peter and Randall that detailed the long list of abuses I felt Wes had committed. Legalism. Image control. Self-preoccupation. False prophecies. Tyrannical leadership. Systematic shunning of former members. Paranoia. Holding himself up as our sole mediator with God. Focusing on the works of Satan instead of on the finished work of Christ.

Frankly, I concluded, Wes had hurt me. I was afraid of him.

I was afraid to submit myself any longer to his abusive spiritual authority.

Lacking a suitable church door on which to nail my theses, I simply hit SEND.

———

Five days later, Teresa bustled about making lunch in her small kitchen in Dallas. I sat on the couch checking email. A message from Dad popped into my inbox. The subject line read simply: "Nate."

Is he dead?

But it was just a letter forwarded from Nate, dated March 14.

    Dear Mom and Dad,

I'm headed out early in the morning for eight days in the field with my Marines, so I apologize for this typed and hasty note. I wanted to thank you for sending me the box of old photos, report cards, and schoolwork. I spent Saturday afternoon going through all of it, accompanied by a mix of smiles, tears, and laughter. It was good to remember the love of my family and to revisit the dreams of a little boy.

In six weeks, I leave the Marine Corps to assume a position with a non-profit organization in Atlanta that helps wounded and disabled veterans to find employment outside of the military. After much soul-searching, thought, and prayer, I believe this is where God wants me for the next few years. I'm looking forward to my transition from the military and to the future that God has in store for me.

If you are willing, I would like to talk to you about our separation, what God has been doing in my life, and if it is possible to reconcile. Thirteen years of hard lessons have matured me, grown me, and shown me areas where I have clearly sinned against you and need to ask for your forgiveness. Perhaps you feel the same way. I'm sure that I will be back in Maine at some point this summer, but even a phone conversation may be beneficial.

I hope this letter finds you well. I prayerfully await your response.

Love, Nate

I knew what my response would be.

I lowered my head.

And I wept.

———

Two days later, Randall called.

I held the phone tight against my ear, blocking out the music blaring from my roommate's speakers. "Hi Randall, how are you?"

"I'm weary," Randall said. "It's been a long day. Wes was just committed to the local psych unit."

A psych unit?

"Because of his obsessiveness and perfectionism, he was unable to function. But even in the hospital, Wes was still trying to control Peter and me when we visited.

He failed to take the medications his doctors prescribed. He was consulting 'the Lord' to decide whether or not to take a pill. He was hearing voices in his head. The doctor had to lock him in his room so he couldn't escape."

I tried to imagine the dignified man I'd known for twenty-five years reduced to a shivering shell, his silver hair—always perfectly combed—flopping across his forehead as he rushed the two deacons retreating down a hospital corridor.

Randall sighed. "Steve, this morning in Sunday school, Peter and I shared your letter with the entire congregation. It did some good. The vote was unanimous."

"Vote?" I asked dumbly.

"Yes," Randall said. "We voted to remove Wes Harris as pastor of Faith Baptist Church."

Warm sunlight blasted through my soul.

———

In May, I waited for Nate inside my seminary apartment. We'd be going together to Atlanta. He had just separated from the Marines and I was going to help him move into his new place.

What if I don't recognize him?

In a panic, I rushed to my fourth-floor window and scanned the street below for his blue Ford Ranger. Only a few small cars sat in the May heat.

I walked into the bathroom and glanced in the mirror. My brother stared back at me. I grinned. We'd been separated for thirteen years, but no one had ever been able to take his face from me.

In the bathroom, a green bar of soap lay on the counter. It smelled clean and bright.

In a flash, I was back at my grandparents' house in Eddington as a three-year-old boy.

Sunlight flooded through the kitchen windows and spread across the floor. I watched a block of light advance over the white linoleum. Above me, porcelain animal figurines marched across the sill in a miniature safari: elephant, rhino, buffalo, turtle.

A bar of green soap lay on the counter.

Someone was scrubbing shampoo into my hair—my grandmother, probably—and it felt wonderful. Warm water lapped around my belly. As I rocked to the motion of her fingers, the water rose and fell and when it ebbed it left a thin equator of wet skin that cooled deliciously until another small wave leapt up to warm it. Warm, cool, warm, cool, a private tide in my own private sea, and the light flooding through the windows as a cuckoo clock struck some bright morning hour.

On the floor, in that square of light, Nate played with a yellow Tonka truck. He wore only a cloth diaper. His long hair lay damp from washing. He moved the truck into and out of the light as if the dividing line were a concrete barrier, darkness like a living thing that could block the big rubber wheels and send the truck spinning against the wall.

From the sink, I watched him grip the truck with both hands, his small arms locked straight with tension, his face determined. Then he crashed it through the shadows and into the sun. Brilliant shards of light glanced off the toy's windshield and scattered across the ceiling. Nate thrust out his chin, put his lower lip over his upper lip, and nodded with satisfaction. He let go of the truck and leaned back on small haunches. Then he looked up at me and grinned.

Standing in front of my apartment mirror, I saw that same wide smile.

I glanced down at the street. A blue Ford Ranger pulled into a space on the opposite side.

I raced downstairs and walked out to the gate. It swung wide and clanged against the fence. The windshield of Nate's truck sent light splintering around me.

My twin climbed out and jogged over. "Hello brother. It's been awhile."

Then he crushed me in a war-hardened embrace.

Our long captivity was over.

PART IV
EPILOGUES

Beauty, strength, youth, are flowers but fading seen;
Duty, faith, love, are roots, and ever green.

George Peele, *A Farewell to Arms*

Nate | February 2012 | Baxley, Georgia

"It's good to know that I'm not alone."

A half dozen dark-suited men nodded with fraternal understanding. They stood under a gray sky, clustered next to a cemetery in quiet intimacy. The speaker was one of their own, a decorated Marine veteran of multiple combat deployments to Iraq. Recently, he had struggled to assimilate into the culture of a prestigious university.

Combat had been difficult, but he expected that. It's what Marines do. But school? School was an entirely different beast. School was where you were supposed to chase girls, party, and maybe go to class occasionally. Fresh-faced kids straight out of high school did it by the casual thousands every fall. So, what was his problem? Why did he have such a difficult time fitting in?

The gusting winter wind snatched a humorless laugh from the speaker's lips.

"Every night, I drink myself to sleep. And I think that I have to be the only one. That no one else could possibly have the same problems that I have. Panic attacks. Trouble sleeping. I push everyone away, only to realize how much I love them once they're gone." His downcast eyes focused on the gray pavement of the country church parking lot. A handsome, extroverted man like him was unaccustomed to feeling outcast.

"I talked to Rooster's mother last night at the viewing. She described his symptoms, how he fought against PTSD since he got back from Iraq. It sounded like she was talking about me."

He raised his chin in the direction of the gleaming casket.

"That could've been me." Then, more slowly, "That could be me."

"Rooster" was killed by a State Police SWAT team on the steps of his house early on a quiet Sunday morning in Baxley, Georgia. The Purple Heart recipient left

243

the Marines after his third combat deployment to Iraq and went on to earn his MBA. But friends and family noticed a sobering difference in the once-gregarious veteran. Rooster had left the service, but the effects of his service hadn't left him.

Rooster sought treatment from the Veterans Administration for his post-traumatic stress disorder, but was unable to shake the constant anxiety and depression. On 19 February 2012, Rooster decided to end his struggle by walking into the bullets of law enforcement. He was as much a casualty of the war as any service member who died in Iraq.

I served with Rooster during the bloody desert campaigns of Al Anbar Province in the spring and summer of 2005. Although we served in different platoons, his thick drawl, easy laugh, and perpetual shock of unruly hair always made Rooster stand out. He was a friend to many, and a good Marine.

The loss of such a dynamic, joyous personality to the cumulative effects of PTSD was a tragedy that should sound warning bells in a society that has very little idea how to handle its returning legions.

One of the reasons America fails to properly reintegrate returning veterans relates to a flawed understanding of the nature of combat-induced PTSD. We, the military included, treat it like some strange psychological malady, as if it's a mystery why normal men sent into abnormal circumstances come back changed. Science documents and history confirms the cause and effect between combat and PTSD. Despite this ancient link, our medical and psychological professionals have only begun to understand the disorder in a way that might yield effective treatments.

Behavior modification is the signature "limp" of veterans who struggle with PTSD. I walked with that limp for years. Veterans with PTSD often aren't sure what's "wrong." They only know that things aren't right. As common situations trigger the same unbidden, unpleasant response, they adapt behavior to avoid those triggers. When they can control a situation, they feel safe. When they can't, they often avoid it or sedate themselves. For veterans, PTSD is inherently an antisocial disorder.

You may spot veterans suffering from PTSD as they sit uneasily in the back of classrooms, shift uncomfortably on the edge of church pews, or nervously scan the room at family gatherings. Alcohol often becomes the unofficial medication that allows veterans with PTSD to feel normal or to relax.

Shortly after I returned from Iraq in 2007, I visited a local home improvement store near my new duty station in Washington state. Excited for my project and carrying a list of needed materials, I thought nothing of entering the store as I had a dozen times before. But this time, something felt different. I was uneasy, on edge. I pressed on, ignoring the increasing sensation that I was unsafe.

As I walked down a narrow aisle filled with yard implements, my entire world suddenly shifted under a pulsing wave of nauseous fear. The comfortable space around me disappeared as my self-confidence and sense of security crashed to the floor like abandoned armor. I felt unprotected, out of control. Every person became a threat. Sounds, smells, and the glaring overhead lights passed unfiltered through hyperaware senses to assault my brain in overdrive.

One instinct overrode any rational thought: *Get out.*

I shoved unpurchased items onto a shelf and bolted for the exit. Ten minutes later, I huddled in my truck, tears streaming down my face as I drove home.

I couldn't understand what had just happened.

Episodes like that one became more frequent in the ensuing years. I became a functional recluse, avoiding social situations and new experiences that might trigger a panic attack. Friends and acquaintances became accustomed to me declining invitations to socialize. Eventually they stopped asking. I drank heavily and destroyed romantic relationships in a depressing cycle of thrilling novelty, fear of entrapment, and cold dismissal.

After three years of struggling with the symptoms of my unknown malady, I chose to leave the Marine Corps. On my way out the door, the VA diagnosed me with combat-induced PTSD. I moved to Georgia and began work at a veteran employment organization while pursuing a graduate degree.

To my surprise and frustration, education became a grueling experience. Trapped in a classroom for hours at a time, I fought the urge to get up and pace. I found it difficult to focus and frustrating to deal with concepts and ideas when all I wanted to do was act. When I looked around and saw students happily engaged in conversation and the process of learning, I fought the urge to compare myself to them. Yet we were different.

I had a disability from combat.

They didn't.

Pretending to be unaffected by my time in combat was like expecting a man in a wheelchair to get up and walk.

———

In time, love restored much of what had been damaged by war.

God's love was unwavering, unassailable, and my only sustainment near the end of my military career when long months passed without a touch of human affection. My faith faltered but never failed, though for a season in Iraq it was anesthetized by violence and hard decisions. Glimpses of Providence abounded like shafts of light piercing the squalls of depression and anxiety that I navigated following my deployments.

I regularly went to church, even if that meant hovering in a doorway or sitting on the steps or in a balcony to overcome my fear of being trapped in a crowd. Good-hearted people of faith welcomed me into their lives and homes.

I began to heal.

Healing flowed also from the steady process of reunification with Mom, Dad, Christine, and Steve. During the first few years of separation, I had walled up family memories and affection, plastered them over to avoid the pain of rejection and their whispered messages of inadequacy. Relatives and wonderful families wrapped me in mantles of love in ways that were beautiful, remarkable, and boundless. Nevertheless, from time to time I felt a telltale throb. Behind the plaster was an undying need for the love of my family.

It took work to rebuild what had been destroyed when I left home. That work began when I left the service in 2010.

Steve helped me move to Georgia during my first week out of the Marines. All awkwardness melted away as we shared several days of tactile communion, manhandling boxes and dismantled furniture in a hot, airless apartment. At our core, we were one flesh bound together by a set of shared memories that time, distance, history, and antipathy could not sever. He left for Maine once I was settled into my new place and new job. I followed several weeks later.

My homecoming, in bright sunlight under an old crabapple that had marked my departure thirteen years before, was hedged with a self-protective assurance that bordered on arrogance. I don't believe any filmmaker would've fought to capture the moment when I reconnected with Mom, Dad, and Christine. Years of hurt and distrust don't evaporate with a hopeful greeting and clinging embrace. But over days, and weeks, and months, words of life and forgiveness settled into my soul like a gentle spring rain.

And an old love, buried deep, returned.

———

I visited the graves of Larry Philippon and Billy Koprince within a few months of their deaths.

In 2005, Larry's was easy to find, resting in a row of marble crosses thatched with new sod in Arlington. Picking my way through the quiet green of a September morning, I found Larry's cross and stood guiltily, unsure whether to grieve or repent. An Iraqi sunburn still colored my neck and, in my mind, I saw Larry being carried into the smoking street. The memory and the reality were related yet irreconcilable. I looked up to gain my bearings. My eyes fell upon a familiar name etched in the next row. I looked around. There was another name that I recognized. And another. And another.

Falling to my knees, I sobbed for Larry and for lost friends and for a twenty-five-year-old who didn't know how to reconcile this harvest of war with a country at peace.

Billy was harder to find. When I turned off a western highway near Knoxville and followed a dirt trace to a small cemetery in April 2007, new leaves gave the surrounding hills a feathery look, but the grass between memorial plaques still showed signs of winter. The cemetery was empty and lacked a directory. Not knowing where Billy had been laid to rest, I picked my way over a gentle slope and scanned for signs of newly turned earth. I couldn't find him. As minutes passed, I grew agitated and quickened my pace, crossing and recrossing the areas that seemed to hold the greatest promise.

After some time, the realization that I'd be unable to find Billy's grave and pay my respects reduced me to tears. I mouthed a prayer for forgiveness and a blessing for Billy's family, then walked dejectedly to my truck and departed for my new duty station on the West Coast.

A decade later, I returned to the Tennessee countryside and, after a careful search, finally reunited with Billy. Shreds of ribbon and oxidized medals clung to a wire frame above his grave, remnants of memorial road races that testified to a mother's undying love. An American flag snapped in a stiff breeze across the field, but I barely heard it. Staring up at me in weathered bronze was the grinning face of a boy who had left home to visit Iraq on his way to heaven.

It doesn't all have to make sense, I realized.

"The Greatest Generation" chain-smoked and carpet-bombed their way to victory in Europe and the Pacific, then introduced the image of the happy returning GI into the zeitgeist of mid-century America. Indeed, Steve and I elevated our own grandfather, Gray, into the pantheon of sepia-tinted heroes in this exact same way.

The war in Iraq, on the other hand, was predicated on a falsehood—that Saddam Hussein possessed weapons of mass destruction—and prosecuted with schizophrenic aims. Setting aside the fact that humanity is better without Saddam Hussein, I must ask: can a messy war of choice ever drape a mantle of noble sacrifice over the shoulders of the fallen?

It cannot.

Only cultural sentiment can do that.

And America seems to have decided that the war in Iraq was a bit of unfortunate adventurism in an otherwise justified global campaign against the enablers of the 9/11 attacks.

I'm not proud to have fought in Iraq. The policy was muddled, and the strategy was vacuous. The middling result was upended by ISIS anyway.

But I'm proud as hell to have served alongside the likes of Larry and Billy and a thousand others who, in the words of Joshua Lawrence Chamberlain, "set aside the near advantage, the momentary pleasure; the snatching of seeming good to self; and act[ed] for remoter ends, for higher good, and for interests other than [their] own." Men who will risk their lives in service of their country are national treasures.

———

True healing from the effects of war and the effects of my long separation from my family came when I fell in love with a vivacious, dark-haired Georgian with a Midwest grounding and extraordinary perception. As my wife and partner, Christine's limitless love, fierce loyalty, and deep respect for my military service were the mainspring of my recovery from post-traumatic stress. As mother of our three beautiful children, she gave me an unmatchable gift of life and hope that overwhelmed any lingering vapors of doubt, depression, and fear. I'm in awe of her strength and love.

The men we lost are forever in my heart. Their examples of selfless sacrifice are an eternal legacy that compels profound reflection on the measure of our own lives and choices.

Steve | November 2010 | Dallas, Texas

I sat at a carrel on the second floor of the seminary library looking over the towering stack of books. It was the day before Thanksgiving, two years to the day since I'd been conned. I was finishing a research paper. It was my last task before Teresa and I headed to Houston for the holiday.

I rubbed my eyes and pulled my hat low over my forehead. So tired.

"Is there a Bible anywhere that I could read?"

Startled, I looked up. A fat man with thick lips, puffy bald head, and an overcoat stared down at me. My blood ran cold.

Holy crap. It's Josh.

I couldn't believe it. He was back on campus looking for another seminary student to scam. And just before Thanksgiving too. In a beautiful moment of clarity, I realized that he didn't recognize me with my hat and glasses.

Perfect.

"Uh, yeah, actually there is," I said, assuming the same flat affect I'd mastered as a member of a Bible cult. "Downstairs in the reference section."

Josh looked nonplussed. I could tell that he wanted to draw me in, to play on my seminary student's interest in evangelizing the lost. "Great," he said. "I'm really wanting to learn more about the Bible. I have a lot of questions about Jesus Christ and whether I want to give my life to him—"

"Awesome," I cut in. "You'll find everything you're looking for downstairs in the reference section. Now, if you'll excuse me, I need to finish this paper." I pulled my hat lower and started to type.

Josh stood for a moment, then turned and ambled off toward an open area where other students studied. Two years before, when I had filed my police report, the campus police chief said that a man matching the description I'd given had conned at least two other students out of thousands of dollars in the past. He seemed to strike every two years.

Not anymore.

As soon as I heard Josh engage a different student, I sprinted downstairs and pushed open the library's front door. A campus police officer patrolled past. I ran up to her. "Hey," I said. "I'm the student who got conned two years ago and I just saw the perpetrator inside the library."

The officer cocked an eyebrow. "You sure it's him?"

"Yes ma'am. Positive."

She radioed for backup.

I reentered the library with two officers just in time to see Josh rushing toward the periodicals section in the back. He'd seen us.

"That's him," I said.

The officers broke into a trot with their gun belts jingling. Students glanced up in surprise as we jogged past. We split up in the periodical stacks and saw Josh with his head down, ambling toward the emergency exit in the rear.

"Stop!" the police chief shouted.

Josh stopped, a picture of innocent surprise. "What's the matter, officer?"

The chief ignored him. Turning to me he said, "Is this the guy?"

I looked at Josh. He had the same puffy skin, the same thick lips, and the same gray eyes, the same hunched shoulders. "It's him," I said.

How could I ever forget?

"This student says you robbed him two years ago," the chief said.

Josh smiled and raised his hands palms up. "I don't know what he's talking about. I've never seen him before in my life."

I pointed to his left hand. "That's the same serpentine wedding ring I described in my police report. This is the guy."

The police chief clapped a hand on Josh's shoulder. "Alright, sir, let's bring you to the police kiosk to answer a few questions."

As the officers led him away, Josh glared at me with pure hatred.

I smiled sweetly.

Lying bastard.

August 2014 | Columbus, Ohio

I could take you to the exact spot where I learned that Wes was dying.

Out walking into the field at a local ballpark, halfway between the pitcher's mound and home plate, brick dust rising in slow clouds around my feet and August sun pressing down hot and hard. I flicked through my newsfeed and there it was: my former pastor, the man I'd once chosen as my eternal guide, was dying. His son asked for prayers as he made the long journey to the hospital bed in Maine, not knowing what he'd find except confusion and pain. Wes remained unrepentant to the end.

I stopped and read the paragraph over again. Then I put my phone in my pocket, looked up at the trees, and felt the sun. I looked down and shuffled my feet in the dust.

Four years had passed since my Bible cult fell apart and Wes was removed from his tarnished office. In a touch of poetic justice, I'd preached the final sermon from the pulpit before the church doors closed forever.

Since then, I'd done a lot of healing. Nate and I had reconciled from thirteen years of separation and would serve as best men in each other's weddings. I'd sent a letter of forgiveness to my pastor and received an unapologetic voicemail in reply. So, I set up boundaries to avoid more hurt. I married Teresa and had a son. But I was wrong to think that my pastor's death would bring me peace.

What was broken in life cannot be mended by death. Death has no power to heal, to restore, to resurrect. You can't unbend your twisted life on another person's casket. A gravestone is no anvil.

I'd cherished a secret notion that when the man who had mistreated me for twenty-five years was dead, a burden would be lifted; I'd buy some ice cream and push a quarter century of trauma into the nearest fifty-gallon trash can.

It wasn't like that. Moreover, good people who'd gone through much worse had already told me it *couldn't* be like that. But we all have to figure these things out for ourselves.

No, the death of your abuser can give you neither peace nor joy. But it can make you sad with a sincere sadness that wishes no harm on your tormenter.

It can also make you grateful that you were the one wronged and not the agent of wrong.

And it can bring you life, if you let it.

If you have the courage to remember.

If you have the courage to die a little bit to forgive. Because when you say "I forgive you" and commit yourself to him who judges justly, you take into yourself a small piece of the death of the one who said, "Father, forgive them, for they know not what they do."

I'd like to say I had this all worked out in the brick dust on that ball field. But I'm not that good, and anyway, I like nursing my grudges as much as anyone. About all I came to that August afternoon was an awkward prayer that someday I'd see my former pastor in heaven and not in hell.

It's not that much, I know.

But then again, maybe it is.

28 July 2015 | Eddington, Maine

A year after Wes's death, Teresa and I pulled onto a narrow gravel track that led to a rise where a black marble tombstone lay. Two small American flags fluttered on either side of it. I'd never visited the little cemetery above the Penobscot River, but it felt familiar. Like I was remembering it. Like I was coming home.

It was a beautiful July day. Bright blue sky, puffy clouds, and a breeze stirring sunsoaked trees by the river. Teresa held our three-month-old son, Josiah. My twoyear-old, Oliver, ran in circles after the long drive; I let him run. It was a graveyard after all. Surely the dead had no objections.

"Do you want me to take the boys for a little while?" Teresa asked. "So you can be alone?"

"Sure," I said gruffly. "I only need a minute."

He'd found a good spot, Gray had. The cemetery was only a few hundred yards from the old house. The river lay out of sight behind the trees, but in winter, when the leaves were down, it would sparkle and shine, and even now I could hear its wet sigh and feel a water-kissed breeze. It was a good spot for a navy veteran.

Kneeling in front of my grandfather's grave, I saw myself reflected in its polished black surface. When I saw his name and my own face in the stone, something inside me broke. I lowered my head and sobbed. "I'm sorry, I'm sorry, I'm so, so sorry," I said, repeatedly. "Please forgive me. I was so, so wrong."

Oliver broke from Teresa's grasp and stood beside me. "What matter, Dada?"

I felt his tiny hand on my shoulder. I wiped my eyes. "Daddy just feels sad," I said. "This is my grandfather's grave. I never said goodbye."

"That okay, Dada," Ollie said, his purity an absolution. "You play me?"

Still on my knees, I looked at the tombstone and saw my son in its face as he tugged at my shirt, free and full of joy. The years had not been wasted.

Nothing is ever wasted.

A breeze blew up from the river. The tree stirred.

"Thank you," I whispered. "Thank you so much."

Ollie tugged at my shirt. "Dada play?"

I rose to my feet and picked up my son.

I knew what Gray would want me to do.

———

Down by the Penobscot River, water gurgled around boulders. I smelled the old familiar scents of wet vegetation and sunbaked stone. Grasshoppers chirred in the tall grass.

The dam was gone now and so was its elemental rumble. The river ran strangely quiet between wide banks, swishing and chattering over the gravel shoals I remembered as a child. Ollie and I walked along my grandparents' frontage, throwing stones into the water, hooting with joy when the splashes wet our shoes.

I glanced up at the small, white house that watched over us from the riverbank. I knew that there was something I had to do.

"You know, there are Indian spears and arrowheads all along this bank," I told Ollie.

His eyes widened.

"It's true," I said. "Maybe we'll find one."

Ollie bent over and studied the flints at his feet. "Look Dada! Arrow!" He picked up a flat rock.

It was nothing of the sort.

I took the stone from his hands and appraised it with a critical eye. Ollie's mouth hung open as he looked up at me. Beside us, the river ran as it always had, swift and clean and true—down toward an endless sea.

I handed the stone back to Oliver. "Son of a gun, if that don't look like an arrowhead," I said. "Let's put it on the shelf when we get home."

The boy in front of me and the boy inside of me were one.

There had been no intervening years. The story flowed as it had always been meant to flow—as it had been ordained—toward a kingdom full of goodness and light and unquenchable joy.

Made in the USA
Columbia, SC
23 April 2024